Gittin' Western

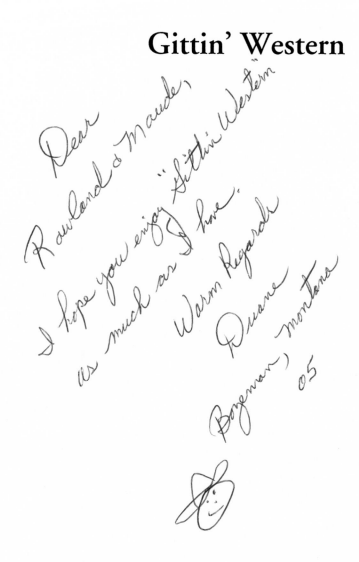

Dear
Rowland & Maude,
I hope you enjoy "Gittin' Western"
as much as I have.

Warm Regards
Duane

Bozeman, Montana
05

Gittin' Western

✦

A True Adventure of Spirit, Mind, and Body

by
Duane Wiltse

iUniverse, Inc.
New York Lincoln Shanghai

Gittin' Western
A True Adventure of Spirit, Mind, and Body

Copyright © 2005 by Duane Wiltse

iUniverse books may be ordered through booksellers or by contacting:

iUniverse
2021 Pine Lake Road, Suite 100
Lincoln, NE 68512
www.iuniverse.com
1-800-Authors (1-800-288-4677)

ISBN-13: 978-0-595-34722-3 (pbk)
ISBN-13: 978-0-595-79465-2 (ebk)
ISBN-10: 0-595-34722-3 (pbk)
ISBN-10: 0-595-79465-3 (ebk)

Printed in the United States of America

With sincere appreciation and affection, this book is dedicated to all the members of my family, past, present, and future.

Contents

AUTHOR'S NOTE xi

PROLOGUE 1

WESTWARD HO 3

WYOMING CHALLENGES 17

CABIN CREEK 24

A HORSE CALLED THUNDER 37

THE PRINCE'S TENT 49

WIN SOME—LOSE SOME 60

RUFUS & SINGER 73

NO PIES FOR SUPPER 83

DAD'S LAST LESSON 89

EPHRAIM 95

A WOMAN'S TOUCH 108

WOMEN & WILDFIRES 115

PLENTY WOMAN 126

GRINGO 132

DAN'S DREAM 139

BAD EYES 146

CRAZY FRENCHMAN 155

HOME AGAIN 161

RANGERS & RADIATION 176

TENNESSEE 190

EPILOGUE. 205

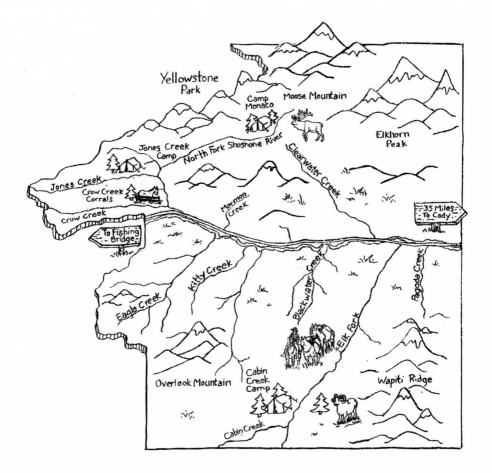

AUTHOR'S NOTE

The recollections and statements made in this book are the opinions of the author. It is my attempt to express my feelings, emotions, and understanding of the events at that time. If anyone is offended by anything written here, I apologize.

ACKNOWLEDGMENTS

Throughout my life, many people have helped me achieve personal goals. This book is a prime example. It would never have gotten out of my mind and onto paper if my cousin Elaine Zielinski hadn't insisted I start it. There were several helpful folks in the adult education classes I took to learn the mechanics of writing. Class members Warren Gehl and Jenny Thornburg's sincere input was invaluable and has led to an ongoing friendship. Jenna Caplette's nurturing instruction and tireless counseling has been and continues to be of immeasurable benefit. Kathy Tyers, a published and busy author, took time to read and edit my manuscript and provided me with insight and encouragement. Wendy Despain worked her amazing computer magic in order to prepare everything for publication. Of course, nothing would have gotten beyond my misspelled longhand account were it not for Plenty Woman's tireless two years of editing and typing.

I express again to all of you my heartfelt thanks.

PROLOGUE

I am the most fortunate of men, having lived the adventures of my childhood dreams. It was never easy and at times seemingly impossible. I am a common man, whose love affair with the West enabled me to guide many guests, friends, and family to life-long bonding experiences through Wyoming's high country.

Yes, it's true I grew up believing in heroes. During the 1940s and 50s, there were many such people, like Gene Autrey and The Lone Ranger, for a young country boy to hear on the radio. Their code of conduct was reinforced by the disciplined example of my parents and extended family. Yet, I was blindsided by an unexpected mid-life crisis. Foolishly, I turned it into a devastating train wreck before I could fully understand and implement those lessons into my own life.

Join me in your imagination. Let me guide you on a true-life adventure of pleasure and pain, of success and failure, from Michigan's rich farmlands to Wyoming's majestic Rocky Mountains. You'll meet great horses and mules I've known, talented cowboys I've ridden with, and marauding grizzly bears that decided not to kill me. I haven't borrowed material from anyone. I wrote it like I lived it. Your trip through this book will invoke many emotions; boredom will not be among them.

So, let's ride, Pard. We're burnin' daylight. You're about to learn what gittin' western is all about.

WESTWARD HO

My name, "Wiltse," is a gift and a burden from my father, Earl. During the 1960s, Dad was well known as the hard-driving President of Bricklayers Union Local 12 of Flint, Michigan. As was expected by Dad, being his eldest son, I followed in his brick-laying footsteps after graduating from Kearsley Agricultural High School in 1954. Yet during the spring of 1971, an irresistible restlessness overtook me.

I was convinced my success as a young mason contractor was due in part to Dad's prestige. My C&W Mason Contracting business was providing my wife, five children, and me with a very comfortable lifestyle. We had all the trappings of success—a large, three-bedroom brick home with two natural brick fireplaces, brick patio surrounding a large in-ground swimming pool, all sitting in the middle of forty acres of prime real estate, a cottage "up north," and a new green Ford station wagon—all paid for.

Still, I wanted to follow my own dream—to become successful at something entirely on my own, in some place where no-one knew the family name.

John Steinbeck wrote in his 1933 novel *The Red Pony,* "Westering has died out of the people. Westering isn't a hunger any more." It was with me! I had always been a fair hand at poker. At thirty-five years of age, I had come to the point in my life where I needed to bet or fold. I pushed all my chips into the pot.

◆　　　◆　　　◆

"So, now that you've bought yourself a ranch, you're going to need a horse, aren't you?"

I've wanted a horse for as far back as I can remember, I thought. *Of course I'm gonna need a horse.* But, just what did this windburnt old-before-his-time rancher have in mind?

We sat across from each other at his old oak table. The mid morning Wyoming sun streaming through the dusty kitchen window ricocheted off the scarred table top and filled his soon-to-be-mine old log house with its brightness.

We had just shaken hands in an agreement that made me the proud owner of an eleven section, run-down ranch in the shadows of Wyoming's Beartooth Mountains. The light June breezes carried the sweet aroma of new mown hay through the torn screen door.

"What do you have in mind?" I asked cautiously.

Ol' Harvey studied me for a couple of minutes with his bloodshot right eye. The smoke from the last half of his Marlboro curled up between his eyeglasses and his closed left eye. In a dry raspy voice somewhere between a whisper and a mutter, he answered "I've got a big bay gelding out there that'll teach you everything you need to know about riding."

"Out where?"

"Up on the upper range along Rocky Creek."

"What's he doing up there?"

"Just livin'."

At the time, I thought *he* thought I was greener than *I* thought I was, but I've come to realize that he was closer to the truth. Anyway I didn't want to act any greener by asking a lot more questions, such as "Is he broke?" "How do I catch him?" or "What's his name?" Incidental things like that don't need to be brought up at such an important occasion as buying your lifelong dream of a western ranch. *Heck*, I thought, *I've got a couple of pretty stout twelve- and thirteen- year-old sons. We can surely figure out one old range horse.*

"How much?" I asked.

"Well, being's how you and I are gonna be neighbors now, and being's how I sorta like you a little, and being's how the horse market in Cody is down a little right now, and I won't have to catch him and move him off your place, aaaaahhhhh, $150 cash."

Not wanting to appear too anxious, I hesitated a couple of minutes and doodled in my spiral notebook some, all the while thinking, *Duane, there is a lot you don't know about this horse or this man. 'Course, you've already bought his ranch. You might as well buy his horse and get on with your upcoming education! Besides, you have a plane to catch and it's a hundred-mile drive to the airport.*

"What's his name?"

"Cimarron."

I stood up, shook his hand, looked him in the eye, and said "Deal."

He walked me out onto the front porch and said, "Let me know when you want to move in."

"Be about three months," I replied over my shoulder as I hurried down the stone steps.

Later, while I cruised the friendly skies at 30,000 feet above the land of Butch Cassidy and the Sundance Kid, my mind whirled, caught up with the events of not only the last three days, but of the previous thirty-five years as well.

◆   ◆   ◆

My Mom and Dad had each been raised on hardscrabble farms cut out of northern Michigan pine forests. A year and half after their marriage in October 1935, the folks decided they wanted to offer the family they were planning more opportunities than were available in northern Michigan at that time. So, with much apprehension and some excitement, they said their goodbyes, packed their meager belongings and me, their new farm-born son, into their mortgaged second-hand 1935 Chevrolet, and set out down the dusty gravel road to a new way of life in the factory town of Flint one hundred miles to the south.

The strongest, most influential man in my male-dominated life was my father. Dad was a dark-complexioned, brown-haired man of medium build. He was strong-willed and physically strong as well, handsome with especially well-cared-for, attractive hands. The long, strong fingers and bulging veins were a rich tan color from a life of year-round outside work. No matter the task of the day, be it repairing the family car, laying brick, gardening, hunting or fishing, he thoroughly scrubbed his hands with hot water and Lava soap every evening. Dad was a great believer in self discipline and respect. He also believed there were only two choices in life—his way or the wrong way.

Dad was an incurable risk taker, not reckless but calculating. His motives were always to make life better for himself and his family. He worked very hard and turned every risk he took into advancement. He left the security of the family farm in northern Michigan for a job in the auto factory in Flint and rapidly was promoted to supervisor. Five years later, he was drafted into the Army, but World War II ended two weeks prior to his departure for boot camp.

As the building boom began after the great war, Dad left the auto shop for what he considered a better opportunity in the building trade. After a few years of struggle to master the masonry trade, he became a very successful and sought-after brick foreman. He would have as many as thirty men working for him on many of the biggest building projects in the booming Flint area.

My parents Earl and Dorothy Wiltse. The first professional photo they could afford. Picture made in 1945 to commemorate their 1935 wedding. Mom is wearing her wedding dress.

Good thing, too, because Dad now had six children at home to care for. He had come a long way since he first arrived in Flint some twelve years earlier. Jobs of any kind were hard to come by in 1937, and Dad was fired from the first one he landed. The Creamline Dairy didn't take kindly to Dad drag-racing their old ice truck against Catsman's coal truck down Flint's main street. Dad's outspokenness would get him fired from numerous jobs over the years.

But his compelling personality and considerable talent would get him hired as fast as he was fired. Since I was the eldest, Dad expected a lot from me and reminded me many times how I was to be a proper example for my younger two brothers and three sisters. Dad was a true believer of the old adage, "spare the rod and spoil the child." He was not slow to anger and seldom spared the rod.

In 1941, when Dad built our Sears Roebuck house, it was common to have a coal-fired furnace in the basement. We had one of those behemoths with octopus-arm duct-work snaking under the floor joists into the far corners of the upstairs. The accompanying dark, scary coal bin was a small, 8x12 unlit room, tightly sealed to keep coal dust from permeating the house when the coal man slid coal into it from his truck down a chute. When Dad was mad at me, instead of a whipping, sometimes he would banish me to the coal bin. My sisters stood in corners when they misbehaved. I was never sent to a corner. It was either a whipping or the coal bin. I always stood rigidly still in the total blackness. I didn't want to get dirty and incur further punishment from Dad, nor alert the bogey man I was sure lurked in the inky void. It was a very dark place, physically and emotionally.

He did cut me some slack one day, though, when I was three years old. Shortly after moving to Flint and before any of the other kids were born, we were living in a tent at a small campground behind the old Nightingale bowling alley, east of town. Mom and Dad had bought an unfinished kitchen table and four chairs. Evenings after work, Dad sanded and painted the furniture with oil base white enamel and trimmed it in red. There were no water-based paints in those days. I was fascinated by the brilliant beauty he created out of plain wood furniture. As was the custom in those days, Dad rode to work with others the next day. That meant the dull, old black Chevy sat parked under the big maple tree shading our tent. I was more excited than ever that evening. I couldn't wait for Dad to get home so I could show him how I had made the car "pretty."

I'll never know why Mom didn't catch on to me, but I painted the right side of that black Chevy with white enamel as far up as a three year old could reach, and I was really proud of the job I had done. Dad was crestfallen, but all he ever said about the incident was he should not have left the paint and brush where I could get them.

In the 1940s, being left-handed was just one of the things Dad viewed with suspicion. It was right up there with slothfulness, poor penmanship, and being disrespectful. My brother Larry had the misfortune of being born left-handed. It wasn't uncommon for Dad to forget or ignore that "defect." Exasperated, he gave up trying to teach little Larry how to tie his shoes one evening when I cautiously pointed out Dad's right-hand method was backward to Larry's left-hand mind.

Under Dad's strict tutelage, in the mid-50s I began my apprenticeship in the masonry trade. At eighteen years old, I was expected to perform and produce at a level of professional excellence that would stand me in good stead the rest of my life.

Dad and I had a special connection, a special relationship based on mutual love and respect that lasted a lifetime. We shared everything with each other—our hopes, our dreams, our successes, our failures, our frustrations.

We didn't always agree, but always spoke candidly and respectfully with each other as equals. Though he never spoke the word, there was a deep and abiding love for me that flowed from his sparkling brown eyes regularly. That look of love was indescribably empowering.

◆   ◆   ◆

With my nine-year-old hand, I shaded my tired eyes from the glare of the hot, late afternoon August sun. I had just stepped out of the old red brick Greyhound bus station in West Branch, Michigan. The driver had dutifully stopped in every town on M76—Saginaw, Bay City, Pinconning, Standish, Sterling, even Alger—since leaving Flint some six hours earlier.

I had long since eaten the sack lunch Mom sent with me, and I was hungry and tired of people I didn't know asking if they could help me. Uncle Ross was supposed to meet me here but was nowhere in sight. No matter. I just wished I hadn't brought so many clothes. It was going to be a job lugging the heavy old cardboard suitcase the two miles to Uncle Ross's creek-side home.

I had just taken a few steps when a familiar voice rang out, loud and clear enough for all the bus passengers to hear the dreaded, "Hey Shagnasty!!—Uncle Ross's favorite nickname for me.

Everyone was looking at me and laughing, especially Uncle Ross, as he stepped from his shady hiding spot behind an ancient maple tree across Main Street.

I lived for and considered it a great privilege to spend two weeks each summer visiting grandparents, uncles, aunts and country cousins "up north." Mom and Dad took all six of us kids "up home" for holidays, and Dad included me on his many hunting and fishing trips with his brothers and renegade brother-in-laws.

But these personal trips were different. Somehow they were special adventures just for me. All the relatives readily welcomed me into their homes and daily lives. From these multitudes of sources I was constantly and sternly cautioned not to become a teenage delinquent.

As a youngster and a teenager, I learned much about life and work through this large extended family. But my favorite place in the all the world in those years was Uncle Sam's. That's where I took my turn milking cows while listening to the announcer chant on an old radio in the dusty corner of the cow barn, "IT'S—THE—GRAND—OLE—OPRY!!! LET'R GO, BOYS!" Then we'd hand-milk those cows to the rhythm of Roy Acuff's "Wabash Cannonball," Lester Flatt and Earl Scruggs' "Foggy Mountain Breakdown," Hank Williams' "I'm So Lonesome I Could Die," Hank Snow's "I'm Movin' On," and a long list of other country legends of the golden age of country music.

I learned to skim the foam off a full bucket of milk with the back of my hand so the milk could be divided evenly in other buckets to feed the calves, and always be careful to keep a couple buckets of clean milk, the ones the cows hadn't stepped in, for Aunt Myne's kitchen. Cousins Bud and Dale were reasonably patient with me as I struggled to crank the handle on the old cream separator in the cellar. It was important to gain and maintain the proper rhythm so the separator bell dinged and the cream flowed uniformly. The cream, after all, was a prized portion of their family income. This was an era of great change in rural America, from the simpler, pastoral horse culture prior to WWII to tractors, electricity, telephones, indoor plumbing, milking machines, and even ball point pens after the war. No one I knew had a television.

I seemed to have one foot in each era. I relished the opportunity to be present at one of the last threshing bees, where I was part of the oat-shocking crew and took my turn at the old hand water pump in the back yard, pumping water for those stout, sweaty neighbors as they drank from their cupped hands and rinsed the chaff from their leathery faces, necks, and muscular arms.

Then we went to the long, heavy-laden dinner table, and I was invited by the men to sit with them as farm wives served steaming dishes of home-raised, deliciously prepared meat, potatoes and vegetables. There were no paper plates or plastic utensils. The silverware was solid, heavy, stainless steel. The plates came with some of the visiting wives, some flowered, many plain, but all solid cookery—except the tin ones. The glasses brimming with ice cubes and homemade lemonade ran the gamut of heavy tumblers to thin, glass, recycled jelly jars. My favorite flowery feed-sack shirt Mom had made me was a perfect material match to the dress the cute, long-haired, blonde girl that kept looking at me was wearing. The man that had invited me to sit next to him grinned and whispered in my ear, "Her name is Jeannie Hagelstein. Her dad owns the big Holstein farm north of here." This was the ultimate gesture of acknowledgment and acceptance, in my fourteen-year-old mind. I blushed and smothered the butterflies in my stomach with lumpy mashed potatoes and chicken gravy.

◆   ◆   ◆

It was hot and muggy that Saturday afternoon—July 28, 1956. My brother Larry, cousin Dan and I stood stiffly in the stuffy backroom of Otter Lake's quaint Episcopal Church. Our white tuxedo coats hung carefully on the backs of metal folding chairs. Our once-crisp white shirts stuck to our backs as we impatiently waited for my best friend and best man, John Stanton, to arrive. It was not like John to be late. We had gone through high school together, run track together, hunted and fished together, even double-dated. John was always dependable, but it was time to start the wedding procession. Just as we entered the small, cool Gothic-style chapel, breathless and a bit disheveled, John joined us.

It had been a struggle the last year to keep Betsy committed to our wedding date, but now as she entered the chapel on her Dad's arm, I thought, *Finally, my troubles are over.* She was a beautiful bride, and I truly felt we were as much in love as a pair of twenty-year-olds could be. I was 5'9," 135 pounds with thick brown hair and hazel eyes. Betsy had big brown eyes, a full figure, and sort of short all the way around—5'4,", short black hair, short on humor, and short-fused. I truly thought that she would soon realize how superior my light-hearted, practical, linear approach to life was and would be anxious to give up her inherited anger.

Early on, in addition to the pleasing way Betsy filled out her sweater, I was attracted to her education. She did well in school. Her Mom was an elementary teacher, and all of her relatives seemed to have or were in the process of acquiring college degrees. She lived in the small town of Otter Lake some thirty miles from our school. She didn't ride the bus to school but rode with her mom and only attended the last couple of years, so no one knew her very well. As I raised her veil for our wedding kiss, I thought I detected a hint of apprehension in her eyes.

In my mind, teachers and college-educated people were special, though none of my family were such. I had been offered an athletic scholarship at Albian College in Southwestern Michigan but wasn't confident enough in my scholastic skills to accept it. By the time we were married, I was in my third and final year as a bricklayer apprentice and had begun to understand that higher education doesn't automatically convert to wisdom.

While Betsy and her family were great at debating current events of political or religious nature, they never seemed to get much done but talk. They didn't even get along very well. Sometimes they'd be angry for months or years over something said or some position taken during one of their endless debates. Betsy's mother and grandmother each carried a lifelong anger and grudge against men. Without warning, the ancestral anger of the mothers was routinely visited upon their spouses and children.

It was at our wedding reception that the wheels began to fall off. I was laughing with some of my thirty-five cousins when Betsy found me and rather sternly said, "You'd better go straighten out those crazy uncles of yours."

"Why, what's the matter?"

"They are threatening to beat up my uncles."

"Where are they?"

"Over by the back door."

By the time I made my way through my dancing and dining clan, things were getting a little dicey at the back door. I got there just in time to hear Uncle Ross invite five of Betsy's uncles outside. Uncle Ross had his younger brother, Darrold, and my Dad with him. Uncle Sam was leaning against the wall nearby, half hidden by the smoke from his ever-present cigar, a mischievous smile teasing the corner of his lips. They had just enough beer in them to believe they were all ten feet tall.

"What's going on, Unc?"

"What's going on? I'll tell you exactly what's going on, Duane. I didn't fight half way across Europe to come home and listen to some loud mouth draft-dodger insult my favorite nephew. I'm gonna whip his ass. I'm gonna whip all their asses," he slurred.

"Unc. Unc. Wait a minute. I need you to do me a favor."

"In a minute. I got business to tend to."

"That's the favor I need."

"Huh?"

"Don't whip these guys tonight."

"But, Duane, you don't know what the son-of-a-bitch said about you."

"It doesn't matter, Unc."

"He said you weren't good enough for Betsy. That she could've done a lot better than you. They got no manners, Duane. I'm taking the lot of them outside for schooling."

Some folks said that Uncle's harsh mood swings were a result of too many days frozen in a foxhole during Germany's last offensive in the Battle of the Bulge. "Unc, listen a minute," I said. "It's my wedding, okay? I need you to let it go this one time. Besides, they're probably right."

"Bull shit."

"Come on, Unc. Let's go get something to eat."

For a moment, Unc stood his ground, clenching his teeth hard as he studied his options. Then the tight anger in his face was washed away by his big country-boy grin as he threw his arm around my shoulder and pleasantly said, "Aaaaahhh, OK, Shagnasty. Whatever you say."

He limped a little, now, on our way to the potato salad and chicken.

◆   ◆   ◆

With hands on her hips, my wife, Betsy, now a frazzled mother of five, asked incredulously, "You bought WHAT?" Her brown oxford slammed the kitchen floor.

I couldn't help but flinch. "I bought a horse."

The parted curtain focused some of the sun's last rays on the left side of her face, amplifying the harshness in her brown eyes. She threw down her dish towel and took a step towards me. "And what in God's name are you going to do with a horse all the way out in Wyoming? How far is that from Michigan anyway? I just knew you going hunting out there would lead to trouble. What were you thinking anyway?"

"I'm thinking it would be a good place to raise the kids."

"Wait a minute. Did you say raise the kids?"

"Just wait til you see that country, Betsy. It's awesome. The sun shines out there all the time, the air is clear, and the sky is a beautiful blue with white fleecy clouds. The creeks and rivers are so clean and pure you can drink out of them. There's antelope everywhere and no traffic. There's hardly any people, and the ones that are there are friendly and courteous. Just like I always imagined the West would be."

"You sound like you're suffering from jet lag. You need a good night's sleep. Get to work early in the morning and you'll be back to normal by the end of the week."

The Michigan sun had set now. I took a moment to visualize the Wyoming sun kissing the snow-capped peaks of the Beartooth Mountains good-night. Knowing I wouldn't be getting any good-night kisses, I took a deep breath and waded on in. "Not exactly."

"What do you mean 'not exactly?'"

"We will need to put everything up for sale, 'cause I also bought the ranch the horse lives on."

Betsy's hands flew back to her ample hips as she demanded, "Have you lost your ever-loving mind? I knew it. I just knew you were going to do something like this. I've seen it coming for a couple of years now. If you think you're gonna uproot me and the kids and drag us out west to God only knows where, you're badly mistaken, Buster. I'm putting my foot down here and now. I'm not going to leave my family and friends. I've lived my whole life here in Michigan and I'm not going to sell my home and go chasing after some half-baked dream of yours."

When Betsy put her foot down, it usually made a pretty good thud. At this point, our marriage had been all about what she needed. I had been trying to please her for fifteen years, but my best efforts weren't making her happy. When Betsy wasn't happy, no one around her was happy either. It was time for change.

This Wyoming ranch acquisition was going to require some time and some very careful family negotiations. *At least she's forgotten being mad about the horse. Now all I have to do is get her over being mad about the ranch.*

I was right about one thing. After a week of her brooding silence, it did take a lot of time to answer her questions, such as—How were we going to pay our bills? Where were the kids going to go to school? Were the schools as good as Michigan schools? What would we do if things didn't work out? What was the ranch house like? How far was it to town?

The children's responses to the plan to move west were as varied as their ages and personalities. The two older boys, Mark(13) and Jeff (12), were hellbent to go. Then there were the three little kids, as they were referred to by family members—Denise (8), Stephanie (7), and John (6). Denise was dead set against the whole idea. She was mad about it and would not be swayed. Stephanie did not like the idea either but was being swept helplessly along by me and the older boys. John just kind of be-bopped along in his own world. What's a six-year-old kid get to say anyway? Besides, his sisters kept him pretty well henpecked.

◆   ◆   ◆

Just before time for school to start in September, 1971, C&W Masonry was dissolved and the first house I ever built was sold. We said our tearful goodbyes to family and friends, which turned out to be much harder and more emotional from both directions than I expected. Especially with my Mom and Dad.

Dad had been dead set against the idea at first. But once we had talked it through, his position became as always: nothing ventured, nothing gained. Mom was just plain upset and no matter what I said, blamed the move on Betsy. Mom claimed because Betsy didn't get along with the rest of my family, she jealously wanted to separate the kids and me from them. Even remembering their own big move thirty-five years ago, they were reluctant to see us leave.

Friends and family have often claimed I could fall in the shit and come out smelling like a rose. I prefer to think that it's easy to make money in America. When I discovered I could buy an older tractor/trailer rig, and haul all our stuff in the forty-foot trailer for the same $3,000 the professional movers wanted, then sell the rig in Billings, Montana, for as much as I had in the whole deal, that became my moving plan.

At first light on September 6, 1971, grinning expectantly like guys on their first date, Mark, Jeff and I confidently climbed into that old green GMC cab-over tractor. The two boys thought it was really neat when I blasted the traditional family hunting signal from the air horn. The signal was usually given by blowing on an 45/90 shell casing and consisted of one long whistle, two short toots, another long whistle.

Then, with my best Ward Bond impersonation, I waved my left arm out the window and hollered, "Westward Ho!" Our great American adventure began as we rumbled out the driveway heading for Cody, Wyoming, some sixteen hundred weary miles to the west. Betsy, with the three little kids, reluctantly followed in the family station wagon.

We crossed the Mississippi our third day west. I couldn't help but think of the pioneers of the 1800s, who had passed this way only a couple generations before me. Their slow-moving wagons were resented and targeted with arrows and gunfire by many of that era's natives. Even though my "wagon" lumbered along at fifty miles an hour into the stiff prairie wind, an unheard-of speed for the pioneers, the current natives traveling on Interstate 80 resented our slow pace and targeted us with horn honking and finger waving. I didn't care. I was straining to see the Rocky Mountains, still two days west.

I suspect many of the pioneers and I shared similar dreams and visions. Hoping to build upon their foundation of self-reliance and accountability, I too sought a better future for my family.

There were only 300,000 people living in Wyoming in 1971. Not a single one of them knew me or my family name. Eighteen years earlier, several old-time brick layers that I had served my apprentice under had insisted that if I was diligent about learning the trade, no matter what happened, I could always support my family. I was about to put their theory to the ultimate test. Many friends and relatives in Michigan believed I was risking too much and soon would return broke and broken.

As we turtled our way across Nebraska, the traffic thinned. The headwinds did not. While Mark and Jeff napped in the hot smelly truck cab with me, our slow pace offered lots of time to think. My mind was full of dreams of the future and thoughts of the past.

How is it that sometimes just a word or a gesture, a smell or sound, can release a flood of memories and dreams that engulf a person's mind? The sweet aroma of new-mown hay, leaking through the battered old screen door three months previous when Harvey had asked, "Now that you've bought yourself a ranch, you're going to need a horse, aren't you?" had triggered just such a kaleidoscope in my mind.

From my favorite grade school stories of Dick and Jane visiting their uncle's cattle ranch in Wyoming to my own visits to my favorite Uncle Sam's farm in northern Michigan during the late forties and early fifties, I had always longed to live in the Rocky Mountains. In later years, the struggle in my mind was how to incorporate the lessons of hard work, optimism, honor, and integrity I saw in that closing era, and apply it to the times now thrust upon me. This was an era of excesses and of "me first"—the sixties, when I must now raise my children with no Uncle Sam's farm to visit.

Now, at thirty-five years old, most of my family and friends considered me to be successful. I had memorized my way through high school. I made a name for myself as a champion in track and cross country. My record time of four minutes, forty seconds (4:40) in the mile run was set a couple of years before Roger Bannister's sub-four-minute, world-record mile. My best two-mile cross-country time was ten minutes flat. Those school records lasted until my brother Larry coached the school to four State Championships some twenty years later.

I graduated third in the state from masonry trade school at nineteen years old, married, and built my masonry contracting into a thirty employee business. Those thirty guys respectfully nicknamed me "Boss."

But even after twenty years, the memories of Uncle Sam's farm and Dick and Jane's Wyoming had not faded away. As my older children began to reach their teens, my dilemma was how to protect them from the excesses of their time—how to teach them of nature, animals, life and death, of honor, integrity, compassion, accountability and self-worth.

If only they could see some of the things I saw while growing up. If they could understand that what they did or didn't do would positively or negatively impact their lives and the lives of every member of their family.

How do I achieve this balance in all our lives? Is it out there in Wyoming?

WYOMING CHALLENGES

Only 125 years earlier in 1896, the legendary frontier scout, big game hunter, hunting guide and entrepreneur, Buffalo Bill Cody, helped found the town of Cody, Wyoming. In time, Bill would establish the local newspaper, the *Cody Enterprise*, and his beloved TE Ranch twenty miles up the South Fork. At the main intersection in downtown Cody stands Bill's famous, opulent Hotel of the Rockies, "The Irma." Named after his daughter, The Irma is still a favorite gathering place for locals and visitors.

Bill had long brown hair and was known far and wide by the Indians as "Pahaska," which meant "long hair" in their tongue. When Bill built his guest lodge three miles outside of Yellowstone Park's East entrance, it became known worldwide as "Pahaska's Tepee." Over the years, the ownership of the profitable lodge changed from time to time, but the name always remained "Pahaska's Tepee." Nowadays, the US Forest Service has a trail head nearby called the "Pahaska Sunlight Trail." If you mount up there and ride twelve miles upstream along the North Fork of the Shoshone River, you come to a beautiful wilderness meadow. This is where Bill had his wilderness hunting camp. From here, he guided many dignitaries on big-game hunts in the early 1900s.

One of his most famous clients was Prince Rainier of Monaco. The prince bagged elk, bighorn sheep, and grizzly bear there with Bill in 1913. In honor of Prince Rainier's visit, Bill christened the site "Camp Monaco."

This was done by flattening an eighteen-inch square with an axe on the south side of a big Douglas fir. The words "Camp Monaco" were painted across the center with the US flag painted above the words, and the flag of Monaco and "1913" painted below.

◆   ◆   ◆

Top: Ranch house at Clark Wyoming. Bottom: Denise, John and Stephanie first day of school. Barn and Beartooth Mountains in background. Clark, Wyoming.

It was this rich hunting heritage and cowboy culture that irresistibly drew me to the scenic Cody country, a natural extension of the generations of hunting traditions of my own family dating back to 1623. When I was just four years old, Dad began teaching me the skills to become an accomplished outdoorsman—to be confident and competent in the woods or water day or night, to accurately anticipate weather fluctuations, and to read the stars as well as a compass. Guns, knives, and fire became tools to me. Little did I realize my knowledge of the old ways would be a big part of my future.

It was late afternoon on September 10, 1971, when I eased the tractor/trailer through the narrow ranch gate. The night before, we had camped at Chugwater, Wyoming, where the wind blew our tent down. The old truck pulled a lot of long tough hills that day. I was very relieved to have made it to the ranch before dark with only nerve-racking, overheating truck problems all day. For me it was not only relief, but a feeling of freedom and great exuberance, almost as if I had been there before—of coming home. I was enchanted with the view of the Beartooth Mountains barely five miles west of us and invigorated with lungs full of clear Wyoming air.

Yes! I was home!

In addition to the one hundred sixty deeded acres and seven thousand acres of BLM[1] and railroad lease, there were several turn-of-the-century buildings on the ranch. The house was built of big logs in 1900. It was two stories, rectangular, with two dormers on the front over a full-length, natural stone porch with stone pillars to support the porch roof. The house faced east; the first floor contained the kitchen, dining area with a coal fired space heater, two small bedrooms, a small bath, and living room with natural wood-burning fireplace. The space heater and fireplace were our only source of heat for Wyoming's -30 degree winters. The upstairs had a large bedroom on each end, with a large bath and storage cabinets in the center. The three boys slept in one room, the two girls in the other.

I set up a triangular tower outside the girls' bedroom window to serve as an emergency fire escape. From the attached TV antenna we could get a couple of snowy channels from Billings, Montana, ninety miles north of us. Sometimes I'd catch the kids climbing the tower late at night, sneaking in or out of the house. Lots of times, I missed the rascals.

---

1.   BLM = Bureau of Land Management, a federal government agency charged with stewardship of millions of acres of public land not governed by the U.S. Forest Service

The old barn, which had been built for milking cows, had concrete walls and floors that barely remembered once being painted white. In the wind, the jittery, rusty, corrugated-metal roof seemed to let in as much rain as it kept out. The low-roofed chicken coop, tool shed, and one-half below-grade ice house were all log with sod roofs. The two-car garage and old, original Clark Post Office buildings were log with cedar shake roofs like the main house.

Historically, in rural western communities, it was common for a post office building to be established on one of the more accessible ranches. The small, two-room building still had the mail slot in the door and an outside-entrance stone cellar that the rattlesnakes had claimed. I shot the snakes and built shelves in the cellar to store canned goods. Of course, having seen the snakes in there, none of the female members of the family would ever go down in the cellar again. Upstairs, I built two double bunk beds, a small bath, and kitchen. With an old pot-bellied stove I'd found abandoned in the chicken coop, the upstairs of Clark, Wyoming's old Post Office turned into a comfortable bunkhouse for guests—and later, even some hunters.

When we got to Wyoming, it was like going twenty years back in time. The scattered neighbors were all farmers or ranchers, friendly and helpful. Everyone gathered at the school regularly for dances, picnics, softball, and horseshoes.

One day, I asked Tom Laird, the old prospector, what the big straw stack behind his cluttered cabin was for. He took me through a hidden entrance and into the hollow stack that hid his working whiskey still. Talk about "white lightnin'!" The ol' boys in Tennessee had nothing on Tom.

Before we got our own milk cow, we got milk from the Denny's, a farming family about three miles downstream. I bought an old, used hand-crank cream separator from them. The kids weren't all that keen about hand-washing all the little screens and strainers, but they sure looked forward to the fresh cream on their Saturday morning fruit and pancakes. The kids thought I'd come unwrapped when I declared Tuesday evenings to be electricity-free nights. We used kerosene lamps, talked with one another, read books, played parlor games, did homework together, and went to bed early. Soon, the kids eagerly anticipated Tuesday evenings.

So far, my plan to realign our lifestyle was working.

As with all of life's decisions, there were plus and minuses to our move to Wyoming, and it didn't take long for the minuses to start shouldering their way to the front. I am not qualified to judge the accuracy of all the many tales describing Wyoming's strong, seemingly ceaseless winds, but I can attest to seeing it blow my three little kids off their feet as they tried to make their way back to the house after finishing their barn chores. They bounced around like little tumbleweeds, but I knew they would always come back. The wind would blow away large chunks of black top from the edge of the road we lived on, or soak me with water blown from the Clarks Fork River as I rode horseback three hundred yards from the river bank. The ferocious winds repeatedly froze the water pipes in the house during our first winter and knocked out our electricity regularly. In fact, our first Easter at the ranch, Betsy ended up cooking dinner on our little old Coleman camp stove. The wind even tipped over our forty-foot trailer before we got the furniture completely unloaded. With the help of our new neighbor and his backhoe, we uprighted the trailer with minimal damage. Then, according to plan, come Spring I sold the tractor/trailer for what we had in it. Yup, it's easy to make money in America.

The kids were settling in at school but having to play catch-up. It turned out the schools in Wyoming were more advanced and demanding than in Michigan. A school bus stopped near the house and took the three youngest to the Clark School about two miles from the ranch. It was a well-equipped two-room country school that taught through the sixth grade. The kids did well there. Another bus took the two older boys to the farm town of Powell, some thirty miles away, for junior and high school. Eventually all the kids did well in school and sports and graduated from Powell High School.

By and large, we were all having a ball. Denise and Stephanie were even beginning to accept our new lifestyle. There were times, though, when I came into the house all black and blue from trying to ride that damn Cimarron horse and found Betsy sitting on the couch crying.

It probably didn't help that during our first full summer—1972—we had eighty-two guests, most of them unannounced, all of them my family or friends from Michigan. Some showed up before others left. It was like a big, revolving, summer-long family reunion. Most of them stayed several days, touring Yellowstone Park and soaking up the ambience of the ranch and surrounding country. One day while in Cody buying supplies, I even unexpectedly ran into family members asking directions to our place. It was out of control.

Of course, all the guests wanted their picture astride some of the new horses I'd bought for the kids. Some of the brave ones even rode out with me to drive our small herd of black baldy cattle to fresh grass. They would laugh nervously and hang tight to the saddle horn whenever Cimmaron took a notion to dump me in the sage and prickly pear. His success rate had fallen off to about fifty percent. Whenever he did buck me off, he would just stand around smugly watching to see if I would get back up. Once I had gingerly eased back into the saddle, he'd calmly go about our business. He'd had his say. It seems we were both beginning to understand and respect each other's stubbornness.

◆   ◆   ◆

By that fall, our financial reserves were severely depleted. Betsy wanted me to get a 9-to-5 job in town. One of the reasons I had left the rat race in Michigan was because I noticed a lot of the rats were winning. I had come to Wyoming for a more fulfilling lifestyle. I didn't see it clerking in some store from 9 to 5. So, over her strenuous objections, I invested the rest of our savings in a KOA ranch camp franchise and the materials to build a camp ground.

Bill Dansby, one of the favorite teachers at the Clark school, was also a pretty fair carpenter, who built small homes and such during the summer. Bill agreed to bring a carpenter friend of his, Hanson Murray, and spend his Christmas break from school to help me get the campground building built. It was a simple 32x60 rectangle that housed the convenience store, washers, dryers, showers and toilets. We completed most of the building during the holidays and had all forty sites completed by the time tourist season began. Like most new businesses, it started slowly. It took three years of hard work to show a profit.

During that time, I fell back on my masonry trade to pay the bills. Every member of the family worked hard and contributed to the success of the Kampground. We soon discovered the profit was in recreation and food. My experience at Uncle Sam's farm as a kid, plus the response of our many guests to our animals and lifestyle, convinced me there were many families out there looking for just such an experience. I decided our Mountain Dew (D.E.W., named for my initials) Ranch Kamp would become a dude ranch for campers. We developed a five-day plan around a different and special horseback trip each day. We had a daily family float trip on the nearby, pristine Clark's Fork River; we had evening steak rides overlooking the river; we had sourdough pancake breakfasts. Everyone was encouraged to participate in daily ranch chores, from milking the cow to feeding the old sow and her baby pigs, even watching calves being born, branding, haying, everything. We did it all.

KOA's corporate office is in Billings, Montana. It wasn't long before we began to get visits from curious upper-management types. Their records showed that while we were one of the smallest campgrounds in the system, our guests spent more money with us per head per day than almost any other of their operations. They ended up using our recreation program as a model for their new recreation plan for all KOA campgrounds.

After laughing at me that first summer, the next summer many of our neighbors invited us to bring our "dudes" over to their places as well to help with their chores. Sharing our large, 30x50 swimming pool, showers, washers and dryers with our neighbors was greatly appreciated by them. On many Saturday nights, we and our guests were treated to some great old-time sing-along music by these same neighbors. Some traveled twenty-five to thirty miles to play their banjos, mandolins, guitars and accordions around our campfire. The secret ingredient that made all this work so successful was my energetic and imaginative kids. Just like the kids in my Dick and Jane grade school books, my five kids loved to race their horses over the range and rode like wild Indians any chance they got.

John rode his sorrel Shetland pony bareback and was sensitive to the bigger kids on their bigger horses with saddles making fun of him. John defiantly named his pony "Razor Blade" because John insisted, as only a seven year old can, that Razor Blade was the sharpest horse in the West. Contrary to his mother's strict instruction that he was never to ride alone, he repeatedly slipped off by himself. Late one afternoon John came walking stiff-legged, with arms held away from his hurting body, to the house for help. There were literally hundreds of prickly-pear needles sticking out of him. As Betsy gingerly plucked with the tweezers, John sobbingly related how he fell off his horse at full gallop and landed in a patch of cactus.

Betsy asked him why he had been riding by himself and where the fall happened. John wisely ignored the first half of the question and answered, "You just go along the fence out there behind the barn til you come to the bald cactus. That's where."

They were always bringing some orphan animal to the barn. Baby antelope, raccoons, fox, you name it. They were having the times of their lives and learning a lot, too—not just from nature and the animals they cared for, but from the many and varied guests they met and spent time with at the campground, adults as well as kids from all over the United States and some foreign countries. Many of these families came back year after year, and we became very good friends.

However, the adventure that would be life-altering for each of us was about to begin

CABIN CREEK

It began on a cold, blustery day in January 1973. While in Cody running errands, I stopped into the old Cody Saddle Shop to check on a saddle I had left for repair some weeks earlier. The owner, John Thevenoff, busy at his work bench in the back, assured me he'd be getting to it soon. John had a big old pot-belly wood-burning stove off to one side of the store, which was a favorite warming spot for cold customers such as myself. This time of year, there was usually a number of locals sitting around the stove discussing weather, turns of events, etc.. Current-event subjects in the Cody Saddle Shop usually consisted of cattle and horse prices, prices of hay, rodeos, and hunting. The five chairs were taken by fellows that by their dress looked to be either ranchers, cowboys, hunting guides, or a combination of all. Bill Venakamp was the only man I recognized. Bill had unbuttoned his Carhartt rancher coat and was standing next to the stove, warming his hands.

I had met Bill when I bought some hay from him earlier in the fall. Bill was a little older than the rest of us there. He had a nice, well-kept little ranch about fifteen miles south of town along the South Fork of the Shoshone River. He ran a small hunting operation from his camp on Fish Hawk Creek, which was about forty miles west of town on the North Fork of the Shoshone River. As Bill's wife was not well nowadays, he was looking to slow down some and stay closer to home, so he had put his hunting business up for sale. He had told me about his decision when I bought the hay from him.

Before heading back to the front of the store, I stopped at the stove for a moment. Bill nodded to me, and I asked if he'd had any luck in selling his camp. He said he thought maybe he had. Some old kid from Oregon was pretty interested and looked like a likely prospect.

I nodded to the rest of the men. Just before I reached the front door, John appeared and asked in a hushed tone, "You interested in buying a hunting camp, Duane?"

"I don't think so, John. I've never really thought much about it," I answered.

"Well," he says, "I know where there's a good one, and I suspect it can be bought right." He pushed the door open for me.

"Thanks, John, I'll keep it in mind," I replied as I leaned into the wind coming off Rattlesnake Mountain and right down Main Street. I tried to concentrate on the rest of my errands, but I couldn't get the idea of owning a hunting camp out of my mind. I remembered as a youngster listening in awe to my Dad and uncles telling hunting stories about my Grandfather Fred's whitetail hunting camp in Michigan's Jack Pine Plains. To me, being an outfitter would be the ultimate achievement.

I had become acquainted with a few big game outfitters and hunting guides besides Bill. In fact, I had been renting extra horses for our campground recreation program from Glen Fales. Glen was highly respected longtime outfitter in Cody. I admired Glen and others like him and longed for a similar lifestyle. But I pushed the daydreams from my mind with some logical questions such as, "Where would I get the money to buy such an operation? I'm a dude from Michigan myself, how would I get any customers?" *I can only imagine Betsy's reaction to such an idea,* I thought as I returned to the saddle shop. I was relieved to find John alone, repairing tack in the cluttered back room.

"It always piles up in the winter time." He gestured to the accumulation of saddles, head stalls and harnesses surrounding him. "What can I do for you?"

"Tell me more about that outfitting business you mentioned that was for sale."

"Well, I don't know a whole lot, except that Bob Adams sold his camp up Elk Fork two years ago to Jack Wolf and hasn't been paid one red cent yet. Bob was in here a few days ago, goin' on about how he was going to have to find another buyer. It's a helluva camp, Duane. Bob's been up there since 1947, lots of game. I bet you could write your own terms with him right now."

I thanked him for his time and information and headed home. I didn't mention the hunting-camp conversation to Betsy or anyone else. Over the next month, I longingly thought about the possibilities of buying Bob's camp and building an outfitting business, yet I knew there was very little chance to make any money in the business. Like ranching or cowboying, it's the lifestyle it offers—not the money—that makes it appealing.

Every scenario I had worked out with paper and pencil came out the same way. If I worked hard and managed well, the best I could hope for was to break even. There's just so much overhead in a wilderness horseback camp that there is little or no yearly profit. I decided if I went into the big game outfitting business, my objectives should be: 1) to become one of Wyoming's most successful and sought after outfitters; 2) to include my children and use the experience to further bond with them; 3) to be able to spend lots and lots of time horseback in Wyoming's Rocky Mountains and at least pay all the expenses for my love affair with the high country.

I hadn't spoken with Betsy or Bob Adams about my thoughts and didn't have any real plans to do so. Then one day I happened to run into Hanson Murray on the street in Cody. One of the first things Hanson said to me was, "Congratulations on buying Bob's camp."

"What do you mean?"

"Well, I heard you bought Bob's camp. Didn't you?"

"No. I haven't even talked to Bob about it."

"Well, it's damn good country, Duane, lots of game, big country. If you do buy it, I'll be glad to help you get started. You know, show you the country, even guide a year or two."

With butterflies of excitement in my stomach, I thought, *Wow, maybe with Hanson's help I could pull this off.* "Thanks, Hans. I'll let you know."

"You bet," he said as he climbed into his pickup.

Forgetting all about why I had gone to Cody in the first place, I headed out to Bob's ranch east of town. I found him pitching fresh hay to a corral full of yearling calves.

Bob had been riding the Elk Fork country for twenty-six years. He had successfully outfitted and guided hundreds of hunters for elk, deer, bighorn sheep, and grizzly bear. But as a result of his growing dependence on square-bottle visions, in recent years his business had dwindled considerably. The two years of inactivity due to the defunct sale finished off what little business may have remained. So he was in a mood to make a deal, yet he still wanted all he could get and offered me the same deal he had with Dick Wolfe, which was $35,000, with $10,000 down and $25,000 balance paid off over ten years at $2500 per year plus eight percent interest on the unpaid balance. Bob would hold the paper.

I told him I'd think about it and get back to him. Later when I explained the offer and my interest in it to Betsy, she was even more against it than she had been about the campground and refused to even discuss the possibilities. In fact, she didn't speak to me at all for over a week. I had a couple of lengthy long-distance calls with Dad about the prospect of buying the camp, the conclusion of which was, "nothing ventured, nothing gained." So, without Betsy's blessings and in spite of her objections, I set out to talk with Bob Adams again.

I figured it was best to catch him in the morning before his drinking caught up with him in the afternoon. Bob had just finished his morning chores and was sipping coffee at the kitchen table when I arrived. What else may have been in his old chipped mug I'm not sure. As he let me in the kitchen door, he graciously offered me a battered enamel cup.

The room was small and old but toasty. I wrapped my chilled hands around the warm cup and backed up to his glowing wood stove. "Thanks, Bob. If you have a minute, I'd like to visit some more about your camp."

"Sure. What would you like to know?"

"What about business? Do you have any hunters booked for this year?"

Bob's bleary eyes seemed to lose focus as his gnarled fingers fiddled with his gray, drooping mustache. "Well, you know that damn Wolfe and his partner Royal had the business for two years and haven't done anything much with it. I can give you some names and phone numbers of guys that used to hunt with me, though."

"How many years ago?"

More mustache fiddling, more coffee poured. Finally, pushing his crumpled, stained Stetson back just a tad, he confessed, "Oh, four or five, I guess."

"How about saddles, pack gear, camp stuff?"

"Oh, hell. I got lots of that shit."

"What about horses?"

"I got twelve of the best damn mountain geldings you ever seen."

"How old are they?"

"Seven year old, kid-broke, and bomb-proof."

"All twelve of them are seven?"

"Well, give or take a year or two on a couple of the sonsabitches, I guess."

"Where are they?"

Bob got up from the table and stepped over to the wood stove, as if to warm his hands. "They's wintering up on Trout Creek. You wanna see 'em?"

"Maybe later. What about the rest of the gear and stuff?"

"It's all out here in the barn. Come on, I'll show you." Bob pulled on his well-worn Carhartt jacket and reset his Stetson.

Well, Bob was sure right about his tack and gear. It was mostly old, worn-out shit. I suspected his remuda[1] was in similar shape.

"How much of a job would it be to see the horses, Bob?" I asked.

"Oh, not much at all. We can just ride up in those hills west of the drainage and I'll fire off a couple a shots from my 45. Jim Beam, Southern Comfort, or Johnny Walker'll come a'running right in," he stated emphatically as he patted his right hip.

---

1.   remuda: extra saddle horses

"I've never ridden that country, Bob. From the road it looks like it's pretty good size."

"'Bout five or six thousand acres, I reckon."

It's going to be a little more of a project to see Bob's horses than he thinks, I thought. *Besides, truth be known, like much of the tack and gear, they probably all need to be replaced anyway. The most important element of this whole deal is the Forest Service permit. No new ones are being issued, and Bob's old original permit covered over a hundred square miles of pristine hunting country.*

With Hanson's help, and Mark and Jeff, I knew that over time we could build a business of satisfied clients. I already had some good tack and horses we had been using at the campground. I could upgrade and replace Bob's old stuff and horses over time as well.

I decided to make him an offer I could live with. I began by pointing out that his deal with Wolfe and Royal, while looking like a good deal for him, had turned sour for everyone.

"I'll tell you what I think I can afford and if you can live with it, I'll make it work for both of us, okay?"

"Sure," he answered.

"First, the twelve horses stay on the pasture where they are til I can use them at the campground June 1 at no cost to me."

"No problem," he said.

"All the tack and gear you showed me goes into the pot, nothing held back. And most importantly, the Forest Service permit transfers and I get my outfitter license before I pay you anything."

"Yeah."

"The total price will be $25,000, no money down, annual payment of $2500 plus six percent interest on unpaid balance, payable January 1 each year. That way I can pay you from the income of the preceding year's hunts. You hold the paper and if I can't make a full payment any year, I can just pay the interest and the contract stays good."

"God Damn, Duane! I had a lot better deal with Wolfe two years ago," Bob exclaimed.

"Yeah, but remember, Bob, two years ago you turned over a client list to him. Right?"

"Right!"

"And all your seven year old horses were two years younger, right?"

Bob sat down on a bale of hay. I detected a sigh and slight sag in his shoulders. "Uh, huh."

"And Wolfe hasn't paid you anything, right?"

"Yeah, but—"

"So this is a better deal for you 'cause you'll get your money from me."

"Yeah, but, how about just a little something down, Duane? Damn!"

"If I had it, Bob, I'd be glad to give it to you. But all I got is a dream and two sons to help me achieve it."

"Hmmmmmmmm." He rubbed his chin and looked directly into my eyes. I looked him right back. I had studied on this project and deal for weeks and was convinced I could make it work. I wanted to make it work. I wanted to become a high country outfitter.

It must've shown, because after a couple of thoughtful minutes, Bob got up and said, "By God, I believe you. Let's drink on it."

"I appreciate the offer, Bob, but I don't drink much. Let's shake on it." He stuck out his paw and said, "Deal."

Mark and Jeff at 16 and 15 years old had grown into a pair of strapping, confident, handsome young men. They wore their tight curly hair in an enormous Afro style that was the envy of their peers, especially the girls. However, they could wrestle and play football, castrate and brand calves or ride bucking horses with the best of them. They were getting very close to being able to out-shoot and out-hunt me. All they needed was a little seasoning to temper and channel their excitement and exuberance during a hunt. Soon we would all be learning the fine art of packing and riding horses in difficult dangerous mountain terrain in all kinds of weather. The boys were thrilled to hear of my deal with Bob Adams.

Betsy was not.

◆   ◆   ◆

As June approached, I made arrangements with Bob us to ride up Trout Creek and gather my new horses. Cimarron had become Mark's favorite mount. He was still the toughest, most experienced horse we had, so I loaded him into our horse trailer and met Bob at Trout Creek corrals.

It was a cold, windy day with occasional darts of rain stabbing our cheeks. We had ridden about an hour and not seen a sign of a horse when Bob pulled up. We were at the upper end of a 6000-acre pasture with most of the hills and broken country below us. I thought Bob looked a little apprehensive as his bleary eyes scanned the country around and below us. "I guess I oughta try a couple of shots," he murmured. Our saddle horses jumped and fidgeted as the echoes of gunfire bounced around the sheer palisade cliffs above us.

After five minutes or so of waiting and watching, it became obvious to even Bob the lost horses were not going to come running up to greet us with their tails wagging, anxious to go to work.

"We can cover more ground if we split up," Bob finally said. "Why don't you go around there to the West and I'll ease around to the East. Gather every horse you can find and drive them down to the corral by the trucks. I'll do the same and meet you there in, say, about three hours."

"Okay," I replied as Cimarron responded to my heels.

For the first half hour or so, I'd see Bob occasionally as I zigged and zagged in and out of coulees and draws and over ridges. By the time I finally found five startled horses, I hadn't seen Bob for some time.

No matter. I figured even though I only had five head, I better get them down to the corrals before I lost them. Bob probably had the rest, anyway. If not, we could always make another circle. I was hoping these five were the wrong ones anyway, small, scrawny pitiful things that they were.

By and by, I got them off the hills and locked in the corrals. Bob not only didn't have any horses in the corral, he was gone. Truck, saddle horse, trailer and all.

That made me mad. What kinda guy leaves his partner up in the hills and goes to town without even so much as a "fare thee well?" I decided right then and there I was having no more to do with Mr. Adams. I had been wondering about a guy who named all his horses after his favorite whiskey anyway.

Now I knew.

The hell with him, I thought as I loaded my horses in the trailer. *The boys and I will do it ourselves.* Sure enough, I spotted Bob's truck parked at one of the bars as I drove through town.

The next Saturday when the boys were out of school, the three of us went up. In a couple of hours, we'd found and gathered the rest of the string. The whole bunch were thin, wormy, and in desperate need of care. We wormed and shod everything and then began to get acquainted through grooming, feeding and riding. There was one horse that began to stand out. He was a good lookin' intelligent guy with a great attitude and personality, a bay with four white socks and a blaze face. We all referred to him as "that blazed-face horse," and he quickly became a favorite of everyone. In a short time, the blazed-face horse became affectionately known simply as "Blaze."

◆   ◆   ◆

In Wyoming, the spring runoff gets plumb serious during the month of June. By the 4th of July, the rivers in the high country are usually safe to cross horseback. So early in July, 1974, with lunch-filled saddlebags, Mark, Jeff and I set out up the Elk Fork trail to find our newly purchased hunting camp site.

As we rode along, we all marveled at the beautiful country, excitingly pointing out to each other features of landscape and places we bet elk could be found. The one spot high up on the mountain that intrigued all of us featured a long narrow waterfall disappearing behind a thick stand of tall fir trees. We just knew there was a hidden sanctuary up there, teeming with game. Some hiker a year before had apparently discarded a pair of socks on the lip of the medium size draw we rode through. The spot is known to this day to the three of us as "Dirty Sock Draw."

Mark was riding Cimarron. Jeff was astride another bay I had bought for him a couple years earlier. The bay moved with a fluid grace that was a pleasure to ride, whether walking up the trail or at full gallop chasing antelope. We called him Lightfoot. Usually we would have Lightfoot up front, as he always set a good pace. But I had an important reason to put Blaze up front on this trip. We just made the fourth river crossing about two hours into our exploration when Jeff said to me, "You never been in this country, Dad, right?"

"Right," I answered.

After a short pause he asked, "So how are we going to find this camp, then?"

"I don't think we are. Blaze will find it. He's the smartest horse in old Bob's string and he's been there many times. I'm betting he'll tell us when we get there."

"Sure glad we brought lunches," Jeff responded good-naturedly. We made the fifth river crossing and Blaze confidently continued upstream, though there wasn't much trail to follow any more. We passed through Bear Gulch, as stated by a moss-encrusted Forest Service sign with the corner bear-bit off. As we came out of the dark timber in the gulch and around a sunlit sage brush hill, a panorama of snow-capped mountains, grassy ridges and sparkling mountain streams opened before us as if by magic. It was like entering a secret enchanted world of yesteryear.

I wanted to stop and soak up the view awhile, but Blaze seemed intent on his mission, and I feared if I interrupted his focus and rhythm he might become confused. On slack rein, Blaze traveled on around the hill, but instead of continuing on upstream, he left what little trail there was and veered to the right. He worked his way down to a small drainage through quakies[2] and junipers until we struck a small, white-water mountain stream shrouded in Ponderosa pine.

We had already crossed eight or ten such streams, but Blaze didn't cross this one. Instead, he headed up through the pines. Ten minutes later, he stopped at a small, secluded mountain meadow on the bank of the stream, dropped his head, and began to graze on the fresh green grass.

"I believe we're here, boys," I said. Before I got Blaze securely tied to a tree, Jeff had already found a small wood stove stashed in some tall sage. Next, Mark found a stone fire ring in the tall grass. By the time I had the lunches out of the saddlebag, they were running around the outside of the meadow, calling out their finds of buckets, frying pans, tables, and so on.

As we ate our sandwiches, we looked at a Forest Service map I had brought along and discovered we were on "Cabin Creek." We heartily agreed that from that moment on we would be known as Cabin Creek Outfitters and Blaze would have an honored position in our new business.

◆   ◆   ◆

At the ranch, the campground was getting busier and busier. Later that summer, Russell Tompkins and family of four from Windham, New York, stopped for an overnight on their way to Yellowstone Park. They ended up staying a week with us. It was one of those rare occasions in life when one is privileged to meet and bond with some very special people. The Tompkinses were such a family. Their children and ours hit it off right away. Wives Bunny and Betsy had a lot in common, as Bunny was a school teacher and was married to an independent non-conformist who made his living logging with horses in the Adirondack Mountains in upstate New York, and who bought and sold horses and mules on the side.

After two years of college, Betsy had done some substitute teaching. Then she'd married a man who considered quality of life and personal relationships more important than a 9 to 5 job. Discussing their personal trials and tribulations brought on by such exasperating men gave the women some common ground.

I always considered Russell to be a bigger rascal than me, though. After all, he was the former Alaskan bush pilot who had his license revoked because he used his wife's urine sample to hide his diabetes from the licensing board. Course they

---

2.   quakies: aspen trees

picked up right away there was no way Russell could be pregnant, so out the door they threw him.

Russell and I appreciated each other's personality, demeanor and abilities. That appreciation lasted after the children grew up and went their separate ways and long after Betsy and Bunny quit writing to each other. For me, it lasted long after Russ's premature death due to his diabetes.

I have many fond memories of Russell in hunting camp during those first years. The best horse wrangler I ever knew, he could read horses like a book. I never worried about the remuda or was short a horse when Russ was in camp. Even though he was nearly blind near the last, I could tell he really appreciated me driving all the way to Windham to spend a couple of days with him. The drive from Wyoming to upstate New York was long, but the drive back to Wyoming was long and sad.

◆　　　◆　　　◆

Jeff Wiltse and Scott Heny packing in to Cabin Creek camp.

Upon returning from finding our camp site on Cabin Creek, I bought a book entitled *Horses, Hitches & Rocky Trails*, written in 1959 by an old-time packer from Dubois, Wyoming, Joe Back. Initially, the boys and I read and reread this book. It became our packing bible. For several years, one of us always had it in his saddlebags.

Now, even after thirty years of packing, I not only couldn't improve on it, I appreciate and understand it more than ever. In anticipation of my first professional elk hunt, which was set to begin on September 10, 1974, I decided to pack some canned goods into camp in mid-August. The plan was to get a little experience packing and a head start on the upcoming hunt.

One of the "horses" we got from Bob Adams was a mule of questionable mental capacities. In an effort to find out more about this no-name mule, Mark, Jeff and I led him into Cabin Creek laden with about one hundred pounds of canned goods. We tied our saddle horses to trees and while Jeff held the mule's lead rope, Mark and I gingerly removed the lash rope and were congratulating each other on our fine job of packing.

Suddenly, bellering and bucking, the mule went ballistic. Jeff dug his heels in and hung to the lead rope with both hands and was holding his own at first. But every time the mule bucked, he jettisoned several cans of peaches, tomatoes, blueberries or Crisco high into the air. Shortly those damn cans started raining down on us. One of the first creamed corn bombs creamed Jeff, hitting him on top of the head and knocking him flat.

The "retard" was now loose and bucking a circle around the meadow. From the rear, he reminded me of a WW II destroyer shooting off depth charges. Jeff sat on the ground holding his head and said, exasperated, "God damn! Look at that counterfeit idiot buck!"

When the mule had finally bucked off all but his pack saddle, he quit as suddenly as he started. It was not uncommon for guides or wranglers to stumble upon an occasional treasure of canned goods scattered in the most unlikely places for the next couple years. From that day, the no-name mule was known as "Nitro."

My love affair with Wyoming's Rocky Mountains began to get serious during my first western hunting trip in 1968, and I am not over it yet. To finance the courtship, I went into the outfitting business, which was about to begin with disastrous results.

Duane riding Sage Fire leading grandson Luke and brother Larry across the swollen Elk Fork river. Heading into Cabin Creek camp.

A HORSE CALLED
THUNDER

As good as his word, Hanson met me at the Elk Fork trail head early on the morning our first elk hunt was to begin. Hanson was an experienced packer, and in no time we were headed into our previously set-up camp. Though we only had two hunters this time, all of us needed experience. Betty Gray, a neighbor, would be our cook. Art Clark, a friend from church, would tend camp in exchange for a chance to kill an elk for his own freezer. Russell Tompkins would wrangle horses just because he wanted to.

The hunters, Don and Dave, were brothers from California, a couple of really nice guys. Hanson would guide Dave, and I would guide Don. That, we felt, should allow us plenty of spare time for Hanson to show me how to get from place to place up there.

On our first evening's hunt, Dave bagged a nice, fat spike bull. Don missed a five-point bull four times. Around the supper table that night, we all boasted about our early success and felt sure we would fill Don's tag soon. The next day dawned clear and bright, as we eagerly set out to pack in Don's meat. We decided that Hanson would take Dave plus Russell and Art, each leading a pack horse back to the kill site, and load the two pack horses with the meat, while I took Don around the other side of the drainage in hopes of finding more elk to hunt.

We had split up for over an hour when I unexpectedly heard gunfire from Hanson's group. Studying them through my binoculars some three miles across the drainage, I could make out one man who appeared to be sitting on the ground with another standing just above him. Further up the hill were the other two men with the horses. About that time, I saw white smoke puff from the rifle of the standing man. A minute later, we heard the shot. I couldn't tell what was wrong, but one thing was clear. Your hunting partner doesn't idly fire into the air when you are trying to hunt unless he has a big problem. I told Don to follow slowly and safely as he could, but I needed to get over there fast. Something was damn sure wrong.

On the way over, I remembered Don asking me at church one Sunday morning, "Duane, would my heart bother you if I went to the mountains for elk season with you this fall?"

"Of course not, Art. Why should your heart bother me?"

"Well, I mean because of my heart attacks, you know."

Now that flip answer offered so easily weeks ago thundered into my mind as I stared at Art's crumpled and twisted body lying in the jumble of rocks at my horse's feet. I had ridden Surprise, my big Appaloosa gelding, unmercifully hard the last hour to get to the scene of the wreck. Still mounted and panting from the exertion that accompanies all efforts at 9,000 feet of elevation, I exclaimed, "What's the matter, Art?"

Opening his eyes, he gasped through clenched teeth, "My damn leg's broke, Pard."

"What do you mean, your leg's broke? What happened?"

"I mean it's busted. Smashed to smithereens and hurts like hell. Damn it. Get off that horse and give me a hand. I'm hurt bad." Relieved that it wasn't his heart, Hansen and I splinted his leg with sticks and neckerchiefs. I remembered Art had barely survived the last of his three heart attacks, and that was when he was at home in Cody, only minutes from the West Park Hospital. Now he lay on a steep, boulder-strewn mountainside in the head of Burnt Timber Creek, some thirty-five miles west of Cody by car and another fifteen miles south up the Elk Fork River by horse. If he suffered another attack up here because of shock, excitement or fatigue, he would die for sure. We were many hours of hard horseback riding from the nearest phone and further yet from any medical assistance.

We used sticks to scratch out a reasonably level spot to lay Art and discussed what we'd have to do to save his life. The accident had happened about noon, and it was 1:00 p.m. already. Darkness and the early autumn chill that comes with it to the high country in September promised to be our immediate enemies.

Quickly, we decided Hansen would stay with Art. I would ride to camp and return with blankets, food, water, and most importantly, Art's heart medicine. Russell would make the grueling three-hour ride to the telephone to call the Park County Search and Rescue helicopter stationed in Greybull, about sixty miles east of Cody.

Art grabbed my pant leg. "Duane, whatever you do, don't forget my medicine. I am not feeling very good," he whispered as I prepared to mount up.

His steel-gray eyes were moist with pain and fear. Art was fifty-six, not a large man, maybe 5'8" tall and 150 lbs. soaking wet, but very tough, both physically and mentally. He'd been orphaned at an early age, played semi-pro baseball around the Big Horn Basin during his late teens and early twenties, worked on farms and ranches and hunted elk in the Big Horn and Beartooth Mountains all his life. Right now, he needed help—medical help, and lots of it. With every passing moment, his situation grew more critical.

I spurred Surprise. He sensed my urgency and responded instantly, leaping and clawing at the mountain, sometimes nearly out of control, as we headed back down the mountain and toward camp too fast. *There's going to be a lot of good horse flesh abused before this night is over,* I thought.

I knew Art didn't have much of a chance surviving the torturous hours that lay ahead, and my heart ached for him. My human limitations frustrated me. If only I could fix it for him, like he was always fixing broken things around camp for me. *That's where he should be right now,* I thought, *around camp fixing things and catching trout for supper. Not lying out there in the cold rocks all busted up, gritting his teeth against the pain racking his body and worried sick about his pump quitting.*

We had gotten carried away with yesterday's hunting success. When Art said he'd like to go up and help pack out the meat, I hadn't given it a second thought. Now we were in a real jam.

The rest of our horses were peacefully grazing on the flats along the Elk Fork River. As Surprise and I came off the mountain in a cloud of dust and rolling stones, they threw their startled heads in the air, with alerted eyes and ears riveted on the exhausted, foam-covered Appaloosa and sweaty rider.

I gathered the remuda and rode into camp at a high lope. The horses thundering into the corral brought Betty to the hitching rail with concern on her face. As I dismounted, a quick glance at my watch reinforced my concern. It was 3:00 p.m. already.

Shouting, "Art's hurt," I thrust a list of supplies I needed into her hand, tossed her a pair of saddle bags, and told her to hurry.

We had changed the name of the horse Bob Adams called "Johnny Walker Red" to "Big Red." Big Red always made catching him a contest. But this afternoon he stood still in the camp corral as my first loop settled gently over his head. It took me barely five minutes to throw a fresh blanket on him and switch my saddle from Surprise, who hadn't moved from the spot where I dismounted. He just stood spraddle-legged, head down, his sides heaving in and out. I threw the packed saddlebags over my shoulder and swung into the saddle. I asked Betty to take care of him as I spurred Big Red through the timber and towards the long climb back up to Art.

Russell had been riding a young, green-broke colt that morning, so he was a few minutes behind me coming into camp for a fresh horse. Before I rode out of sight I saw him catch a medium-size black horse we called "Thunder." Thunder was half Morgan, half Mustang and all heart—exactly what Russell would need for his race to the trail head. There he would jump into his truck and drive to Hansen's cabin on Green Creek for the nearest phone, over some fifteen miles of narrow, twisting mountain road that followed the North Fork of the Shoshone River. Everything was going to take time—too much time, I feared. Russell left camp about 3:40 p.m.

His choice of Thunder for his pony express ride was another example in a long list that illustrated his good judgment of horses. Russell has that indefinable quality that all exceptional racehorse jockeys have—knowing how to 'rate or pace' a horse so he finishes strong but spent. His plan was to save forty minutes in the first ten miles, then after the last river crossing, go for broke over the remaining five miles.

Thunder had been rested for two days, so being fresh and full of green grass he was anxious to go. But Russell, knowing he had five river crossings to make and fifteen miles of rough country to cross, wisely held him to a fast walk for the first half mile. Thunder was warmed and loosened up by then so Russell let him out just a little into a nice ground-eating lope. The trail follows the Elk Fork River, which splashes and wanders its way from its birth in a little green meadow surrounded by sheer cloud-shrouded cliffs at the base of Rampart Pass. The headwaters are secreted behind a very wild, narrow, and steep canyon with a thunderous water fall right in the middle.

The fish, game, and scenery in there are akin to my expectations of heaven. Sometimes tranquil enough to bathe in, most times wild, white and free, the river travels through about thirty miles of some of North America's most majestic mountains. At its origin, it is ankle deep and narrow enough to jump across. By the time Russell would make his fifth crossing, she'd be fifty yards of deep, white water crashing over, around and through all size rocks and boulders. The streams and rivers rise dramatically during a sunny day in the mountains. By late afternoon and early evening, a lot of snow has melted and traveled down the twenty other streams that feed the Elk Fork. It was mid-afternoon when Russell left camp. Thunder would have to swim portions of the last crossing.

As they approached the first crossing, Thunder naturally dropped back into his trot, then to a slow walk as he stepped into the water. Russell allowed a pause for a short drink. The first three miles were uneventfully behind them.

As they came out of the river, Thunder responded willingly as Russell nudged him back into the lope. He felt good under Russell—relaxed, alert, breathing deeply as he wove in and out of the timber from shade to bright sunlight. He maintained his rhythm uphill and down. Under the shimmering golden leaves of the aspen that grew along the river bottom, through the tall green fir, pine and spruce trees that stabbed their cone-clustered tops into the pure blue sky, they rode. The sound of the rushing river only a few yards to their right drowned out the sound of Thunder's hoof beats as they approached the easiest river crossing.

Suddenly the tranquil scene was shattered by an explosion of sound and movement slightly ahead and to the right. Thunder snorted and bolted sharply to the left, leaving Russell clawing leather to stay aboard. Russell just barely gathered the white-eyed, nostril-flared mount under him as two grizzly bear cubs dashed across the trail and up the slope to his left. Then the real grief arrived—a very angry, six-hundred-pound, hump-backed sow grizzly. The silver-tip hair on her neck and shoulders standing on end made it plain she was on the fight. The glare from her piercing yellow eyes and the growly snarl leaking from around her bared fangs as she crossed a few yards in front of Thunder told Russell what was coming next. Time seemed to be suspended, but it was only a couple of heartbeats until she had checked the safety of her twins and with an ominous woof, turned to challenge the intruders.

Russell had only two choices. He could wheel Thunder, who was frozen in his tracks, around and race back up the trail. Maybe Mama would only make a fake charge, as grizzlies sometimes do. But if it wasn't a false charge, she'd catch them all too soon. Russell could probably get up a tree, but he'd lose his horse in the fight and several hours of precious time. Big Mama might even hang around fuming and fussing, requiring a lengthy and time-consuming detour.

The other option called for bold, split-second timing. The crossing looked tantalizingly close, a scant hundred yards ahead—the enraged silver-tip, maybe thirty yards to the left and slightly ahead. The instant she switched her attention to momentarily check her offspring, Russell spurred Thunder and let out a rebel yell.

Nothing, but nothing runs at a grizzly. Startled by the sudden aggressiveness of her intended victims and hampered by naturally poor vision, the bear stood up on her hind legs for a better view. Her hesitation gave Thunder the edge he needed to get past her with powerful thrusts of his massive hind quarters and dash for the crossing.

But the griz recovered quickly. Fifty yards, forty yards, then thirty yards remained to the ravine where the trail crossed the river, but the bear was closing fast. At twenty yards, the trail turned left within ten yards of the riverbank—a good twenty feet above a deep pool.

The bear was snapping at their heels. She would pounce the moment they entered the ravine. Russell held Thunder right, spurred, and yelled again. The edge of the undercut bank crumbled beneath them as Thunder leaped into space. In a shower of black dirt, green grass and mountain flowers, they struck the water about midstream. They were both swimming before either surfaced. As they struggled up the stony bank on the other side, the sow, standing at the freshly scarred bank, gave them one more spine-chilling growl, turned and ambled back to her cubs. Both man and horse breathed a sigh of relief as they warily watched her slowly dissolve into the timber, growling and snapping, her massive head lolling from side to side.

The grizzly was gone, but Russell was more worried than ever. Thunder was now a tired, hurting animal. The all-out 100-yard dash and swim after nearly six miles of loping spent the reserves Russell was saving for the last crossing and final five miles to the truck. Worse yet, Thunder was favoring his right front shoulder. They rested only a moment as Russell sat on a rock and poured the water from his boots. Then he walked, giving his horse a chance to rest. When Thunder was limbered up again, Russell caught a stirrup and swung into the saddle.

"Fun and games are over for a while at least, Thunder. Let's get back to work," he said as he urged Thunder along the trail.

◆   ◆   ◆

It was 5:30 p.m. by the time I had returned to the scene of the accident astride a tired and lathered up horse. It had been slightly more than four hours since I left for water, medicine and other survival supplies. Intense, unrelenting pain and paralyzing tension had already taken a terrible toll on Art's physical and emotional reserves. Before Big Red could come to a complete stop, I dismounted and stumbled over the steep, boulder-strewn site, canteen in one hand and heart medicine in the other.

Together, Hansen and I raised our ashen-faced friend's head and shoulders off the cold, stony ground. He gratefully gulped the cool water and pills and questioned me urgently about the helicopter. I had no answers for him. As he sank back to the stones, he said, "I don't feel very good. I hope they are in time. Promise me one thing, Pard," he whispered.

"Of course, Art. What is it?"

"If the helicopter can't get into this canyon and I don't make it, you'll pack me out horseback. You won't let the coyotes have me."

I turned to Hansen. "What the heck is he talking about? Coyotes getting him?"

"He's been hallucinating the past half hour or so."

"Well, there's sure not going to be any coyotes or any other critters pick his bones, I'll promise you that," I replied emphatically. "What the hell happened here, anyway?"

"Frosty blew up on him. Course, it was Art's own fault. He got the lead rope under Frosty's tail."

"Yeah. So?"

"Well, he was leading that old gray mare pack horse you call Hungry. The one that's always got to have every clump of green grass along the trail."

"Go on," I urged.

"Well, she'd jerked the lead rope out of Art's hand several times, making him dismount and catch her. Gave him a couple of bad rope burns in the process, too. So he got mad and wrapped the rope around his hand so she couldn't get loose."

"That was a damn fool greenhorn thing to do, Hansen! Why did you let—"

Hansen flung out his hands. "Just a gol darn minute, Duane. I had my hands full with my own pack horse switchbacking up this steep sucker. I didn't know he'd done it until it was too late."

He continued to explain. Evidently, as he made one of those sharp switchbacks, Hungry swung her head out for some grass and slipped the rope under Frosty's tail. Without looking back, Art jerked the lead rope to retrieve her head and attention. But with that rope taut and tight under the root of Frosty's tail, Art got more of Frosty's attention than the mare's, and the rodeo was on. With that rope wrapped around his hand, Art was in trouble instantly. By the time he got shed of the rope and pack horse, Frosty was burnt so bad he thought he was afire and bucking for all he was worth trying to put it out.

There were a lot of rocks and boulders kicked loose and rolling down the mountain when Art was thrown. He landed on his butt and back, with his left leg braced against a big solid boulder to keep from going all the way over the edge, but another boulder about the size of a washtub came crashing down on him, missed his head by inches, and smashed his leg to a pulp just above the ankle.

"I could hear the bones breaking from clear up there where the elk lay," he finished.

As Sheep Mesa to the west of us devoured the sun, our spirits and chances of getting the helicopter in before dark began to dissolve. Art seemed to be feeling a little better. Just having his medicine was comforting. At least he wasn't talking about coyotes anymore.

Hansen built a fire to be used for warmth as well as signal while I gathered a good supply of dry firewood. We had estimated that Russell would arrive at the truck parked at the trail head about the same time I had returned with the water and medicine—5:30 p.m. That should put him on the phone to the S & R boys by 6:00 at the latest. It gets dark up there about 8:00 that time of year. Allowing some scramble time, plan time, and flight time, the helicopter should arrive around 7:00 with an hour of light left to load and fly Art to the hospital.

But it didn't. 7:30 came and went with no helicopter. 8:00 brought deepening dusk as well as signal howls from various coyotes echoing off the canyon walls as they gathered for the night's hunting, but no helicopter.

Art was afraid he wouldn't be able to hold any food in his sick stomach, so he hadn't eaten since his 5:00 a.m. breakfast. Now he lay on a foam pad wrapped in blankets next to the fire, staring into the blue-black sky. As if by magic, little sparkly bluish white stars began to appear. Pain and anguish were clearly visible in the whites of his eyes. The passing of only five minutes now seemed to be at least an hour to him as he repeatedly asked the time. 8:30 p.m.—still no helicopter.

By now, we were worried about Russell also. Something must have happened to him too. Hansen and I sat hunched on the steep slope, our down vests and down coats pulled tightly around us, our feet to the fire, and waited and prayed and waited.

◆　　◆　　◆

Meanwhile, by the time Russell had led Thunder back to the trail, the horse's breathing was nearly normal and the limp was slight. But the vigor was gone out of both of them as Russell caught his left stirrup and swung into the saddle. Both the coal-black horse and his rider took a good look behind them. Again Russell walked Thunder for a ways, hoping the horse could regain some of his strength and composure, get warmed up and go back to his ground-eating lope. But Thunder was a bundle of raw nerves now, no longer tugging at the bit. Russell thought the horse saw bears with big teeth and claws in every branch that rustled in the breeze, every shadow, every songbird that burst from the grass along the trail. Shying and snorting, he aggravated his shoulder with each encounter. His lope was no longer strong and fluid, but labored and gimpy. The further they went, the more often Russell got off and walked, leading the head down, limping horse.

It was 5:30 when they crossed the river the fourth time. The water was high and swift. Thunder was just barely able to keep his footing. Russell knew there would be no such luck at the last crossing, so he got off and walked Thunder the entire two miles between crossings to rest him as much as possible. By the time they reached the swollen fifth crossing, Thunder's mental attitude was pretty much back to normal. He was still very tired and sore but he knew the corrals, hay, grain and rest were a scant five miles away and he was anxious to get there. As he lost his footing just short of midstream and began swimming through the boulder-strewn, riley water, Russell slipped out of the saddle on the upstream side and held tightly to the saddle horn with his left hand while fending off sharp, slippery boulders with his right. They were swept nearly twenty yards downstream before gaining their footing again along the other bank.

By the time Thunder caught his breath and Russell poured the water out of his boots for the second time that afternoon, it was 6:15. He gathered his horse under him, gave him his head, and said, "We've got to be at the corrals by 7:15. Thunder, can you do it?" We never knew if it was his empty stomach or the urging in Russell's voice that Thunder responded to, but pain or no pain, that fantastic mustang heart took over and he went back to work. Yard after yard, mile after mile, he ate up the distance. Head high, eyes flashing, mane flying in the wind, the little black horse covered with white lather burst into the corral area at 7:14 on the dot. He stood in the middle of the corral, head between his front legs, sides heaving, waiting to be unsaddled and cared for.

◆   ◆   ◆

At 8:45 p.m., the chopper made a pass over the signal fire that was so tiny in this vast, black wilderness. Art was nearly beside himself with relief and excitement. Hansen and I couldn't help but jump up waving and shouting in the dark. It was a spontaneous reaction of relief and expectation.

What we didn't expect was for the chopper to keep right on going. If they'd seen our fire, why hadn't they dropped a flare? Or if they hadn't seen us, why weren't they flying around out there looking for us, like you read about?

"What's the matter now?" Art raised up on his elbows. "Are they landing? I can't see shit from here."

Hansen slumped down beside Art and answered, "Take it easy, ol' Pard. I think they've gone back for fuel."

The air whooshed from Art's lungs as he fell back on his foam pad. "Damn!" was all he said for a long time.

All we had was a signal fire. Without some kind of communication such as radios, successful rescues are very difficult and rare. Everyone was engrossed in his own thoughts. The slow passing of time was heavy on our minds. It was now 10:00 p.m., and the only thing that had happened since the chopper left was it had gotten darker and colder.

By 11:00, Art was getting feverish and we were all very restless. Where was that helicopter?

Art took the last two aspirin we had at 11:30 and reminded me of my promise about the coyotes. There was a faint light beginning to glow in the sky to the east of us behind Wapiti Ridge. Slowly but surely, the big, bright, beautiful, orange harvest moon began to grow above the 11,000-foot ridge that encompassed us. It seemed so clear and close one should be able to reach out and touch it. We watched in reverent awe as it grew into its full roundness and bathed us in its beautiful terrestrial light.

Within fifteen minutes, we could hear the helicopter returning. So that was it! They had to wait for the moon to get high enough to illuminate the rescue area. Within a few moments, they landed on a small plateau about six hundred yards above us. Soon, Art's personal physician from Cody and another medic were at his side, checking vital signs and administering the professional care he needed before they could move him. They quickly replaced our makeshift splint with one far more adequate and strapped him into a stretcher. By 12:15 a.m., the arduous ascent to the chopper began.

The accident had taken place one-half mile short of the head of Burnt Timber Creek. We were on the north side of the drainage, about six hundred yards below the top of the ridge that intersected Wapiti Ridge, forming the main canyon. The climb to the landing site looked deceptively easy. Very few hunters, carrying only rifles, could make the climb in less than one hour.

A stretcher, heavily laden with an injured man and carried by four tired men in the dark, was no small load on this steep terrain. You could stand flat-footed, stretch your arm out, and touch the ground with your fingers at eye level anywhere en route to the chopper. On hands and knees we carried, pushed and pulled Art, inch by inch, foot by foot, yard by yard, over boot-shredding rocks. No one escaped the cuts and bruises to hands and knees that the mountain demanded as penance that night. As we struggled on above timberline, our temples throbbed, our lungs burned, and our rubbery thighs screamed for oxygen from the rarified 10,000-foot air.

The mountains ask no quarter and grant no quarter, and are as unyielding to men's demands as they are beautiful to our senses. It was 3:00 a.m. when the exhausted rescue team gained the plateau. There was very little talk or exhilaration. The Search and Rescue men were professionals and tired, and Art's condition was still very unstable. As soon as the stretcher containing him was secured to the struts outside the chopper, they all disappeared into the night amidst a whir of flashing red and green lights.

Art's heart survived the ordeal, none the worse for wear. He was on the operating table from 4:00 to 8:00 a.m., though. As surgeons gingerly inserted three stainless steel plates with fourteen stainless steel screws to repair the shattered ankle bones, they assured him he was going to lose all flexibility in his ankle and He could never hunt the mountains again—and he was lucky to be alive. I wonder what they would have thought if they had seen him the next fall, hobbling up the sage brush draw behind our elk camp, taking pot shots with his old 30–30 Winchester at a camp-robbing coyote. He looked like Chester of the old TV western, "Gunsmoke." Once the steel was all removed from his ankle, he regained about ninety percent flexibility, and he hunts and fishes the mountains as well as ever.

There will always be a special place in our hearts and memories for Thunder—the proud, half-Morgan half-Mustang horse with the big heart. Thunder died that night.

◆   ◆   ◆

Hanson and I arrived back at camp in time for breakfast. Russell rode in on a borrowed horse about noon. We all spent that day resting and getting reorganized to continue our elk hunt the following day. As per our instructions, the hunters had returned to camp with the elk quarters the day before. Betty helped them unpack and unsaddle the horses and turned them out to graze. Don and Dave spent the afternoon skinning, trimming and cleaning up their meat—which was good, except for one thing. Wyoming Game & Fish regulations require evidence of sex on all carcasses. That means, as Hanson and I had explained to the hunters previously, a testicle must be left attached to each hind-quarter and the head provided for the front quarters.

Well, the brothers forgot the testicle part. During their meat-cleaning project, they removed and destroyed them.

In Cody, there is a Wyoming game check station manned 24/7 during hunting season where all hunters, outfitters, and guides must check in and out. Upon checking out, all kills must be presented for visual inspection and compliance with regulation. So now, on my very first professional elk hunt, I was faced with my first ethical decision. Did I hide the meat in duffels and ignore the check station stop, or did I pull in, explain the extenuating circumstances, and rely on the understanding and compassion of the Game & Fish man? Weighing heavy on my mind was the regulation that allows for the revoking of an outfitter's license if he receives even two violations on his record. Nonetheless, I determined not to begin what I hoped would be a long outfitting career by knowingly breaking the law. We would stop at the check station and explain what happened.

Meanwhile, we still had several days to hunt and a license to fill. Hanson and I took the brothers out daily for the rest of their time. Don shot at bulls every day and missed them all.

All four of us stopped at the check station. Upon hearing our tale of woe regarding our lack of evidence of sex, the lady at the check station asked us to wait while she called Dave Bergonia, the Game Warden. We dozed in warm sunlight til he showed up.

Dave patiently listened to our story while checking our meat and licenses, nodding appropriately. "Yup," he said. "I have no doubt you boys are telling me the truth. However, the book calls for evidence of sex to be attached. Since there's none attached, I'll have to write you up." After writing Don and Dave each $20 tickets, Dave turned to Hanson and me and said, "I'm only going to ticket one of you guys. Which one wants it?"

Hanson was well aware of the thin ice the law had me on and quickly said, "Give it to me."

Don and Dave were so upset, I never heard from them again. I paid Hanson's $20 fine and carried a needle and white thread in my saddle bags on every hunt after that. In subsequent years, I became quite proficient at occasionally reattaching the required evidence of sex.

THE PRINCE'S TENT

We spent the winter and spring of 1975 busily advertising and promoting for summer Kampground and fall hunting business

I was intrigued and a bit confused by Glen Fales' answer when I asked him, "How do I go about getting clients for my outfitting business?" Glen's response was, "Well you just...ah...or you ah...ah...Let's see...ah. Well, dammit, you just stay in business for twenty years, and it gets easy then!"

I could see that staying in business for twenty years was going to be the challenge, and it was going to be up to me to figure out the details. I continued to do masonry work to support my outfitting habit while I learned through trial and error which magazine ads, sport shows, or sports writers produced bookings. My biggest disappointment was with sports writers and TV people. What a bunch of counterfeit parasites most of them turned out to be. The one big exception in that field was my experience with Paul Burke, founder of North American Hunt Club, and his son, Steve.

In the early days of both Cabin Creek Outfitters and North American Hunt Club, whenever I'd be promoting in Minneapolis, I'd make it a point to stop in the N.A.H.C. offices in Minnetonka. Mark LaBarbar was there then, heading up their fledgling publication department. The four of us would usually go to lunch. They always had time and interest to share information and ideas with me.

Over the years as I began to write my own stories, the N.A.H.C. was very supportive with critical input and publishing. Our relationship grew to be mutually beneficial. I provided hunts and materials for TV programs, as well as my stories, and they provided me with national exposure.

And sure enough, Glen was right. By the time I survived twenty years of icy trails, horse wrecks, bear attacks, forest fires, and government bureaucracy, booking hunters had become the easy part.

Meanwhile, Betsy and I were so busy working at the businesses, the ranch, and the kids, we had little time for fighting with each other.

◆   ◆   ◆

My very next outfitting trip began with a discreet visit from a U.S. State Department rep. in the late summer of 1975. I was being offered this job, I was told, because I was a small, honest, tight-knit family operation and would be paid well for my services.

The trip had to be in early September for Shiras Moose in the Thorofare country. The hunter would be Prince Abdorza, the brother of the Shah of Iran. He would be accompanied by his personal bodyguard, Ramshide Harshinde, and also an American who would act as a liaison. The guests' identity was to be kept secret, and all licenses and permits were provided by the Governor of Wyoming.

I was assured these people were world-class sportsmen who neither required nor sought any special consideration. Tents and stoves would not be needed, and one pack horse would be plenty to pack what little gear these skilled outdoorsmen needed. The hunt's objective was a large, trophy Shiras moose for the National Museum in Tehran.

I naively accepted the U.S. Government's financial terms of one-half up front and the balance upon completion of the hunt.

Given this trip's Spartan nature, I called on a friend of mine, Red Arthur, to cook for us. Red is a man of medium height and frame, with a head and face full of fiery red hair, and a disposition to match. He's an experienced campfire cook who thinks for himself.

This would be my first trip into Wyoming's world-renowned Thorofare country, so again I asked Hansen to guide for me. As the Thorofare is a highly sought-after place to hunt, Hansen didn't hesitate to sign on.

It is thirty-five miles into the Thorofare, a two-day trip with pack horses from our jumping-off spot at Eagle Creek corrals. I was going to need a horse wrangler who could think and speak horse fluently. I was greatly relieved when Russ Tomkins agreed to drive out from upstate New York for the task.

In the farm town of Powell, it was not uncommon for high school kids to be excused for a week to help their parents during fall harvest. When school started that fall, over Betsy's objections, I made arrangements with the school principal to allow Mark and Jeff a week off to help me in hunting camp.

Mark was seventeen, strong and capable. He would be lots of help around camp and packing horses. The experience to be gained on this trip would far outweigh what he missed in school, I reasoned, and so he rounded out our crew. I saved Jeff for a later hunt.

Two days earlier, I had sent Hansen, Russell, and Red in with two horses packed with grub, and even two 12x14 wall tents to establish a comfortable camp and scout for moose.

The hunt was scheduled for ten days. While Hansen guided the Prince, the rest of us planned to do the camp chores and catch up on our trout fishing. The morning the trip began, Mark and I were busily saddling horses as we awaited the guests' arrival at the Eagle Creek trail head.

Five saddle horses were saddled and dozing at the hitching rail. I was adjusting the britching on the third and last pack horse when I heard Mark say softly, "Uh, oh, Dad. I think we're in trouble."

I followed his gaze to the overloaded yellow Jeep station wagon that was inching its way up the old dirt road that ended at the corrals. The rear bumper was dragging in the potholes and ruts. Presently, the Jeep jarred to a sagging, sighing stop opposite us. Three men wearing crisp African safari clothing stepped out and approached us—the bodyguard, the Iranian Prince, and a loud American. The American introduced us, briefed us as to proper protocol in the presence of a Prince, and informed me they had a lot more gear than could ever be packed on only three horses. The Prince was of medium build and a tad short. He barely acknowledged us.

The bodyguard was big, very big, and he carried a Colt .45 automatic on his hip. He briskly marched up to one of the dozing saddle horses and began slapping the dust off the saddle with his noisy plastic rain poncho. He sure got all of the horses' attention, don't worry.

The American was just plain medium but diligently trying to impress and please the Prince. He allowed as how we were not to address the Prince directly, but to convey all communication to the bodyguard first, and to refer to the Prince as "His Highness." Under no circumstances were we to be in the Prince's presence without the bodyguard.

Hmmm, I thought. *You may be right, Mark. This could prove to be a very educational trip for all of us.*

The guests were already unhappy with me for insisting they needed to reduce their plunder by at least two-thirds. While they were painfully deciding which one-third of their heavy gear we could actually pack into the wilderness, a Forest Ranger in a light green Chevrolet pick-up truck pulled in with an urgent message for me.

"Boy, am I glad I caught you," he said as he handed me a crumpled scrap of paper and curiously eyed the Prince.

Hastily scribbled on the scrap was a message from Hansen. "Make your over-night camp short of Eagle Pass" was all it said. If I followed Hansen's instruc-tions, our overnight camp would be far short of halfway, resulting in a short first day's ride and a very long second-day ride to the main camp. Getting a message to me at all required a great deal of effort on Hansen's part, so I figured it must be important. I reluctantly decided to follow his advice.

Earlier in the summer, Hansen had given me an old green 9x9 umbrella tent to use as a latrine tent in our elk camp during the fall hunting season. My plan was to experiment with the old tent on this trip and see if it would really work as a latrine. I didn't want to wait until I had a long line of urgent elk hunters to dis-cover a snafu.

That day, we used the old green tent for a pack cover on the last pack horse and we tightened our diamond hitch around it. Shortly thereafter, we were all mounted and on our way up the Eagle Creek trail. I led the way. The three guests followed and Mark brought up the rear, leading our three pack horses. Occasion-ally the Iranians visited with each other in Arabic, but otherwise, there wasn't much conversation.

The pass was still about an hour's ride ahead and the sun about three hours from setting when we rode into the last little meadow that afforded any grazing for our horses. I wanted to make a few more miles that afternoon, and we had plenty of daylight to do it in. The stout, colorful Appaloosa gelding that I was riding anxiously strained at the bit, throwing his head as he pranced around. His neck bowed as he tried to coax me to go on. But Hansen's message had been emphatic. If I got over the top of the pass and for some unknown reason could not find enough grass to adequately feed my horses, they would suffer physically and I would suffer mentally. So, I signaled a stop and dismounted near a stand of tall, protected pine and balsam trees. Shortly, the horses were unpacked, unsad-dled, belled, picketed and turned out to graze on our little half-acre meadow.

Meanwhile, the three guests had been walking around on the carpet of pine needles, stretching their legs and enjoying the fragrant solitude. The bodyguard strode over to where Mark and I were organizing our gear and covering tack with pack covers. "Where is the Prince's tent, Duane?" he demanded.

Dumbfounded, Mark and I looked at each other. Several thoughts chased each other through my mind. We never set up a tent for ourselves for just one night on the trail. We had been told that the Prince would live just like the rest of us, that he enjoyed roughing it in spike camp. I should have suspected something when I was told a week before the trip to be sure to bring several gallons of bottled water for the Prince, because he wouldn't drink the creek water. I had the old green umbrella soon-to-be-latrine tent, but no sleeping tents.

With a poise and confidence that surprised both Mark and me, I stepped over to the musty old green tent and said, "Right here. We'll have it up for you in a jiffy."

"How does this thing go together, Dad?" Mark asked as we carried it to the flat spot that the Prince had chosen to spend the night.

"I don't know. Hansen was going to show me when I got to camp. We'll just have to fake it," I replied.

No sooner had we gotten the Prince's tent up than the bodyguard asked for his tent.

I was confused for just a moment. There was plenty of room for four people to sleep in the Prince's tent, even more if they were family or of the opposite sex. Slowly, I began to understand my station in life as seen through the eyes of Persian royalty. I tossed him a little orange pup tent. My kids played with that tent and because it had a floor and zipped shut, I had brought it along to secure our groceries from mice and rain. Mark quickly set up the little orange pup tent for the bodyguard.

When Mark returned to the cooking fire I was tending, he mischievously asked, "Where is my tent, Dad?" I almost beaned him with the chunk of firewood I threw, but he was too quick and ducked behind the big Balsam tree we planned to sleep under that night. Then he came over to the fire and began emptying his pockets of candy wrappers and tossing them in the fire.

Upon seeing this, I sternly asked, "What the hell you doing eating all that candy? Where did you get it anyway?"

"Wasn't me, Dad. It's those Iranians. They've been eating candy and throwing their wrappers on the ground. I've been picking up after them all day."

"What's their buddy Doug been doing?"

"He's as bad as they are," Mark answered.

"Hmm. It 'pears this bunch bears watching, huh?"

"Yep."

The sun was setting the next evening when we all rode across the marsh on the west end of Bridger Lake. At a fork in the trail, a lone rider—Hansen—materialized from the darkening timber sixty yards to our right.

The bodyguard drew his .45, startling me.

"What's the matter with him?" Hansen asked, nodding toward the bodyguard.

"You ain't seen nothing yet. Why are you coming in from that direction?"

"Too much activity up on the other end. Something fishy is going on up there, so I picked a campsite back yonder in the timber. More privacy," Hansen answered.

A fifteen-minute ride through green-black timber brought us into a secluded meadow. Camp was a peaceful scene of grazing horses, two wall tents and a small fire that produced glowing coals for Red's excellent slit-trench style cooking.

The hands figured we would all sleep in one of the 12x14 tents and the guests would all sleep in the other one, but the Prince immediately claimed the empty 12x14 tent for himself. After making some disparaging remarks about not having a stove or a bed, he disappeared inside.

Hansen's eyebrows rose, but he said nothing as we set up the fine old green umbrella tent for the bodyguard.

When supper was ready, the bodyguard served the Prince in his tent and then retired to his own tent to eat in private—a practice they followed for every meal of the hunt, except one.

After supper, the rest of us gathered around the cheery warmth of the campfire and brought each other up-to-date on our experiences of the last two days.

Russell reported the horses were in fine shape—no sores or injuries from the trip, and he would have several well-rested, well-fed horses saddled long before daylight to begin the next morning's hunt. Typically, Red wanted to know what the hell he was expected to do with the gallon of bottled water he had unpacked.

"The Prince must have pure water to drink. When that gallon is gone, refill the plastic container at the creek for him. He'll never know the difference." I said.

The reflection of dancing flames in his eyes and the slight grin that parted his red beard can only be described as devilish.

I asked Hansen to explain the message the Forest Ranger had delivered and why we weren't camped at our appointed campsite.

"Well," he said. "We stayed up there the first day and night, but there was a steady stream of people stopping by wanting to see the Prince. The Forest Service even raked the area and cut and stacked some firewood. I understood the Prince was traveling incognito for security reasons and that area didn't look very secure to me, so I moved down here. The reason for the message," he went on, "was to save you the kind of grief we suffered at the hands of an over-zealous Park Ranger."

It seems Hansen had camped at his favorite site just a couple of miles inside Yellowstone Park's boundary the first night on the trail. It was raining hard, so the boys set up a tent. Just at dark, one of those people that works for the government "of the people, for the people and by the people" (a Park Ranger), on his way to his warm dry cabin, stopped by and demanded they break camp in the dark and rain and get off National Park property.

Opening morning of the hunt, the horses were saddled and breakfast was ready by 5:30 a.m., but no hunter! At about 7:30, the bodyguard appeared and told us the Prince would want his tea first, hot and very sweet. Half an hour later another call for tea drifted out of the Prince's tent, and shortly thereafter, a call for warm water to wash his hair. Later still, he called for his breakfast.

Just before 10:00, the Prince appeared, wearing crisp, clean, new Eddie Bauer duds with his Weatherby 300 magnum wrapped in protective oilskins and tucked under one royal arm. Now he was ready to stalk the cunning and deadly Shiras Moose.

Because they had missed the first hours of daylight, Hansen requested sack lunches. Then they could stay out all day and at least get in an evening hunt, but the Prince insisted on returning to camp at 4:00 p.m. They hadn't seen any moose anyway, he reasoned, and thought maybe they would have better luck the next day.

For four days we followed that same fruitless and frustrating routine.

On the fifth day, when Mark, Russell and I returned to camp with fresh Cut-throat trout for lunch, we found Hansen saddling pack horses. That could mean only one thing. We gathered around Hansen to hear of the kill.

"Did he get a nice one, Hansen?" I asked.

"No. He's just a three-year-old with small antlers," Hansen replied.

"I don't understand," I said, puzzled. "I thought the Prince wanted a good bull for the Museum."

"Seems funny to me, too," Hansen raised his sweat-stained Stetson to scratch his graying hair and squint into the sun while measuring its distance to the horizon. "But, I pushed the bull out of some willows and into an opening within seventy-five yards of the Prince and he put two bullets in his chest cavity. So I guess he must have wanted that moose. Let's eat some lunch and then all of us can go back up there. We have a lot of caping, quartering and packing to do yet this afternoon. Remember, they told us several times not to touch the trophy until they were through with picture taking. I haven't even gutted the moose yet. He's laying right where he dropped."

Hansen led the way back to the kill astride his sorrel mare, Ginger. We were just coming up out of a boggy bottom and rounding some willows when we ran right into the three members of the hunting party. They were a mile away from the site of the kill.

"You'll never believe what happened!" the American exclaimed. "Shortly after Hansen left, as we were preparing to take pictures, the moose suddenly sprang to life and raced off into the protective timber before anyone could do anything about it."

Then they all started talking at once. Now they wanted Hansen to take them over by the lake about two miles in the opposite direction for an evening hunt. We sat on our horses, eyeball to eyeball with the royal hunting party, momentarily stunned by their story.

"I think they're lying, Dad," Mark whispered.

I think so too, I thought, *but how do I publicly call a foreign dignitary, a world-class hunter and a guest of the U.S. Government a liar, without creating some kind of international incident?*

Hansen broke the silence by agreeing to take the two Persians to the lake. The American was to accompany Mark, Russell, me, and the empty pack horses back to camp.

The creak of leather and the jingle of spurs was all that could be heard as we rode along the trail. Each man was engrossed in his own thoughts.

Two-thirds of the way back, I still didn't have a clear plan of action in my mind, but knew that I was going to start with that mousey American. He and I were going to have an understanding, by hell, and we were not going to leave a dead moose to rot.

Two strange horses were tied to the hitching rail when we arrived in camp. Red and two uniformed Forest Rangers were sitting drinking coffee by the camp-fire.

Before I could say anything to the American, the Rangers began questioning me. Did we have a real Prince in camp? Why hadn't we used the campsite they had prepared for us? Where had we been for the last six days? When could they meet the Prince?

The only information they had gleaned from Red was what was for supper and after about thirty minutes of double-talk with me, they were convinced they weren't going to meet the Prince that day either.

As they rode out, the game warden rode in. I thought to myself, *Old Dave is good, but by God, he can't be this good. I don't even know where that moose is yet. What in the world does he want?*

Short and stocky, Dave rides a long-legged Fox Trotter and gets up early every morning. Very little, if anything, gets past him. After a casual, inquiring stroll around camp wherein he exchanging pleasantries with all the hands, he beckoned me over by his horse.

A stream of snoose juice exploded against a rock and was followed quickly by the question, "This old kid you're hunting, does he have a license?"

"You bet," I said. "A government permit."

More snoose juice. "You seen it?"

"Of course. Haven't you?" I asked.

"No, by hell, I haven't. The Governor says it's none of my damn business who he gives those damn permits to." Two shots of snoose juice this time. "I suppose he'll be out hunting till well after dark," Dave said softly.

I nodded agreement.

"But, you've seen his license?" he asked piercingly this time.

"Yes, I have. And it's signed by the Governor and everything," I answered.

After a little more thoughtful spitting and kicking dust, Dave swung into the saddle and reined his long-legged horse toward the main trail.

"Okay. That's good enough for me. I'll see you around. Good luck."

One more spit before he rode out of sight as the evening shadows enveloped him. Dave was barely out of sight when Hansen, the Prince, and his bodyguard rode in from the opposite direction. Dismounting quickly and handing his horse's reins to Russell, Hansen said to me, "Come on, Duane. Let's go get some water."

The creek was about forty yards from camp. Hansen and I seldom pack water, but the seclusion of the stream afforded us our first opportunity to talk privately concerning the runaway moose. I was anxious to hear his thoughts.

"I'm sure that moose was dead, Duane. He certainly looked dead when I left him. Whatever you decide to do, we'll back you all the way to hell and back." Concern showed on Hansen's weather-beaten face.

Hansen had confirmed my suspicions. Now I must act. I had been studying on it all afternoon, and it didn't seem all that complicated. The man had killed his bull. He should tag it and take it home. End of hunt. End of story! It is amazing to me how some people can complicate a simple solution.

The Prince was startled and apprehensive when, uninvited and alone, I entered his tent.

I was angry. Leaving an animal to rot while he hunted for a bigger one went against everything I had been taught by my father about pride, sportsmanship, and conservation. Not to mention it was illegal and I could lose my hunting and outfitting privileges for a long time.

I had been jacked around all afternoon by these foreign dignitaries, then the United States Forest Service, and finally by the Wyoming Game and Fish Department. Now I was having trouble choosing my words carefully.

Looking the Prince squarely in the eye, I blurted out, "I don't believe your story about the moose running away."

A long, stony silence settled around us as we glared at each other.

The bodyguard was alone in his own tent. All of the hands were warming themselves around the campfire. No one knew where I was. I heard Red call supper.

Finally, the Prince broke the silence by stating evenly, "That moose is beneath my status as a world-class hunter. I can't take him home."

"I don't care if you take him home or not," I said, "but the hunt is over. Fill out your tag because we are packing everyone out of here tomorrow, including that moose. If you don't want him, I am sure the hands will make good use of the meat."

Red called supper again.

"There are some other things we could do," the Prince said loftily.

"Like what?"

"I could pay everyone extra to keep quiet about that bull and hunt until we find a bigger trophy," he replied.

I could scarcely believe what I had heard.

"There isn't a man in camp, including me, that would accept any amount of money from you under those circumstances. You would only insult us if you asked."

"Well then, I'll just order everyone to keep silent," he stated emphatically.

"That may work for you in the Middle East, but not here in the Thorofare," I shot back.

Suddenly Ramshide, the six foot plus bodyguard, burst through the tent flap, his black eyes flashing with his cocked .45 leveled at my belt buckle. I stood stark still between the Prince and his bodyguard, not daring to move.

Red disgustedly called supper for the third time.

The two Iranians spoke briefly to each other in their native tongue. Slowly, the bodyguard holstered his .45. I breathed again.

The two of them were engaged in a lengthy discussion in their own language when Red's fourth summons to supper became obscene expletives. He was just outside the Prince's tent and knew nothing about the events of that afternoon. Red was fed up with all the dawdling. Supper was ready and by hell he wanted it eaten while it was still hot.

Everyone was surprised when the Prince joined us for supper around the campfire that night. Before we had left his tent, I agreed to let the Prince make a face-saving explanation concerning the end of the hunt.

The moose had started to sour, but we packed it all out anyway.

There were no pictures, no celebration, and no payment of the fifty-percent balance due me. None of the hands won the $40 pot, betting on when the Prince would get sick from drinking Red's extra-sweet creek water tea.

Although the Prince spent only one night in the old green umbrella tent, throughout the years the latrine tent in each of our three wilderness elk camps was called "The Prince's Tent." And sometimes around the campfire, if the mood was right, our hunters would hear the story in answer to their query, "Why do you call the latrine tent 'The Prince's Tent?'"

WIN SOME—LOSE SOME

As I booked more and more hunters each year, I needed more hands. Hanson had retired after the Prince's moose hunt. Mark, Jeff and I could no longer handle all the guiding. Betsy cooked for a trip one year but created so much stress for everyone that I had to replace her. Hiring experienced wilderness camp cooks and competent wilderness hunting guides was a big challenge.

My reputation for paying honest wages and providing good working conditions began to get around, and slowly, the best hands made themselves available. In a designated wilderness area such as our camps were in, no mechanical devices such as chain saws or generators were allowed. Our camp consisted of a cook tent, a dining tent, a tack tent, two sleeping tents for the guests, and one or two sleeping tents for the guides and wranglers. The cook slept in the cook tent to protect it from marauding grizzly bears.

The cook is the key to a good camp. He/She administers first aid to bruised bodies and egos. For better or worse, the cook sets the tone of everyone's mood each morning with hot coffee and a hearty breakfast. If not, it can be a tough hunt. Even if the hunters don't fill their tags, with the right story-telling attitude, the cook can carry the day. They do it all with gas lanterns, wood stoves for cooking and heating, and water carried from the creek.

Wilderness hunting guides are the "cowboys of the high country." In fact, many of them work on ranches or rodeo the rest of the year. They dress for the elements and the tasks required of them—cowboy boots or packers, long johns, wool pants and shirts, leather chaps, down vests, silk neckerchiefs, gloves, and usually a black cowboy hat. Many of them take their pay in cash and come with descriptive nicknames—"Buck," "Birdshot," "Tramp," "Tad," "Toad Body," "Griz," "Professor," and "Blue Duck" are some I was privileged to know and work with. Much like my sons Mark and Jeff, these young men in the prime of their lives all possessed extensive skills in handling horses, people, ropes, knives, guns, and themselves. Much to my dismay, sooner or later they would meet a nice girl, get "mothered up," and move on to a "real job." I was beginning to understand that in our world today, "Nobody gets to be a cowboy forever."

◆   ◆   ◆

By 1980, the two businesses—KOA Kampground and Cabin Creek Outfitting—had become more than we could handle and still have some family life. The key to our success in the campground business was our children, and they were getting older and looking on to other interests. Mark was married in 1976 and Jeff in 1979, so when we were offered a deal to sell the ranch, I reluctantly agreed before all the kids grew up and left home.

Betsy and I bought a small house on twenty acres close to Powell so the three youngest could participate more in school activities. By 1982, I had finished the basement into an office, family room, and bedroom. I had also built a garage and deck, plus corrals and loafing shed for the horses.

Now, a late spring storm screamed into the mountains of Northwest Wyoming with a vengeance. Just before dark the vet had said, "I'm sorry, but there's nothing more I can do, Duane. I doubt if she'll live another two hours."

Denise insisted, "Let's take her in the house like we used to with the calves, Dad. We can save her. I know we can." the vet didn't know that Denise and I were ready and able to spend the rest of the night to save this little black filly with the distinctive white markings over her hips. She had it all. Her long legs, petite head and overall conformation would make her an ideal brood mare in a few years. For ten years, we had been breeding Appaloosas, the breed preferred and perfected by the Nez Perce Indians, and this was the first filly with so much potential.

Before selling our ranch, we had saved countless calves in similar straits. One method that proved effective when they were born in a storm was to take them in the house and place them in the bathtub filled with warm water, then rub them dry in front of the fire before returning them to their mother's side for nursing.

"She won't die, Dad. This is the way I saved Apple when he was sick, remember?"

My darling daughter, Denise, cradled the droopy-eyed head of my prize Appaloosa filly colt in her lap. She sat cross-legged on the basement floor as I added another log to the fire crackling in the wood stove. She talked soothingly to the stricken colt, who was wrapped in an old blue blanket, while we feverishly rubbed her listless body, trying desperately to restore her natural circulation and body heat. Years ago, through personal determination, Denise had saved our very first colt, which she promptly named "Apple."

I knew if determination, concern for living creatures, and loving devotion counted for anything, we would have a chance with this colt. So I had gathered the helpless colt into my arms and carried her through the house and to the basement. Long, dangling legs dragged across the carpeted living room and thumped down the basement stairs. It reminded me of the blaze-faced, sorrel horse colt that had died in my lap the previous spring, the victim of a similar storm.

I'll never forget the feeling of frustration and despair when I found the mare valiantly trying to shield her newborn from stinging snow with her own ice-encrusted body. I vowed to myself, that black night, that somehow I'd have new corrals and barn before foaling time came next spring. No more foals born in the sagebrush to be killed by coyote, mountain lion or storms.

We scrimped and saved and struggled all winter. By late March, together with the efforts of my five children, we had our new corrals and barn. The very night we finished, one of the mares had used its solitude and protection to give birth without incident to our first foal of the season. Somehow, in spite of our best efforts, this week-old colt had become disoriented and separated from her mom early in the storm. Denise discovered the mare frantically chasing around the corral in the swirling snow, nickering for her newborn. With a quick shout to me that we had trouble in the corrals, she disappeared into the storm. Moments that seemed like hours later, her worried shouts from behind the new barn led me to the snow-covered, shivering colt huddled at the base of some sagebrush.

"Look at her eyes, Dad. Look at her eyes. She's feeling better, isn't she?"

By golly, she did look better. We had been rubbing her so much even her spindly legs were warm. I looked at my Grandfather's old pocket watch I carried. We were beyond the two hours the vet had allowed us. The inside of her mouth was still cold, and she hadn't tried to get up yet, but we were encouraged and talked excitedly as I bathed her mouth with a warm, damp wash cloth.

There are a lot of things said and written about the special relationship between a man and his sons. I have the great privilege of that experience with my three sons, but nothing can compare with the depth of feelings between a father and his daughter when it really works. There is an intimacy and tenderness that big strong gruff fathers need.

Through the years of loving, laughing, crying, teaching, rebellion and learning, Denise and I had grown very fond of each other, and now she was planning to be married in June and I didn't like that. It was only nineteen years ago that Betsy nearly miscarried her. And now she was going to get married already. What about all the calves we'd saved? What about all the trout we'd caught under the bridge? What about all the rattlesnakes killed, the mule deer watched? Now in two months, my eldest daughter would leave me for another man. I had a lot of hopes and dreams for her, too. I was not emotionally ready to lose her.

"Dad, you'd better go to bed. You're not paying any attention, and besides, the clock upstairs just struck midnight. I'll have this colt nursing on her mother by dawn."

I was jolted back to the current crisis by Denise's excited exclamation, "Dad. Look, she's trying to get up. She's going to be alright, isn't she, Dad?" Then suddenly Denise hesitated. "But her eyes don't look right. What's the matter with her eyes, Dad?"

The fear in her own lake-blue eyes reflected the terror etched in the colt's eyes. Her voice broke, the words catching in her throat, "Oh, Dad, she's not going to—oh, Dad. No!"

The hypothermic colt lay dead between us. We stared at each other in anguish and disbelief, tears streaming unashamedly down our cheeks. We had fought so hard and lost again.

◆　　　◆　　　◆

My hunting business had expanded the Cabin Creek camp to full capacity. In fact, I was renting an additional twenty head of horses from Jerry Asey, whose Northwest Outfitters business was going down the same drain as Bob Adams'.

After my 1981 season, I decided to save gas money and time by trailing Jerry's horses back to him instead of trucking them. It was only about 30 miles from my Elk Fork trail head to Jerry's place, but between us there were three tunnels and the town of Cody. My first thought was to use the historic old stock trail, where horses and cattle were brought into Cody for market—but I didn't want to do that before checking with the local cops. They advised me to forget taking the old trail. The sprawl of development had consumed it. They didn't want me to trot twenty horses through a new neighborhood, creating havoc with the flatlanders' lawns, gardens, and sprinkler heads, resulting in a lot of irate phone calls to them. Instead, they said to take them right through town up Main Street, on a Sunday morning.

So as the east began to gray, and with my son Jeff riding point and Mark and John on each flank, from the rear I pushed the excited horses out of the Elk Fork corrals. The edge was off them by the time we reached the first tunnel. We knew we had to push them hard at that critical point so the leaders couldn't double back on us. We did. And they didn't. In fact, halfway through the first tunnel, we engulfed a small rental car containing a startled oriental couple. Their eyes were damn sure round when I rode past them. Going down Main Street, the horses nervously eyed themselves in store front windows but clattered up that yellow line like it was a narrow canyon game trail. The few people waving to us from the sidewalks that morning were either just getting up or fixing to turn in.

Once the horses were safely in Jerry's corral, he offered hot coffee all around.

Sitting on the top rail, the mid-morning sun warming our backs and the hot coffee warming our bellies, I was surprised when Jerry asked me to buy him out.

"I've still got a couple payments left on my own camps, Jerry. I don't see how I can swing it," I said.

"It wouldn't cost you all that much, Duane. Couldn't you at least think about it?"

"You don't understand, Jerry. My wife doesn't like the outfitting business."

"Tell me about it! Mine left me a year ago. You wouldn't have to pay me anything. Just take over my payments, Pard. Get the bank off my back. They're killing me."

"How much money we talkin' about?"

"I don't know. I think it's around a hundred thousand dollars."

"A hundred thousand dollars! Are you crazy?"

"But that's cheap for two camps and a cabin, plus all the horses and gear and stuff. Hell, you been using my horses. You know they're good. Besides, I got a big summer trip booked you can have. Would you please just come to the bank with me and talk? Even if you don't buy the camps, that would at least buy me some time with them."

I was watching the horses mingle and visit with each other, and I was thinking. Thinking about all the unhunted six-point bull elk roaming Jerry's country.

I hopped down, ignoring the boys' encouraging nods from behind Jerry. I handed him my empty cup and said, "Okay. I guess so."

The banker, Dennis, was surprisingly helpful by explaining the camps' value and their willingness to be patient. He was a hunter himself and brought out maps so I could see the prime locations of the cabin, corrals and tack shed from which Jerry operated.

◆   ◆   ◆

Duane at the historic Camp Monaco tree. The big fir was killed by the Yellowstone forest fires of 1988. The carved, painted section of the trunk was salvaged and is displayed in a typical wilderness hunting camp setting at the Buffalo Bill Historical Center, the famous museum in Cody Wyoming.

Both camps were located on the upper Shoshone River along the east boundary of Yellowstone Park. They provided access into over one hundred twenty square miles of elk-hunting country long known for producing trophy class bulls. In fact, one of the camps was the famous Camp Monaco, established by Buffalo Bill Cody in the late 1800s—a National Historic Site.

The bank's appraisal of Jerry's Northwest Outfitters value was $50,000 for each camp and $35,000 for the mountain cabin; a total of $135,000. The balance due to the bank was $107,000. They not only had no problem with me taking over the payments—they were hopeful I would.

Four of my kids and I were thriving. We embraced the challenges presented by the dry windy climate, the Rocky Mountain environment, and the cowboy culture. Every time the weather, mountains, or horses beat us, we learned valuable lifelong lessons, dusted ourselves off, and made a new plan. But sadly, Stephanie seemed bewildered at our lifestyle. Maybe it was her birth order, but whatever it may have been, she became unnaturally quiet and kept to herself. At school, she excelled in track and basketball but struggled in the classroom. It wasn't until after she graduated that we discovered she is dyslexic.

Betsy, too, struggled to understand and appreciate the western lifestyle. She wasn't able to grasp the physical "grab it & growl" or "let 'er buck" philosophy of Wyoming rural life. I suspect that her heritage of formality, debate, and regular weekly paychecks, which was no longer a part of her lifestyle, left her feeling isolated and insecure. She was never comfortable in the company of construction workers or horsemen. Their boots were usually muddy, and they tended to be plain-spoken people with strong, independent attitudes, expressed with a drought of conversation.

Betsy and I celebrated our twenty-fifth wedding anniversary on July 28, 1981. I was forty-four years old and I remember quite plainly wearily giving up at that time on us ever agreeing on anything or having the kind of close, soul-mate type relationship I had always hoped and longed for. Betsy's long-term disdain and disrespect for me, my lifestyle, and my family produced an accumulated negative impact on our relationship and our family.

An unknown force had highjacked my first love, Betsy. I spent a couple of years grieving for our lost love. It was as if we had both died. In her place was this mean, vindictive woman my mind now knew as "Elizabeth." I didn't know who I had become yet. Consequently, I didn't pay much attention to her harsh objections to my thoughts of expanding Cabin Creek Outfitters by absorbing Northwest Outfitters.

I continued with my research. I talked with U.S. Forest Service personnel, Wyoming Fish & Game Biologists and Wardens, plus interested clients. I received positive feedback and encouragement from all these sources. But the final piece of the puzzle came from a man I never met.

While attending a sport show in Las Vegas that winter, I received a phone call from a Mr. Fred Wischlacz. Fred explained he was an avid sportsman who lived in the Minneapolis area. He had heard of Cabin Creek Outfitters and my efforts to expand into this new hunting area next to Yellowstone and would like to help, if I was interested.

Am I interested? Does the sun come up in the east? Is the Pope—"You bet," I answered. "What do you have in mind?"

"I'd like to invest in something that is more fun for me and my family than the stock market."

"I can appreciate that."

"I'll put up the cash money to pay off the bank. In exchange, I and my two sons and their families have access to Cabin Creek Outfitters' cabin and camps for our family summer trips and fall hunts at no charge. Okay?"

The butterflies in my stomach were chasing each other around so fast I was getting dizzy. I sat down on the edge of the bed, leaned my elbows on my knees to quiet them down, then all of a sudden I had to go to the bathroom. In my best horse-trader manner, I tried to sound nonchalant. "Okay. Anything else?"

"We'll have an accountant structure the deal so I have some tax advantages each year. And if you ever sell the business, I get my original investment back. Oh, and I'd like to be allowed to book some clients for you and help out some in camp."

I knew I'd heard what I heard, but I couldn't believe it. Remembering the old saying, *There's many a slip...*I answered cautiously, "Well, I'd like to think about it and meet you to discuss the details in person."

"Good. Is it alright if I meet you in Cody when you get back?"

"You bet."

When Fred and I met in Cody a couple weeks later, we immediately liked each other. It only took a few days for the accountant and attorney to draw up the necessary papers for Cabin Creek Outfitters to absorb Northwest Outfitters and Fred's interest to be secured.

◆   ◆   ◆

John and Jim pulling a stump at new Jones Creek campsite.

Fred was a little older than me. He was a successful executive with Rydell Shoes in Minnesota. During the first few years we shared a lot of good times together. Fred even got a sheep license one year, and we had a great hunt. We booked lots of hunters together. I stayed with him and his wife in their beautiful home on the banks of the Mississippi River when passing through on the way to sport shows back east. I visited him in the Minneapolis hospital when his heart went bad. He wasn't able to come to the high country after that, but his son Doug would bring his Boy Scout troop from Duluth for summer pack trips each year until he was struck with brain cancer. They were a great family that made a significant contribution to the ongoing success of Cabin Creek Outfitters.

Early summer of 1982, my seventeen-year-old son, John, and a college professor friend of mine, James Allen, from NWCC[1] of Powell, Wyoming, were helping me set up camp at our new site at Jones Creek on the upper Shoshone River. The big summer group of fathers and sons that I had inherited from Jerry Asay would be arriving in less than two weeks.

Everything was going along well until I looked up and saw a rider approaching from a quarter mile upstream. I recognized him as my son, Jeff. Jeff is easy to recognize at any distance horseback because no one sits a horse as well as he does.

My Dad and Mom had spent a couple of weeks with us every fall since we moved to Wyoming, visiting and hunting. Dad hadn't been feeling well for nearly a year. Doctors had been treating him for an ulcer, but he had been steadily getting worse, so they scheduled exploratory surgery.

I knew Jeff would not be taking off work and riding all the way up here unless he had some important news for me. I left the edge of the timber where I had been staking a tent and strode across the meadow toward him. As we drew close, the look in his eyes caused my throbbing heart to lodge in my throat.

Jeff dismounted, dropped his reins, grabbed me in a tight hug, and spoke hoarsely into my ear. "Grandpa's full of cancer, Dad."

He held me close for a couple of minutes while I blinked away tears and tried to rein in my thoughts and emotions. Because of my tight schedule, no one in Michigan was expecting me to make the trip back. I thought about all the work to be done in preparation for the Father and Son pack trip coming up shortly.

I gazed for a moment at the vast panorama of green mountains and blue sky that surrounded me and knew if I was to be of any value to the Fathers and Sons next week, I had to visit my father in his time of need this week.

---

1. NWCC = Northwest Community College, changed in 1989 to Northwest College

Jeff helped me saddle my horse and asked if I wanted him to stay and help with the camp setup. Jim and John said not to worry, they would handle things. As I swung into the saddle, Plenty Horse responded with his smooth, long-legged lope.

I stopped at home in Powell just long enough to shower, shave, and toss a duffle bag of fresh clothes in the back of my pickup, and I headed east over the Big Horn Mountains toward Michigan.

Two days later, needing a shower and a shave, I stepped into Dad's hospital room. He was propped up in bed reading a magazine. When he saw me, he lowered the magazine. With pain and fear in his eyes, he reached for me and said, "Old Lucifer has reared up and got me, son."

Mom, quietly sitting beside Dad's bed, stood and in her gentle loving way embraced me, saying, "Thanks for coming, Duane."

◆　　　◆　　　◆

For forty-seven years Mom had been supporting Dad. She worked just as long and hard as he did to provide for themselves and their family of three daughters and three sons. Before we had a freezer, the mason jars lining our fruit shelves were filled with the bounty of our large vegetable garden, berry patch, fall hunts and spring fishing trips. Dad's favorite place to fish for Brook trout was the Little Two Heart River in Michigan's Upper Peninsula. The best fishing, he claimed, was in the spring when the Tag Alder leaves were the size of a mouse's ear.

When we got the big chest freezer in 1948, Mom filled that too. As a youngster, I felt a strong sense of security and independence, helping prepare and seeing all the stored food.

During World War II, I planted all the vegetables in my own personal victory garden in the shape of a big V, much like the formations of war planes I occasionally saw flying overhead. When rationing began, we ate more venison and trout than ever. Like many other women, Mom rolled her sleeves even higher and spent a year in the factory with Rosie the Riveter's crew.

No matter what issues she had been dealing with during the day, thirty minutes before Dad was expected home from work, all us kids were set firmly in chairs in different rooms of the house so she could clean up, brush her hair, and get "fixed up" for Dad. Dad's coming home from work was always a special time for us kids. It was special in part because Mom made it special.

◆   ◆   ◆

The doctor's findings were bleak: pancreatic cancer, which had spread to other organs. Dad had three to six months to live. After I cleaned up, ate and slept, I spent all the next day with Dad—most of it alone, to give Mom and the others a break. Some times we sat in silence, some time laughing, some time crying, always remembering. Naturally, Dad didn't want to die—he was only sixty-six years old. There were a lot of things he wanted to teach his six children and twenty-two grandchildren. Setting a proper example and teaching life's natural truths had always been important to him.

After analyzing his remaining options, Dad agreed with my observation there was only one more lesson of life for him to teach us. That was simply how to die with dignity. Voice choking with emotion, he said, "But, Duane, you know how sometimes I can be such a pain in the neck?"

"Yeah, Dad, I know. We all can be at times."

"Right, but ah, I mean especially during these last months. I don't want to be, you know. I don't want to be a burden." With tear-streaked face he added, "Too many times I've been too hard on your Mom. I want to be a good patient. I don't want to cause trouble. I'm worried about going to the bathroom. You know? Messing myself. I hate the thought of not being in control of my mind or body. God dammit, Duane, I don't know what to do!"

I had a headache from clenching my teeth and trying to be strong for him. "Dad, the doctors tell me it will be several weeks before the pain gets so bad that the narcotic pain killers will mess with your mind. Meanwhile, there are a lot of friends and family who want to spend some time with you. Doctors say you can go home in a couple of days, and you really would be better off there anyway."

"Yeah, I know. Yeah, I want to go home."

"Right, and folks can come and visit you there and…"

"And I can sleep in my own bed?"

"Right. You can sleep in your own bed."

"I'll be okay when I get home, and you can go back to Wyoming and your family. You tell them I love them, Duane, okay?"

"Yes, Dad, I'll go back to Wyoming. Mom, Larry and the girls will help you."

"What girls?"

"Jean and Phyllis."

"Oh, yeah, okay. You know, Duane, they're the best daughters I could've ever had, and Joyce, too. Don't forget about Joyce. You remember how we used to argue at the supper table about niggers and stuff."

"Yeah."

"I did that on purpose, just to get her goat, you know?"

"I know, Dad."

"Like that time you only got one ice skate for Christmas, remember? How old were you then, nine or ten? I don't remember for sure. I do remember how badly you wanted a pair of hockey skates for Christmas, though. That was the only thing you asked for that year. Amidst all the ruckus of Christmas morning, I was watching as you were trying to be so calm and cool when you opened the skate box. But you couldn't hide the excitement dancing in your eyes. You even calmly read the note explaining that Mom and I could only afford one skate that year and you'd get the other next year. When I first thought of the joke, it really sounded funny to me. I mean, whoever heard of getting one skate? But when I saw the excitement in your eyes replaced by disappointment, the joke wasn't funny anymore. Even at that age it was hard to get one over on you. That's why the other skate showed up right after dinner. By then your Mom was about ready to skin me anyway."

Gazing out the half-open window at the setting fireball sun, he murmured, "I have to remember to tell Joyce about that 'nigger stuff,' too."

"You should, Dad, and remember, I'll be back right after hunting season, okay?"

"Yeah, good idea. That'll work."

Dad settled back in his bed and smiled, relieved now that we had a plan.

When we got Dad back to his home on Lake Huron near Au Gres, I headed for Wyoming. The long, sad drive to Wyoming from Russell's home in upstate New York a few years earlier was nothing compared to leaving my best friend, my mentor, my lifelong guide, my ailing father. And that's not all I had to think about. Elizabeth's insensitive and caustic late-night telephone remarks regarding Dad's life and attitudes echoed in my mind and pierced my heart as I drove and drove.

I was in no way prepared for the mess that awaited at home.

RUFUS & SINGER

I read and reread the letter that was waiting for me from the U.S. Forest Service. The Shoshone Forest Supervisor, Steve Mealy, had placed me on probation while I was with Dad. No formal complaint, no hearing, no nothing. I was just flat on probation and subject to losing my new hunting camps. It was late afternoon, so I only had about an hour of impatient waiting for John to return home from work. I was anxious to hear what he could tell me about this probation.

"The only thing I can think of, Dad, is that the bears must've caused some trouble."

"What bears?"

"Well, it all started a couple of days after you left to go see Grandpa…"

It was late afternoon, had been hot all day, and the Shoshone was up and running hard. John and Jim were done setting up camp but decided to stay over the night and leave early the next morning, when the river would be down. So they were just going around camp, picking up tools and trash, when they noticed a rider about three hundred yards upstream with a pack horse at the crossing. They started hollering at him not to cross, but the river was too noisy for him to hear. John couldn't believe it when he headed out into that high water. He was in trouble almost immediately, or rather his pack horse was. John could see right away the pack horse was a young, inexperienced colt carrying box panniers. The water came halfway up the panniers and scared the colt. Once he stumbled on the slippery rock bottom, the water started pouring into those box panniers. The poor colt couldn't get his footing back and the swollen current started to tumble him over and over. The rider bailed off his saddle horse right in the middle of the river. The saddle horse barely clawed his way on across and up the other bank. Meanwhile, the man was trying to hold the pack horse's head above water with little success.

By the time the current swept them down to camp, which only took a minute or two, the packhorse had drowned and the man was about to. John made a lucky throw with one of their lash ropes and hit him right on the head with it. He latched onto that rope like a bear on bacon, and John and Jim were able to drag him out.

Imagine their surprise when John recognized him as our old buddy, Game Warden Dave Bergonia. He was exhausted and grateful for the rope but plenty upset about his pack horse. It was his expensive new colt's first trip to the mountains. The colt hung up on the big gravel bar just below camp at the mouth of Jones Creek, which Dave thought was lucky. At least now he could retrieve his saddle and pack gear. John didn't think that having bear bait located so close to camp was lucky for us, though. John suggested they quarter the horse and pack him out the next day.

But Dave would have none of that. He couldn't bring himself to cut up his new colt. He insisted John use a couple of our big pack horses to drag the colt as far from camp as possible.

"Well, Dad," he finished, "with all the down timber and brush, that only turned out to be a couple hundred yards."

"Did you report the incident to the Forest Service or anyone?"

"No. Dave's the law. Who should I report it to?"

"Never mind, John. You did the best you could. I'll go have a word with Mealy in the morning. I'm glad you were at least able to save Dave. Well done, son."

"Yeah, thanks, Dad"

◆   ◆   ◆

Bright and early next morning, as I marched past Jay's office on my way to Steve Mealy's office at the end of the corridor, I heard Jay call out, "Duane, Duane, just a minute." I turned to look back and saw Jay standing in his doorway, motioning for me to come in. As I entered his office, he shook my hand and gestured for me to sit down. Jay was the man just under Steve, and his signature was on my permit.

"I think I know where you're going and why, Duane, and I don't blame you for being mad. But please hear me out before you go down there and kick Steve's door in. Okay?"

"Okay, but what the hell is going on?" I asked bluntly.

"It all started a couple of weeks ago when some big brass came in from D.C. You know how sensitive the grizzly bear issue is right now."

"Right." I nodded.

"Well, because they've given us the lead on this deal, they wanted to see how we are handling things here on the Shoshone. You have a reputation of running a clean, bear-resistant camp."

"Yeah. So?"

"So, without checking, Steve and I took the four Washington big shots up to your new Jones Creek camp. And, Duane, it was a disaster. Bears had been in it and made the biggest mess I've ever seen. The brass were aghast and Steve was embarrassed and so humiliated, he stormed back in here, issued that letter of probation you're holding in your hand without thinking or checking with anyone.

"I've done a little checking around. Dave told me about his wreck and how your son saved him and wanted to pack the dead horse out. He feels bad now that he didn't. It's plain the dead horse drew the bears into your camp area, and after they finished off the horse with no one to defend your camp, they went through it with a vengeance.

"Now, the good news is that in spite of all this, Steve has been promoted and will be leaving for Washington D.C. within six weeks. I'll be taking over for him. As far as I'm concerned, when Steve leaves, the probation leaves with him. I wouldn't blame you one bit if you went on down the hall and raised ol' billy hell with Steve, but the less attention there is to this matter, the easier it will be for me to bury it."

The next and last time I saw Steve was at his going-away party. We respectfully raised our glasses and tipped our hats to each other. He went on to a successful career in D.C. I went back to Wyoming grizzly country.

I really enjoyed having my daughter, Denise, working with me in camp one last time during that summer on the Father and Son pack trip. All the guests had a great time, and Denise and I explored some of the new country together. We even chased a big ole black bear out of camp one morning by pelting him with rocks.

◆　　　◆　　　◆

With the acquisition of the cabin and two more camps, Jones Creek and Camp Monaco, I could not only expand my outfitting business but my business vision as well. I envisioned each of my three sons, Mark, Jeff, and John, each managing a camp, with me booking hunters and coordinating everything. It was an exciting vision to me, and I set about the task of turning it into reality with long hours of hard work, consisting of endless hours of promotion, upgrading of equipment, personnel, and horses.

I needed at least twenty head in each camp, which meant I was always buying and selling horses in an ongoing effort to assemble sixty of the most reliable mountain horses possible. Finding that many well-trained, bomb-proof, affordable horses around our small community of Cody/Powell was impossible. So I started raising and training my own.

I'd had no formal education in how to train horses. But I'd had enough on-the-job training by spooky, spoiled horses to know what kind of horse I didn't want. I sought to establish a relationship of mutual trust and respect with my colts. I wanted them eager to do as I asked, not forced to do as I demanded. It was difficult at first, but once I quit trying to teach the horses English and started letting them teach me Horse, I was amazed at what a good pupil I became.

As I learned to read them better, our relationships improved. Instead of my having to get some of them in a corner to catch them, they would come to me when I called. Instead of having to reach under one's belly with a coat hanger to get aholt of the cinch for saddling so I didn't get my head kicked off, they learned to stand quietly for grooming and saddling.

◆　　　◆　　　◆

Buying mules was the beginning of Grad School for me. If you'll listen and learn, mules will teach you everything you need to know about animals in general and yourself in particular.

I've owned a lot of intelligent, hard working, devoted mules. Mules named Smoke, Frog, Skeeter, Ruby, Sis, Durango, Nitro, Tramp, Thelma, Lady, Louise, Kate, Jake, Rufus and Singer—the list could go on and on. There are a couple of stories for each of them. Rufus' and Singer's stories are typical.

I bought both Rufus and Singer from Russell Tompkins, though several years apart. Rufus was a big stout John mule, about 15.1 hands, heavy-boned, a draft-type animal of brindle color and tiger-striped legs. When he was nervous or upset, he would grind his teeth, wring his tail, and pace. I was guiding a hunter, who shot a small bull early one morning on the river bottom about three miles upstream from my Cabin Creek camp. After field dressing the elk and preparing the quarters for packing, I returned to camp with the hunter and saddled up Rufus to go back for the meat.

While I was saddling the mule, Birdshot, one of my hands, came over and asked, "Has that ole mule ever packed meat before?"

"Not that I know of."

"Want me to go along and help ya?"

"I suspect it would be a good idea."

Birdshot knew that the smell of fresh meat spooked some animals and they would refuse to carry it. Sure enough, we were still one hundred yards from the meat when Rufus caught wind of it and was not going any closer. Birdshot was leading Rufus, so I told him to tie him up right here and we'd carry the meat over to him ourselves. "Just be sure and tie him high and short."

We tied our saddle horses nearby but out of the way. When we returned with the meat, Rufus was all worked up. He was grinding his teeth, and his tail looked like an airplane propeller.

"How in the heck we ever going to get this meat on that outlaw?" Birdshot asked.

"Good question. Let me have your jacket."

Birdshot knew what I intended to try and helped me get Rufus blindfolded with his jacket. Next, I used an extra lash rope to tie up his left hind leg. Somewhat disabled but acutely aware that we were packing the dreaded meat on him, Rufus sullenly ground his teeth louder and registered his displeasure by hopping three-legged around the pine tree he was tied to.

Once our diamond was tight, I told Birdshot to mount up, face camp, and be ready to ride. Once he was set, I handed him Rufus' lead rope, then gingerly lowered and untied his hind leg. Rufus was standing still, yet all three of us knew things were going to get western[1] when I jerked the blindfold.

I looked at Birdshot. He sat hunched forward in his saddle, a mischievous half-smile on his face. I pointed to the jacket blindfold. He mashed his black Stetson down on his head with his left hand, where the reins of his saddle horse were threaded through his fingers, and nodded like the rodeo bronc rider he was.

In one motion, I jerked the blindfold and jumped behind a big pine tree. Rufus left a hole in the ground where he had been standing. There was dirt and rocks flying everywhere as he tried his best to run away from the meat on his back. But Birdshot was up to the race. He had his saddle horse wide open and stayed in front, steering Rufus back to camp. They were already there by the time I got my saddle horse quieted down enough to mount up.

It is customary, whenever we are at the trail head preparing for a pack trip, that we saddle our riding horses first. Good thing, too, because the next fall while packing up at Crow Creek to set up our Jones Creek hunting camp, Rufus put us to the test again. It always makes good sense to untie a pack horse from the hitching rail when you tighten his saddle cinches in preparation for packing him. That way, if he's in a bad mood and blows up, he won't jerk the hitching rail down and include a bunch of other horses in his insurrection. That morning, the

---

1.   get western = the resulting chaos when the forces of nature and the laws of physics collide where you're standing

minute Rufus was untied for tightening, he bolted and ran off white-eyed into the timber.

"Hey Toad Body. I believe Rufus is serious about quitting the outfit. You better mount up and fetch him," I called out.

"You betcha, Boss." Toad Body grinned as he swung into the saddle. He was the best rope hand I had in the outfit, and he loved to cowboy.

It was a couple of hours later and we were pretty well packed when T-B returned leading the runaway mule. As he handed me Rufus' lead rope he said, "You sure had him pegged, Boss. He was plumb down to the construction zone and cycling right down the middle of the road before I was able to catch up and dab a loop on him."

Rufus knew he'd been had when I tied him high, short and tight to an eight-inch pine tree. He ground his teeth loudly as we packed our two brand-new, disassembled wood heating stoves on him. Once on the trail, Rufus seemed resigned to his fate and didn't cause any trouble during the trip. By the time we'd reached our camp site, he'd even quit grinding his teeth and stood calmly as we unpacked all the other horses first. The minute the diamond was off his pack, he blew again, but this time he didn't run away. He just went to bucking in a big circle all around the outside of our meadow. Pieces and parts to our brand new $150 stoves were flying every which way.

T-B started laughing. "Duane, look at the counterfeit sum-bitch buck. Boss, I believe he got you again."

"Yeah. I believe I've seen this scene before," I grimly replied. By the time Rufus returned to the hitching rail to be unsaddled, he had completely emptied his panniers. As I unsaddled him, I warned, "You just wait, Rufus. I'll get even with you yet."

He wriggled his ears as if to say, "Bring it on, Amateur."

We put our stoves together with what few pieces we could find and went on with camp setup. A few days later, a good friend and fellow outfitter, Jake Clark, rode into camp on his way up sheep hunting. Jake has always run a big string of mules and asked me about the big brindle mule in the meadow. I couldn't see any future in speaking ill of my ole buddy Rufus so I didn't mention how he jumped fences and would never stay where you put him and other such maddening traits. I just replied "Oh, Rufus? He's a helluva mule."

"Can you ride him?"

"Ride him? Hell, you can pack him, drive him and ride him."

"No shit. He broke to drive?"

"Yup."

"I need a mule to pull my carriage over in West Yellowstone next summer."

"Rufus will pull anything you can fasten to him."

"I don't spose you'd trade him, would you?"

"Well, I don't know, Jake. Me'n old Rufus, we got sort of a thing going."

"Yeah, I know. Good mules are hard to part with, but I'll trade you this big old sorrel I'm riding straight across for him, Pard."

"What's wrong with your horse?"

"Nothin.' He's just not a dude horse is all," Jake replied with a straight face.

I knew that could mean anything from *the horse bucks, you can't catch him, won't load, won't stand to get on or off, you can't pick up his feet to shoe him,* or *he's accident prone*. The list could go on and on, but I was fed up with Rufus.

A little earlier, Jake had rode in on a good-looking sorrel horse. A little later, he rode out on Rufus. We were both smiling. The sorrel turned out to be a pretty good horse, after all.

◆　　◆　　◆

I was surprised to see Jake ride in again the next fall.

"You got any coffee, Pard?" he asked.

"Sure do. Step down and have some lunch with us."

"Thanks. Don't mind if I do."

There were a half dozen or so of us setting up camp again, so we fixed some sandwiches and coffee. After joking through lunch, Jake turned to me and said matter-of-factly, "You didn't mention that Rufus could jump any fence he was put behind."

"Well, he does have a mind of his own," I admitted.

"Mind of his own! Mind of his own! Let me tell you what that rascal did to me last summer over in West Yellowstone. He started the summer pulling that carriage like an old pro. We were all over town. Everybody knew and loved Rufus. I mean, he owned that town. He just wouldn't stay in the pasture at night, but we all learned to live with his gadding about. Then I got a call early one Saturday evening.

"Three guys had been celebrating a wedding and needed to be picked up in front of the Mint Bar and taken to their motel, as they were in no condition to walk or drive. We were about to pull up to the curb in front of the bar when the drunks came stumbling out to get in the carriage. Rufus took one look at that smelly lot, snorted, and just went right on. I hollered at the surprised guys to just stay there and jump in when I came back around.

"When I came around the block the second time, Rufus was watching for them and barely slowed at all when we blew by the bar. By now, several pedestrians were watching the show and cheering for Rufus. I was determined to bring him around again, and this time we were going to stop and pick those fellows up, or else.

"Let me tell you guys something. When we turned the corner and started back down Main Street, I got the ride of my life. Rufus grabbed the bit, lined up on the center line, and went high-stepping past those drunks so fast that even they were cheering him on. I was braced up in that driver's seat, a rein in each hand, and hanging on for dear life. I never knew a mule could travel so fast. He didn't stop til he was back to the corral."

We all had a good laugh and shared with Jake the many lessons Rufus had taught us. In time, I would acquire and put together a string of sixteen pack mules. It was always a thrill and sense of pride to see that hard-working string of animals following each other up hill and down, through swift rivers or deep snow, packing supplies into camp and elk out of camp. I loved them all, but my all-time favorite was Singer.

Singer was a medium-size bay mule who moaned and groaned and bobbed his head in time with his gait when he was packed or ridden. Hence his name, "Singer." Singer was intelligent, capable and accommodating. Whenever I'd explore new country, I'd always ride Singer, because I knew he would get me back out no matter what.

Due to the several miles between my camps, it was necessary to ride a lot after dark. Singer was my mount of choice, as he never got surprised by moose or bear. Many times when it was so dark I couldn't even see his head, he'd take a few steps off the trail and stand still while I listened to something pass on the trail beside us.

For some reason, coyotes made him nervous. When they would begin to sing too close to camp, he'd just come in my tent with me, and I'd better make room cause he was coming in. Singer never let me down, and sometimes he did extra work to make up for someone else's shortcomings—like the night I nearly lost him.

I had my string on rented winter pasture a couple miles from home that year. When the feed got short toward spring, after work each day I'd take a bale of hay to them just before dark and make sure everyone was alright. That particular night all the horses were there, but no Singer. It was just not like Singer to be off by himself, especially at suppertime.

I took a quick drive around the hundred-acre pasture fence to see if he was hung up someplace. Before it got plumb dark, I hurried out to the road to see if he'd gotten out there somehow. On my way out, I passed a bad bog hole about fifty yards to my left. It was about ten yards in diameter and had a good fence around it. I didn't have my binoculars with me. In the fading light, I could see there was nothing there except a small piece of log out in the middle.

Before I got home, the early March wind was blowing cold rain drops across my headlights. I was restless and barely slept that night. I couldn't rid myself of a sickening feeling in the pit of my stomach. I tried to remember if I'd ever seen that small log in the center of the bog before.

It wasn't quite daylight when I returned to the pasture gate the next morning. As I got out of the truck to open the gate, a sudden impulse hit me to call out Singer's name. I cupped my hands on both sides of my mouth and hollered as loud as I could. I immediately got an answering "Hee Haw" from the direction of the bog.

"Oh my God—he's been in that bog all night, but he's still alive!"

Something had told me to bring the horse trailer and extra lash ropes with me that morning. As I bounced through the sage, driving faster than I should toward the bog with the 4-horse trailer banging and clanging behind me, there were two thoughts on my mind. First, I was sure glad I brought the trailer and ropes. Second, I was very upset with myself for being so negligent as to leave the poor animal in the bog all night.

I backed the trailer as close as I dared to the bog and tied one end of a lash rope to it, and the other end to my waist. I really didn't want to wade out in all that muck but I had no choice. Singer's ears, eyes and mouth were all that were visible. By the time I struggled out to him with a halter and rope, I had sunk to my waist and was treading water to keep from sinking further. I guessed we were in quicksand. All I know is it was scary, and Singer was plumb happy to see me. He had been murmuring to me on and off since I had arrived. After I got the halter on his head, I pulled myself out, hand over hand up the rope I had tied to the trailer.

When I clucked and pulled on Singer, he lunged. We only moved a couple inches. I clucked again. Singer lunged, but to no avail this time. I could see this would never work, so back in the bog I went. This time, after an exhausting struggle, I got another lash rope under Singer's haunches. Hand over hand, I dragged myself out again, tied one end of Singer's butt rope to the trailer, clucked, and pulled hard.

When he lunged this time, we made some progress. We both rested a minute and tried again. The best thing about this whole experience was Singer did not panic and expend his energy wildly floundering around. He remained calm and patient, enabling us to work together. And work together we did. Not only that day, pulling and resting, pulling and resting, but for many rewarding years thereafter.

Rufus and Singer talking war at Jones Creek camp.

NO PIES FOR SUPPER

As the doctor had predicted, Dad enjoyed a few weeks at home visiting with friends, but now as fall drew near, he became weaker and thinner, unable to eat much. I talked to Mom on the phone regularly. Larry, Jean and Phyllis were helping her a lot and looking forward to me getting there after hunting season.

This was my first year at our new camps, and I had hunters booked in all three, so it was going to be a busy season for me. Once it ended in mid-November, I promised I'd go back to Michigan and help care for Dad.

Don Juby was a short, grizzled sort of character who had cooked in the Jones Creek Camp for Northwest Outfitters for many years and had agreed to continue to cook there for me. I liked Don. He was a hardworking veteran of the South Pacific Campaign during WWII. Likeable as Don was, he was also excitable and tended to ricochet from one crisis to another daily. Bears and bureaucracy were especially hard on Don's nervous nature.

During our first elk hunt that year, Don had climbed about fourteen feet up a big pine tree to hang some food out of any marauding bear's reach. In the process, he leaned out too far, lost his balance and fell heavily to the ground. He hobbled back to camp, and I fashioned a pair of crutches for him from a couple of crotched poles. He gimped around camp for the last three days of that hunt, but instead of staying in camp the two days between hunts to prevent any raids from bears, he decided he should go home and soak his aching hips in a tub of hot water.

Don was last to arrive on the morning our next group of hunters were to leave Crow Creek corrals. After his old pickup clattered to a dusty stop in his customary parking place, Don came swinging over to me on brand new, store-bought crutches.

"Duane, if you'll saddle my horse for me and bring him over to my tailgate, I'll get these hunters on into camp."

"Sure, Don. Are you okay? How're you feeling?"

"Yeah, I'm fine. Soaking in that hot tub helped a little but I was still hurting pretty bad, so I went to the doctor yesterday. He said, 'It's no wonder you're hurtin', you old goat, you've cracked your pelvis.'"

Don patted his left shirt pocket as he continued, "Doc gave me some pain killers and said to stay on the couch for a week or two. Guess he don't know what time of year it is. Don't worry, Boss, I'll stick my crutches under the diamond on the pack horse. I'll be just fine. Besides, I brought me along a jug of peppermint schnapps."

With that explanation, Don headed back to his truck and crawled up on the tailgate to await his saddle and pack horses. Shortly thereafter, he stuck his peppermint schnapps in his saddle bags, mashed his hat down securely, and gingerly eased off the tailgate and onto his saddle horse. He headed up the trail with our four awed hunters following his crutch-bearing pack horse.

A couple of hours later as the group entered our camp meadow, the hunters were startled to hear Don exclaim, "He's hit us again! If that damn bear has crapped in my sleeping bag again, you boys can just get yourself another cook cause I'm going home."

Fortunately, the bear had not bothered Don's bed at all, just destroyed everything around it. The hunters were quick to understand the situation, hurriedly dismounted and began picking up, cleaning up and salvaging what they could of our food supplies.

Don and I fixed some sandwiches for everyone and sent the clients out hunting with one of the guides. We sent the other guide back to our cabin with a list of supplies to be replaced and instructions to return before breakfast. He got in about 10 p.m. with the eggs, bacon and Crisco so necessary for breakfast and pies.

As I settled into my sleeping bag that night, I began to wonder if that bear could count too. He always came in when everyone was gone. I could just imagine him laying up there on the mountain somewhere, all comfortable and dry under a big spruce tree, keeping track of us with one big beefy paw and planning his next raid.

Well, I had a surprise for him. A big surprise named Bill Lambert. Bill is a tall, raw-boned southern boy from Cape Canaveral, Florida. Bill and his hunting partners, Del, Dave and Ken, had gotten wind of our bear problem, changed their original hunting plans, and booked this second hunt of the season with us, because Bill wanted a big black bear.

The five of us were sleeping in a big Indian teepee I had erected for our summer trips.

For heat, we had a thirty-gallon barrel wood-burning stove in the middle with a four-inch stove pipe going up to the smoke hole in the top of the teepee, and five bunks with foam pads built around the circumference. We had lots of room and were very comfortable.

About four inches of fresh snow had fallen and we were looking forward to another successful elk hunt. Around midnight I got up to tend to nature. I was only a couple of steps away from the teepee flap, half naked, no rifle or anything, and there He was—bigger than life! We both froze and were locked eyeball to eyeball long enough for all the good deeds I'd ever done in my life to flash through my mind, so you know we weren't there long.

It was only a second before he growled, and I hollered and dove back into the teepee for my rifle. In the fair moonlight reflecting off the new fallen snow, I saw him disappear into the timber beyond the latrine. I levered a shell into my Grandpa's old Winchester 32 Special that had been handed down to me and then fired into the air, hoping that would keep him out of camp for the rest of the night at least. With flashlights, we discovered he had been back in the cook tent, but it appeared at first nothing had been touched—so we all traipsed back to the teepee.

Don had moved his gear into one of the smaller sleep tents and hadn't even bothered to get up this time.

Some of the boys were debating the odds of the bear returning that night, but Bill declared with a twinkle in his eye as how there was no way that bear would return after what I'd called him.

"Didn't you guys hear Duane holler 'get out of here, you pot-licking bear'? A pot licker he called him. Nothing can stand up to that kind of verbal abuse," he laughed. "Not even that big old bear."

I could see he was secretly delighted that El-Bear-O had changed his MO and was sneaking into camp while we were still here, thereby increasing Bill's chances of bagging a big bear on this hunt.

Around the dining table the next evening after an unsuccessful day of elk hunting, the talk turned to devising some sort of alarm system to alert us to the bear's presence should he make another pass at us that night. Strings of tin cans around the camp perimeter, horse bells attached to the cook tent, and aerosol cans dipped in bacon grease were all discussed with great enthusiasm but discarded as unpractical.

Don allowed as how, by God, something had to be done 'cause he couldn't keep up with the thievery. If we wanted any pies with our suppers, somebody better damn well shoot that bear.

"What's shooting the bear got to do with having pies?" everyone wanted to know.

"It's plain to see you guys wouldn't make very good bear detectives," he said with a snort. "One of the things I had the wrangler bring back from the cabin the other night was a new can of Crisco, right?"

Everyone nodded in agreement.

"Well, I only used one spoonful from that can and I've searched high and low and it's nowhere to be found. And even you gunsels[1] should know ya need Crisco to make pie crust."

Everyone agreed that was the last straw. "What the hell are you going to do about that rotten bear?" they asked.

"I guess I'll have to resort to tying Singer behind the cook tent," I replied.

"Well, hell, we might as well forget about having any pie on this hunt," the hunters grumbled as they headed for the teepee.

By the time I had belled and double-tied Singer in a little clump of pine behind the cook tent, all the hunters except Bill had turned in. "I admit Singer is good, Duane," Bill said. "In fact, I've never seen his equal anytime or anyplace, but I don't see how you figure he's any match for that bear, even if it's only a black bear. That critter is smart and biiiiggg!" Bill paused to light up a going-to-bed cigar.

Before I turned out the lantern, I told them that if anyone shot my riding mule during the night, it'd cost them $5000.00 cash. There wouldn't be any arguing about it over a dead mule in the morning.

"I've tied him in that little patch of pine behind the cook tent. So don't shoot him when the ruckus starts," I warned.

"What good is that going to do?" someone asked.

"He has instructions to tell me when the bear is in camp" I replied.

"By golly, Duane, you got a deal." Bill laughed. "If any of us shoots your mule, we will pay you the $5000 on the spot. And I'll guaran-damn-tee-ya something else. I came all the way from Florida for that bear, and if he comes back tonight, he'll be leaving via pack horse."

About midnight, Singer's emphatic snort woke me. "The bear's in camp, boys," I said without budging from my sleeping bag.

Dave came plumb across the teepee with his 7mm at the ready, went outside like the flap on his long johns was afire, hit the cold snow with his bare feet and froze right there. Not ten yards from him was Mr. Camp Wrecker Supreme. And, directly behind the bear was Singer.

---

1.   gunsels = incompetents

Dave's hesitation allowed Bill, who was sleeping right next to the teepee flap but had stopped to pull on some boots, to arrive on the scene. Bill had his 44 handgun at the ready. Even though Bill wanted that bear so bad he could taste it, his good sense and sportsman-like attitude required him to wisely defer the shot to his hunting partner.

By this time, Bruno had decided that being between Singer and two hungry hunters was as bad as being between a rock and a hard spot. As he started back his favorite escape route, he presented Dave with a perfect broadside shot. With the snow, the moonlight and the 9-power scope, he couldn't miss.

Bill relaxed. Dave squeezed the trigger, and the firing pin struck an empty chamber with a resounding "click." Dave and Bill swore as the bear disappeared into the black timber beyond the latrine again. Singer shook his head and stomped his front foot in disgust. The three of us still in our sleeping bags laughed so hard our stomachs hurt.

A couple of hours later, Dave's stumbling over the wood stove and knocking down the stove pipe jerked me full awake! I hadn't heard Singer snort, but Bill had. In fact, he told me later that he was only feigning sleep and was now convinced that Singer and I knew what we were doing. He wasn't about to let Dave and his empty rifle come plumb across the teepee and beat him out the flap again. So he was listening intently, and when Singer snorted and stomped his foot, Bill was ready.

Barefoot this time, his 300 Magnum ready, one foot out of the teepee and the other one planted firmly inside the teepee, he was braced for a good clean shot. That's when Dave arrived amidst the smoke, soot and rattling stove pipes. Off balance and expecting to find the entrance empty, Dave was not prepared to apply his brakes that soon and crashed into Bill, who was at that moment settling his cross hairs on Mr. Destruction's shoulder.

The momentum of Dave's journey carried them both out of the teepee and into the snow on their hands and knees, on a level with the somewhat startled and nervous bear. Two Magnum rifles roared as one, the flame from their barrels lighting up the night and singeing the hair on the big marauder as he went to the Happy Hunting Grounds.

The next night, we stuffed ourselves on bear steak and fresh apple pie for supper. Some of the apples were saved out, and everyone took his turn affectionately feeding Singer his favorite reward for a job well done.

The empty Crisco can and other litter from somewhat more successful raids were found later under a large dense spruce tree with a perfect view of the camp below.

The bear turned out to be the biggest black bear taken in Northwest Wyoming that year. He was thirteen years old, and his teeth were worn down to nubs. His left canine tusk was completely hollow and abscessed. The poor old devil was in a lot of pain, hungry, and at the end of his rope.

So Bill took home a beautiful trophy that wouldn't have lasted out the winter. With our camp gone, he would have died the long slow death of starvation and may have hurt someone in the process.

The fellows all had personal reasons for wanting to return next year. Del claimed he saw a bull elk with ivory plumb to his ass and wanted to hunt him again. And Ken saw a mule deer buck he swore was big enough to bugle.[2] Even though we spent many hours hand-sewing our tents back together, the cook tent couldn't be saved, and we burned it right there on the spot when we left. There are plenty of paw prints on the dining tent, however, that will always remind us of Singer and the Bear.

Twelve years later, I stroked Singer's head in my lap as he died of liver cancer.

---

2.   bugle = the mating call of a bull elk, which is much larger than a mule deer

DAD'S LAST LESSON

My first night with Dad in early December was challenging indeed. Everyone was relieved that I had finally arrived and could now take my turn providing care. They were all wore out. Phyllis and Larry went back home to Flint. Mom went to her own room for some much needed sleep. I went to bed in Dad's room.

He had developed a habit of getting up in the middle of the night and wandering around the dark house. This was unacceptable, as he might fall and break a bone. Dad was very frail and gaunt now, slowly starving to death as the cancer continued its unrelenting attack on his vital organs.

In an attempt to confine Dad to bed, the family had laced sheet ropes to the side of the hospital bed back and forth over him. He looked quite secure. I told him I would be sleeping in the other bed, and that if he needed anything he should let me know. Then I naively fell asleep.

About midnight, I roused myself to check on Dad. His bed was empty! The laced sheets were all in place, but Dad was gone! I was about to panic. The first night I was in charge, Dad disappeared. *There is no way this is a good thing. I needed to find him and find him fast,* I thought as I raced quietly throughout the house. And I sure didn't want to wake Mom up during the search. What do you suppose she would have to say about my negligence?

Shortly my worst fear was realized. Dad was not in the house at all! I dashed into the attached garage. The light in Dad's back corner work shop was on. I barely felt the cold, damp concrete floor on my bare feet as I rushed toward the door with a sickening feeling in the pit of my stomach. Just before I reached the patch of light streaming out beneath the workshop door, Dad calmly appeared. Over his PJ's, he had donned his old work jacket. His steely gray hair stuck out around the edges of his aluminum hard hat. He had his brick laying trowel in his hand and was barefoot just like me.

He seemed a bit startled to see me. When I asked what he was doing, he answered quietly, "Nothing."

"I'm tired, Dad. What do you say we go to bed?"

He shrugged his shoulders and replied simply, "Okay."

There was no way he could get back in bed until I had unlaced the sheet ropes. How he got out I'll never know. But I did know one thing—I was going to have to watch the tricky old devil much closer. Sure enough, about twenty minutes after we both settled down and I was feigning sleep with one eye half open, Dad suddenly sat straight up in his bed and stared hard at me. I didn't move until he started to throw off his blanket. Then I sat up and sternly told him to quit messing around and go to sleep.

He seemed resigned to the fact that I was on to him. I think he went to sleep. I didn't, though. I spent the rest of the night thinking about ways to make his and everyone's life a bit easier. It was obvious Dad didn't like being cooped up in that sick room twenty-four hours a day. I couldn't blame him and decided I'd get him out of it come daylight.

So next morning after his bathroom break, I asked if he'd like to go out and sit in the family room for awhile. His eyes lit up as he emphatically responded, "Yes."

Walking was difficult and dangerous for him, so when he needed to go to the bathroom—which was only a few steps from his room—I'd have him stand on my feet and I'd walk backwards. He could hold onto my shoulders, and I'd hold onto his waist. For the trips to the family room and back, I tucked him into an old rocking chair with pillows and blankets and skidded him around like a sled.

Dad enjoyed having some activity back in his life, and he spent hours looking out the sliding glass doors to the marshes, where for years, he had thrilled at hunting duck and trapping muskrat. I would sit nearby and read. Sometimes I'd read aloud to him. Dad had no interest in TV but did enjoy going to different rooms in the house. When he would tire, I'd skid him back to bed for a nap. That became our daily routine for the next couple of weeks. I even removed the sheet restraints from his bed. They didn't work, anyway. Dad never attempted to wander off again.

He didn't talk much nowadays, but one cold sunny afternoon, he told me how hungry he was. Again, I found myself nodding my head and clenching my teeth to keep from breaking down. He asked if we couldn't please go into town for supper. I didn't know what to say. I felt like bawling. My head ached from the strain and I answered hoarsely, "I don't know, Dad, maybe. What would you like for supper?"

He was sitting straight up in bed now and answered. "A big T-bone steak, medium rare, with baked potato and salad with french dressing."

"That sounds like a lot, Dad. I wonder if—"

"But I am really hungry, Duane. I haven't had anything to eat in a long time, son."

"I know, Dad. I know. Let me check with Mom, okay?" I managed to whisper.

I needed to leave the room for a moment to regain my composure. Dad hadn't been able to eat solid food for weeks. The last several days he wasn't even able to get jell-O or apple sauce down. The doctor had told us he would eventually starve to death right before our eyes and all we could do was treat his pain with the strong laudanum he had prescribed. As the dosage was increased to keep pace with the constantly intensifying pain, Dad would become less and less communicative and coherent.

I knew all that when I returned to him with a bowl of apple sauce. I fed him small spoonfuls as I told him if he was able to handle the apple sauce, we'd see about getting him a T-bone steak a little later. I was amazed and encouraged at how well he was doing, and the bowl was half-gone, when a sudden look of despair and fear flooded into Dad's eyes as all the apple sauce I thought he'd been eating began to leak out of the corners of his tightly clenched lips.

He sat quietly as I cleaned the mess off him and then with a resigned sigh lay slowly back on his pillow. Dad seldom spoke again after that day. For the rest of my life, I've avoided T-bone steak.

Though Dad's skeleton-like smile was hard to recognize, the cancer was unable to steal the love and compassion that shone in his eyes. He seemed especially grateful one afternoon as I held his hand and prayed for him and our family. I never felt so inadequate and powerless in my life, and so frustrated that I couldn't fix things.

That evening around 7:00, he became agitated and motioned with his eyes towards the door. I looked, but no one was there. Dad kept motioning. So I went out of the room for a couple of minutes, got a drink of water from the kitchen, lifted the cover off the pot of homemade chicken noodle soup Mom was cooking for supper, then returned to Dad's room. He was gone.

All those great years of working, hunting, fishing and growing together. He was gone. The weeks and months of tender loving care. He was gone. It seemed to happen so quickly and quietly. I could hear Dad's brother, Uncle Alvin, visiting with Mom as she prepared supper as if everything was normal. But Dad was gone. The most important man in my life was gone forever.

I reached up to close Dad's beautiful brown eyes for the last time, but the lids wouldn't stay down. You see people do that on TV—what a crock. In real death, it doesn't work that way.

The mortician arrived with his gurney in about an hour. He said he didn't need my help to get Dad's body into the hearse. But I insisted on going all the way with Dad. He'd gone all the way with me for forty-six years. It was December 16, 1982.

My sense of loss was immense, and for several years, I fretted that initially there may have been more we could have done for Dad. A better doctor. A bigger hospital. Was there something we missed? Those concerns were put to rest a few years later when I read that like Dad, actor Michael Landon had been diagnosed with pancreatic cancer and survived less than a year. I'm sure that "Little Joe Cartwright" could afford and had access to the best medical minds and treatments available. But the results were the same. I felt bad for Michael and his family.

◆   ◆   ◆

I dealt with my grief by losing myself in my work. I attended several sport shows that winter from Anaheim, California to Kansas City, Missouri, and booked all three hunting camps full for the fall of '83.

I received an interesting offer that spring from Ted and Judy Blair, owners of the Cody Holiday Inn. They had made a deal to host several hundred Taiwanese tourists throughout the summer. The Taiwanese would arrive via plane in groups of 30 to 35 people twice a week. They would need transportation from the airport three miles out of town to the Holiday Inn, shopping tours of Cody, and transportation to and from the Cody Nite Rodeo. The Blairs were looking for a mode of transportation with a western flavor.

They were enthused about my suggestion of a team and wagon and offered me space for my headquarters in front of their lobby, currently occupied by an old swimming pool. All I had to do was fill in the swimming pool, build a small office building, build a covered wagon that would seat thirty-two people, buy a team and harness, and learn to drive them up and down Main Street. We shook hands and I started to work immediately.

The first group of Taiwanese were scheduled to arrive in thirty days!

The project went so well that summer that the next year, the Blairs offered me use of some acreage they owned on the west edge of town to set up a string of saddle horses for hour rides. We were across the road from the rodeo grounds, and it was the only place in town for tourists to ride a horse for an hour or two. Consequently, my twenty head of saddle horses and three wranglers were kept very busy. That same year, I was awarded the contract to provide forty head of horses and four wranglers for the Pahaska Teepee Lodge at the East entrance to Yellowstone Park.

Duane driving Tom and Jerry heading up to the Cody airport to pick up another load of Taiwanese tourists.

Good as they were, I didn't trust any of my wranglers to drive the team in traffic with thirty-plus guests on board. So, in addition to keeping both saddle horse concessions running smoothly, I always drove the team. My days usually began about 5:00 a.m. and ended about 11:30 p.m.. I lived on bologna sandwiches and Mountain Dew.

Even though it was long days of hard work, I enjoyed meeting many new people. I had all sixty head of my horses earning their keep and getting in shape for hunting season.

Home life was practically nonexistent. As was her custom, Elizabeth dealt with her frustrations, disappointments, and demons by spending lots of time in bed. She would usually get up by 7:00 or 8:00 a.m., putter around the house or run a few errands. After lunch, she would nap until the girls got home from school, insist they help her with household chores including fixing supper, then watch TV until 10 p.m. bedtime.

EPHRAIM[1]

There were a number of consequences in having Yellowstone Park as a neighbor of my hunting camps, not the least of which was striving to survive the collateral damage of their policy-changing decisions, such as in the late 1970s, when they abruptly closed the bear feeding stations that generations of bears and tourists had been habituated to. In the late 80s, they adopted a let-burn policy regarding forest fires. And the big one everyone in the United States is now paying for—in 1995, over the objections of eighty percent of the residents of Wyoming, Montana and Idaho, the Federal Government reinstated the animal kingdom's second most feared predator, wolves.

When the Park closed the bears' supplemental feed grounds on the basis it wasn't natural, it became natural for the grizzly to leave Yellowstone for the easy pickings of camp grounds, lodges and back country camps like mine. So I had three new things to worry about: fires, bears, and wolves.

◆　　　◆　　　◆

"By God, Cap'n, you gotta do somethin' about that damn she-bear."

As I stepped down from Plenty Horse, I could plainly see that Don, my trusty old camp cook, was mad as hell. It's easy to tell when something is bothering Don, because he'll come striding across the Jones Creek camp compound to where I am tying my horse. Wiping his hands on his apron and red-faced, he begins a loud sentence with "By God, Cap'n."

Don, a little burnt and crusty around the edges, runs the camp with an iron hand but has a heart like your mom's cherry pie. Right now, he was splashing through the mud with rain bouncing off his high forehead and fire in his eyes.

"As soon as I turn this horse loose and get in out of the rain, we'll figure it out," I said. "Okay, Don?"

"Yah, right," he mumbled.

1.　Ephraim = a respectful name for the grizzly bear used by original mountain men

As I hung my yellow rain slicker behind the dining tent stove, I asked, "Isn't the fence working, Don?"

"I'll tell you exactly how that damn electric fence is working, Duane. Number 104 and her three cubs have been in here two nights in a row demanding something to eat. You can't expect them guides to hunt elk all day and fight griz all night. They gotta have some rest."

"But what about—" I tried to ask, but Don interrupted, anticipating my question.

"I know. I know! The electric fence was supposed to be the answer to all our problems. When you and the Forest Service isolated the cook and dining tents with two strands of hot wire, I figured I'd have some easy sleeping. Instead, those cubs start to crawl through the fence, get a jolt, let out a bawl, and come on through the fence. We end up eyeball to eyeball with those furry little trash compactors while Mama bear huffs and pops her teeth at us just outside the wire. By God, Cap'n, I tell you it's enough to drive a man to drink. You gotta do somethin'."

It takes special country for grizzly bears to call home. It must be as remote, wild, and big as the bears themselves. We consider ourselves fortunate to have a permit to camp and hunt elk in such a pristine wilderness. You can drink from the streams, catch whatever native trout you want for the next meal, and have fresh-picked wild strawberries or raspberries on the side.

The grizzlies teach us something new every year. One of the first lessons we learned years ago was to never leave a camp unattended overnight. Someone must sleep in the cook and dining tents to prevent heavy losses and damage.

The grizzly bites everything, whether there is food in it or not, leaving holes about the size of a 38 slug in pots, pans, coffee pots, Dutch ovens, and the bases of Coleman lanterns.

They seldom enter a tent through the manufactured flaps, preferring instead to create their own private entrance anywhere else. I think they dearly love to hear canvas being shredded by their long, sharp claws because they never use their entrance as an exit. No, siree; an exit calls for a slash with the other paw, and just in case the griz may have overlooked a lantern or cast iron skillet, he'll go in and out until there are nothing but six inch ribbons hanging from the ridge pole.

Over the years, I've found it costs me an average of $1500 for each successful bear attack. So, after a sleepless night of hoping to counter Number 104's endless forays on our larder, I saddled up and headed for a telephone to call in reinforcements.

The U.S. Forest Service and Wyoming Game & Fish each sent two hands to help save us from the bear and the bear from us. Just like #104, they slept days and stayed up nights to entertain her by shooting off guns, fire crackers, Roman candles and nauseating scents. She must have really enjoyed the nightly shows because she came in about 9 p.m. for nine nights in a row.

The first thing the battery of experts decided was the electric fence had to come down. Being trapped inside the 20 x 40 foot fenced area with the griz was hard on everybody's nerves and disposition, they reasoned, so it was replaced by an eight-foot-high chain link fence.

That seemed to stymie old #104, and the last two days of our hunt were uneventful. We all headed to town to pick up our next group of hunters, secure in the illusion that our camp was finally grizzly-proof and no one needed to stay in camp to guard it. Hunters and hands rode the four miles downstream to our end-of-the-road trail head where the vehicles were parked. They were all anticipating a hot shower and a reunion with their wives.

If I live to be a hundred, I'll never forget the sight that greeted us when we rode into the trail head. A gaping hole, big enough to drive a pickup truck through, had been clawed and splintered into the side of the wood-plank barn. I had stored the extra horse grain in that area of the barn because there were no windows or doors on that side, and I figured the grain would be safest there.

The signs revealed that a big, and I mean big, grizzly boar had ripped that hole, eaten what he wanted of the hundred-pound sack of grain, and had taken the rest with him. When something like that happens, you think, "Oh my God, what are they going to do next?"

I didn't have to wait long for the answer to that question. We had just returned to camp. I was tending to some of the pack mules when I heard Don shout from the cook tent, "By God, Cap'n, you ain't gonna believe this."

And I wouldn't have believed it if I hadn't seen it with my own eyes. That old barn-wrecking boar had padded up the other side of the river and gotten back to the camp before we did. Finding our chain link fortress locked up tight, he devised a way of unlocking it. He had brought his own set of keys, the same keys he had used on the locked barn—six-inch claws. He reached up, got hold of the top of the chain link fence, and with unimaginable strength, smashed it down to size so he could crawl over and get inside the compound to raid the cook tent. Then it was a simple backhand slash to remove the rear corner of the tent and begin his smorgasbord.

A big griz on patrol.

Ephraim up close and personal.

I won't bore with you an endless list of what he ate and how much he ate. Suffice it to say the wrangler and four pack mules were dispatched immediately for fresh supplies.

Another lesson to remember is that a bear never forgets where he got a meal, so he comes back night after night. Even a year after the meal, he will return just to be sociable. By the next night, we had sewn the cook tent back together, braced up the fence, and staked a dog on a short chain leash just inside the point of attack.

"I wish that damn dog would quit whinin' and whimperin,'" one of the guides remarked during supper.

"I'll give him some elk roast gravy," Don volunteered as he ducked out of the dining tent to get our cherry pie from the cook tent.

In a minute we heard, "By God, Cap'n, you better take a look at this sucker."

The scene that slowly came into focus as my eyes adjusted from the lantern-lit dining tent to the inky black night looked like something from a comic strip. Backing away from his assigned guard area, the twenty-pound dog had literally plowed a trench into the ground with his paws, and his leash was stretched so taut you could have played a tune on it.

The motivating force for all this digging, straining and whimpering was six hundred pounds of grizzly boar sitting just outside the chain link fence with his nose thrust through one of the little openings in the fence. That boar showed up for five more nights and sat outside our fence to panhandle. Needless to say, he sat wherever he wanted and we rerouted our midnight trips to the latrine.

I understand if a person loses his sight, somehow he can compensate for the loss by magnifying his other senses. It has been my experience to enjoy a similar sharpening, quickening, and magnifying of all my senses while living in griz country. I became acutely aware of everything around me.

Early one crisp October morning, as I approached my Monaco Camp on horseback, I spotted the most beautiful grizzly I had ever seen. About a hundred yards through the timber, in the upper end of our camp meadow, was a silvery-blue grizzly grazing with eight of our horses. Plenty Horse hadn't seen the bear yet and was impatient to get on into camp. But I wasn't about to ride mindlessly out into the open until I checked things out. A little craning of my neck revealed that camp was intact and secure. The grazing horses were much more relaxed than the prancing Paint I was riding. Obviously, the bear's attitude and body language wasn't threatening to them.

Cheryl, my daughter-in-law, who was substituting for my injured camp cook, was sitting beside a small campfire, darning socks, with a rifle laid across her lap.

I rode gingerly out of the timber into the meadow. The griz spotted me before I had cleared the timber and turned to face me, revealing a striking V of white hairs on his massive chest. His luxurious silver-tipped hair rippled in the slight early morning breeze. Our eyes locked as I passed within forty yards of him. I will be eternally grateful for that moment of beauty, power, and respect we shared as we looked deep into each other's being.

"Did you see Ephraim?" Cheryl asked as I unsaddled my horse.

"You bet," I replied. "Tell me about him."

"He's been up there for the last three mornings. He drifts up into the timber about 10 a.m. then returns about 4 p.m. every afternoon. So far, he hasn't bothered camp."

While splitting wood that morning, I watched my mule, Singer, with outstretched neck, flattened ears and bared teeth, charge the griz three times. For reasons known only to Ephraim and Singer, the bear dutifully ran up into the timber each time, only to return a respectful fifteen minutes later.

The hunters and hands nervously enjoyed the mule/bear exchange and took advantage of some rare photo opportunities, even cutting their daily elk hunts short to be back in camp before dark.

Ephraim disappeared as quietly and mysteriously as he appeared. Over the last fifteen years, there have been lots and lots of black and grizzly bears check out our camp without doing any damage. In fact, it is not uncommon for hands to feign sleep when they hear a bear in camp, hoping someone else will leave their warm sleeping bag to brave the chilly night air and spook off the intruder. But the sound of pearly white bear teeth puncturing a six-pack of Coors and the accompanying slurping of the chug-a-lugging thief causes a class-A commotion. Six-guns in one hand, flashlights in the other, barefoot guides in longjohns bail out of the tent to run off the revenuer.

After the warning shots fired into the air invariably you'll hear an exchange something like this.

"You were holding the muzzle of that hogleg pretty level weren't you Pard?"

"Well Goddamnit! I hate it when they do that. That was the last of our beer you know. Look at it now washing down the creek. Hell, the trout'll all be drunk by morning."

"Aw, quit your whining. That'll just make them taste better for breakfast."

Shivering back into their sleeping bags they'll stab their flashlights into one of their boots and their six-gun in the other for easy access in the dark, within minutes the snoring resumes.

Don McConnell, my regular cook in Camp Monaco, is a salty character that I call "Bandit." He is about 5'7" tall, with a black droopy mustache and just the right looks, habits, and attitudes to have played one of those lovable bandits in the B-western movies of yesteryear.

Don is a stove-up cowboy, old beyond his sixty years from riding and shoeing too many snakey broncs. If it weren't for the plastic joints in each of his knees, I'd never be able to keep him in camp cooking. He'd be out guiding. No matter what happens, Don can always make do. He can make more good meals out of the fewest ingredients than anyone I have ever known.

Cheryl subbed for Don. He'd had a bad horse wreck the fall before, as he was taking a hunter with his gear and his elk to town. Don spent nearly an hour pinned under his downed saddle horse. While he was twisting and straining to free himself and his horse, he pulled one of his plastic knee joints apart. He rode the remaining ten miles to the trail head, unsaddled the horses, and then drove the fifty miles to the nearest hospital with the equivalent of a broken leg. After many hours in the operating room, the doctor insisted that Don do absolutely no more horseback riding for at least one full year. I've never known Don to get excited. He always seems to be calm and in control, regardless of the wild goings-on around him. He is the kind of man you feel comfortable riding the high country with.

Several years ago, as I led my six excited elk hunters into Camp Monaco, Don walked around the cook tent to welcome us all. It was our first hunt together and I had sent Don and a couple guides into Monaco to set up camp the week before. The guides had come out a day earlier to help me pack up and get the hunters safely into camp. Don was left alone in camp to finish up the details. I was anxious to see how everything was and asked Don if things had gone well for him while he was in camp alone.

"No problems," Don replied.

Relieved, I rode over to the corrals. Before I stepped off my horse, I spied a rolled up skin from a freshly killed black bear tucked up against the trunk of a big shady spruce tree.

While the hunters were settling into their assigned sleeping tents, I eased back over to the cook tent where Don was preparing home-made soup and sandwiches for lunch.

"I thought you said there were no problems, Don. What about that black bear skin under the spruce tree behind the corrals?"

"Oh, you saw that, did you? Well, that bear wasn't any real problem. I just shot him before he became a problem," Don answered.

"So tell me about him."

"Well," Don began, "it was barely light yesterday morning. I was still in my sleeping bag when I heard what I thought were horses in the grain. I jumped up and ran outside in my long johns to run them off, but there weren't any horses in sight. It was just another calm, quiet mountain morning. I started back inside the cook tent, wondering if I was hearing things. Then I heard that sickening rip, you know, when a bear is tearing up a tent. I turned around just in time to see that black bear coming out the side of the empty guides' tent. As he ambled up towards the tack shed, I went back to my cot for my rifle."

We generally stretch a large tarp over a ridge pole, leaving the ends and sides open for easy access. This is our tack shed, where we store our riding saddles, bridles, pack saddles and assorted paraphernalia while we are in camp.

As Don rammed the 180 grain soft nose home and closed the bolt on his ancient 06, the black bear was helping himself to his first mouthful of molasses-sweetened rolled oats. Gingerly tiptoeing barefooted through the frosty pine needles, Don took a deep breath and rested on our wood-splitting stump. He settled the cross hairs of the scope on the oat-augering culprit and touched her off.

Don jumped up in surprised astonishment as the bear came roaring out of the tack shed right at him as fast as a runaway freight train. By the time Don rammed another live round home, the sixty yards between man and bear had dwindled to forty. By the time the 06 cracked the second time, the bear dropped, rolled, and skidded to a stop just thirty yards away.

I think I'll just put one more slug in him from here for good measure, Don thought, but he carefully squeezed the trigger on an empty chamber.

"Damn!" Don said to himself as he high-stepped back to the tent for more bullets. "I only put two in this morning?"

Shortly, he was sneaking around the other side of the tent for a better angle—he claimed later. But I say he just didn't want to go back to where the bear had seen him last. Good strategy too, I might add, when you are in a bear fight.

As Don sought to deliver the "one for good measure," he discovered that much to his dismay, the return to the warm tent had fogged his scope up and he couldn't see a thing through it.

Luckily, the second shot had finished the job. The first shot had just nicked the bear under the chin and gone on to destroy the brand new latigo on the only saddle in the entire tack shed—Don's.

Don McConnell: bear fighter, camp cook supreme.

On a big horn sheep hunt the next fall, Don and I lost lots of latigos in a bear confrontation that resulted in the worst horse wreck either of us ever had the misfortune to experience. I think one of the most dangerous factors an outfitter has to cope with while hunting or riding in grizzly country is his saddle horse and pack stock. About half the time the horses pay little or no attention to bears. It's the other half that ages you so quickly and thoroughly—the half when just one horse believes with all his heart the very demons of hell are about to latch onto his tail. When that happens, you'd better take a deep seat, 'cause stuff is going to get broken, your plunder will be scattered from daylight til dark, and your nerves will never be the same.

We were on a sheep trail, threading our way along a boulder-strewn hog back ridge at about 9,000 feet one beautiful September afternoon. The ridge was so narrow at this spot that while on horseback you could easily see off both sides. To our right, it was nearly straight down several hundred feet to a jagged rock outcropping. We looked down on the lance-shaped tops of distant spruce trees. To the left of us, a tree-covered slope fell off as steep as the one our right.

Don was in the lead with three pack horses and I was following with another three-pack-horse string. Behind me rode our somewhat apprehensive sheep hunter.

The trail made a sharp right turn, and Don's saddle horse clawed his way to the top of an especially steep and rocky portion of the trail. When he reached a flat spot at the top, the lead ropes of all three pack horses were taut and strained nearly to the breaking point. The horses strained every muscle to make the grade, their massive lungs screaming for more oxygen. I was resting my pack string at the base of the ascent waiting for Don's string to clear the top of the ridge.

Suddenly, he yelled, "I can't hold them, Duane!"

Don's warning reached me just before the falling rocks, and a heartbeat before the three rolling, plunging, crashing pack horses. With no room to maneuver my saddle horse, I quit him just as he was broadsided by a 1,200 pound horse-flesh bowling ball. I hit the ground running at a right angle to the cascading rocks, branches and horses. The second horse knocked me flat but rolled over me so fast I was only bruised and scratched. I was on all fours and digging for the safety of a big pine tree as the third horse bounced over my legs.

From the tree I was anchored to, I could see Don on the trail above me, still horseback and peering into the cloud of dust. He called to me.

"I'm all right, Don. But what the hell happened up there, anyway?" I shouted.

"It was a griz. He stood up and popped his teeth about twenty yards in front of me."

"Well, you may as well get comfortable up there because I'll be a while cutting these horses loose and getting back on the trail."

A few yards below me, all the pack horses were hung up in the timber. Two of them were upside down against the trees, and the third was folded around a ponderosa pine with all four feet off the ground.

When the pack horse Don was leading saw the upright bear, he just reared back and Don had to drop his dally[2] or get himself pulled into the melee. After that, gravity took over and things got western in a big hurry. Of course, Don came back down, and in a couple of hours, we had all the cinches repaired and the worried horses repacked and heading up the hill again.

◆   ◆   ◆

Speaking of western, it doesn't get any more western than when you startle a grizzly sow with a cub. One of my elk guides, Richard Mason and his brother Dennis, experienced just such a close encounter of the worst kind.

We were between hunts, so the boys went up above Jones Creek Camp for some personal hunting. It was a bright, crisp mid-October morning as they dismounted and tied their horses a couple hundred yards below a springy, aspen-lined meadow. They had just split up to begin their hunt. The gentle breezes brushed their faces as they approached the lower end of the twenty-acre meadow, about thirty yards apart.

The She-Bear was in full charge with her sights locked on Dennis when the unsuspecting young man saw her. Richard's response was instant, aggressive, and probably saved his brother's life, but greatly jeopardized his own. There was no time to think, no time to shout instructions, barely time to do or die. Lunging a step toward the enraged grizzly, Richard shouted and fired his rifle in the air to spook her off.

Richard has survived several false charges by grizzlies with similar antics and has considered himself somewhat grizzly proof. A very physically capable, macho young man in his mid-twenties, he is good with his rifle, rope, horse, pack string, and the six gun that he wore. Richard was an accomplished boxer/slugger in high school. About 5'10", built solid and strong as an ox, he grew up accompanying his father in this very drainage on numerous elk hunts. But this was not a false charge!

---

2.   dally = to wrap your rope around your saddle horn

In response to Richard's action, the bear changed her angle of charge. In a heartbeat, the five hundred pounds of anger bore into Richard at full attack speed.

Her piercing yellow eyes, her open fang-filled mouth, and her grunting, sickening-smelling bad breath were in Richard's face before he could lever his Winchester and bring it into play. Richard went over backwards from the force of her impact, scattering pine cones and needles as they hit the ground.

When she struck him, Richard instinctively grabbed each of her laid back ears, using his strong hands and forearms for leverage. He was able to thrust his own face to the right and her bristling, snarling, wrinkled-up nose to his left. The desperate maneuver saved the vital throat area, but the pain was white-hot as her massive jaw forced her teeth through his heavy down jacket and into his left shoulder.

For what seemed an eternity, Richard struggled to draw his six-gun, but the weight of the bear and the intensity of the attack prevented it. She was all over him—biting, shaking, swatting, mostly his head, neck, and shoulders. He was helpless. It was only seconds before Dennis ran over. He fired two shots while she was mauling Richard around on the ground. Luckily, the shots missed both Richard and the bear. Since grizzly bears in Wyoming are currently on the threatened species list, Federal bureaucrats take a dim view of anyone killing them.

With a parting swat and growl, the sow left Richard bloody, bruised, and forever wiser.

The boys hustled down to their horses, rode the ten miles to a phone, and reported the incident to the Wyoming Game & Fish Department. Then they drove to the Cody Hospital for a tetanus shot and stitches to reattach his left ear.

The one lesson bears have taught us and reinforce annually is that they are absolutely unpredictable. The old axiom of an ounce of prevention is worth a pound of cure is never more true than when dealing with grizzlies.

As Don Juby would say, "By God, Cap'n. Once you step in it with a griz, there is going to be hell to pay."

A WOMAN'S TOUCH

The huge, cherry-wood bar before me was presented to Buffalo Bill Cody in 1900 by Queen Victoria of England, in appreciation for a command performance of his world-famous Wild West Show. The ornate bar was built in France, shipped to New York City by steamer, then by rail to Red Lodge, Montana, and finally by horse-drawn freight wagon to Cody, Wyoming. To this day, it is a featured attraction in Cody's ever-popular Irma Hotel.

From my seat at the old bar, I saw her in the mirror when she came through the door behind me. She paused as her eyes adjusted to the subdued light in the Irma Café. Obviously looking for someone, her gaze swept the room like a chinook wind and settled on the back of my neck.

I didn't know where the woman was from. I kept one eye on the mirror while I sopped up the last gravy from my hot beef lunch. She wove her way around tables filled with dining tourists jabbering about their western experiences and wondering how they could get back home without going over any mountains again.

Dodging the scurrying waitresses, she homed in on me. Her scuffed boots and tight jeans showed signs of hard work. Her sleeveless shirt revealed taut, tanned arms that were no stranger to heavy work. Long, dark hair framed an attractive, intelligent, high-cheeked face. Maybe twenty-four years old—who knows.

"Mr. Wiltse, I'm Rachel Madison. I hear you're looking for a horse wrangler."

I turned to face her. She smelled of Lifebuoy soap and horse. A pair of elk-skin gloves with holes worn through the thumbs were tucked in her leather belt. She carried maybe a hundred thirty pounds stacked on a 5'7" frame.

"That's true."

Her handshake felt the way it should—firm, polite, and business-like.

"I'd like the job."

"Sit down here a minute. Tell me about yourself."

"I'm bored to death working here in town. I want to go to the hills."

"Boredom doesn't qualify you to wrangle horses in the mountains."

"For two years I've been care-taking a small place up the North Fork, feeding and exercising four horses for their Florida owners. I bicycle and work out in the gym. I'm in good shape. I'm not afraid of hard work."

"Where you been working?"

"I'm the receptionist at Big Horn Realty."

"That still doesn't prepare you for—"

"But, Mr. Wiltse, I can do the job. I know I can. I just need the chance. None of the other outfitters around Cody will hire me because I'm a woman." Her eyes bored into me, not pleading but intent, reminding me of the way my old tomcat, Ricochet, looks at me when he comes back home after I've tried to pawn him off on unsuspecting friends. The chip on her shoulder was clearly visible when she said, "I can wrangle as good as any man. All I'm asking for is one chance. I'll even work for less money."

"I have a policy in my camps that everybody helps everybody. Something goes wrong, everyone pitches in and helps. No matter what the weather or time of day. We don't have a starting time or quit time—it's full time."

"I understand."

"No one really understands til they've been there. Then there are the guides and hunters. If I hire you, they are not going to like having to depend on a woman for their horses."

"I can handle the guides and hunters."

"You don't understand, Rachel. It won't be just your problem. They'll make it mine, too. You got a saddle?"

"Yes."

"How about a slicker?"

"I'll get one."

"Transportation?"

"My pickup."

"I'm not going to pay you less money. If you can do the work, you are worth the money. If you can't, I'll have to replace you. Okay?"

"Yessir."

"Bring what you need to stay warm and dry and that's all. Understand?"

"Yessir."

"You got a good sleeping bag?"

"I'll get one."

"I can't be babysitting you—."

"No sir."

"Be at Crow Creek corrals, 7 a.m., September 5."

I shook her hand and she said, "I do appreciate this chance. You won't be sorry, Mr. Wiltse."

I was pleasantly impressed when Rachel arrived ten minutes early with an old, worn U.S. Army duffel bag only half full. She had not only done her homework, she arrived before the hunters and two of the guides. Later, when I introduced everyone to the hunters, the guides were cool to Rachel. Once we were in Camp Monaco and unpacked, it was standard operating procedure for the guides and me to have a powwow to decide guiding and hunting assignments.

"How come we get stuck with a woman wrangler?" Tad complained. "I'm not doing my work and hers too. Hell, she don't even know the horses' names. How she gonna get the right horses in the dark? If I'd knowed you needed a wrangler, I could've brought one of my friends."

"Hey, she's our wrangler! If she can't do the job, I'll fire her. Then we'll get one of your buddies, if you'll vouch for him. I hope you haven't forgotten what happened with the last guy you recommended."

"Hey, that wasn't all my fault," Tad muttered as his gaze dropped to the ground. The other two guides, Andy and Dave, just stood with their hands in their pockets, kicking the dirt.

"To hell you say. As always, I expect everyone to back up everyone. That includes Rachel. She gets in a jam, don't nobody leave her hanging. Agreed?"

"Yeah. Okay."

As the hunt proceeded, Rachel struggled, but kept up with her grueling duties of rising at 4 a.m., haltering and graining horses the guides had chosen the night before for that day's hunt. All horses that weren't being used on a given day were turned loose to graze and rest between assignments. They might wander a mile or more from camp, so four of them would have bells fastened around their necks. Two horses were always picketed in the meadow near camp, so the wrangler had a horse to ride to gather the remuda each afternoon. After the last guide came in an hour or two after dark, they would tell the wrangler what saddle or pack horses they needed for the next day's hunt and which horse, if any, needed medical attention or shoe work. Those horses would be grained and locked as securely as possible in the corral. The rest were turned out for their twenty-four hours off. No horse was used two days in a row.

On the fourth morning of the hunt, a little after 4 a.m. as I was building a fire in the dining tent stove, Rachel came in and nervously asked if she could see me a minute.

Even though our cook, Don, boiling coffee, was the only one stirring at that hour, it is never a good idea to try to have a private conversation in a tent. You never know when someone will walk by in the dark and overhear. I motioned for Rachel to follow me out of the lantern light into the cold darkness by the wood pile.

"What's the problem?"

"I think I forgot to tie the corral gate shut last night. All the horses are gone."

"How about the picket horses?"

"They're still here. Should I saddle one of them and go after the others?"

"No. It's still three hours til daylight. You don't even know what direction they went. You or your horse could get hurt riding around out there in the dark."

"What should I do?"

"Help Don with breakfast and lunches. Come first light, I'll find their tracks and see where they have gone."

"But what about the guides and hunters?"

"I'll figure something out. It's important you don't say anything to anyone else about not tying the gate shut. You understand?"

"Yessir."

"Good. Now, go help Don. I got stuff to do."

The lantern had just been lit in the guides' tent when I returned from tying the gate shut and breaking one of the top rails on the back side of the corral. Dave was building their fire, Andy was pulling his suspenders over his shoulders, and Tad was still buried in his sleeping bag when I ducked into their tent.

"Got a change in hunt plans this morning, boys. Remember that weak pole I said you shouldn't use when you were building the corral?"

"Don't tell me—" Andy said.

"Yup. Busted clean in two, and all the horses are gone this morning."

A feather-muffled "God damn, where's our horse wrangler" came from Tad's cot.

"She's helping Don get breakfast. I suspect the horses headed down. Just hope they stopped at Jones Creek."

"If they did, old Tift will have them in the corral. He's a good wrangler," Tad muttered as he pulled on his cold, stiff boots.

I followed them out the tent flap. They scattered in the darkness to pee. I looked up at countless brilliant stars and breathed in the tantalizing aroma of wood smoke and coffee for just a moment. "What the hell's a few lost horses to worry about? It's a good day to hunt on foot, anyway," I thought.

"I paid for a horseback hunt. I'm not hunting on foot in this steep country," Richard said.

Leave it to the lawyer in the group to complicate life.

"It's your call. Lunches are ready and the guides are ready to hunt. If anyone wants to go back to bed and rest up this morning, I'm sure we'll have the horses back for an afternoon hunt."

"I don't like the idea of missing a half day's hunt," Richard said.

"Shit happens in the wilderness, Richard. Just put your hiking boots on and you won't miss any time hunting."

"No. I'll wait for the horses, but if I miss more than half a day, I'll be expecting a refund."

"Don't worry—the horses will be here just after lunch."

Right after breakfast, Richard went back to bed. Everyone else went hunting. I checked a few yards of the horse trail with my flashlight. Sure enough, the string had lit out for home on a dead run. It's two hours to the Jones Creek Camp—by then, the runaways would have blown off steam, and hopefully, stopped to talk some of their buddies into joining their mutiny. If so, my wrangler down there, Jeff Tift, would haze them into his corral and wait for someone from Monaco to show up.

The brilliant starlight was beginning to melt into the predawn coldness as Rachel, wearing what looked like all the clothes she brought, disappeared down the frosty trail.

As we were finishing our lunch of bean soup and grilled cheese sandwiches, you'd have thought Richard was back in Chicago in some courtroom when he stood up and said to me, "Well, Mr. Outfitter, you promised me in front of witnesses a horse to hunt from after lunch. It's after lunch, I'd like to go now. Where is he?"

"If you'll step outside the tent, I believe you will hear horse bells coming up the trail," I answered.

Sure enough, by the time I had the corral gate open and stood shaking a bucket of grain, the first of the high-headed fugitives came innocently trotting across the meadow. Rachel was beaming when she stepped off her sweaty horse and began untying her extra clothes from the back of her saddle.

"How'd you know they'd stop at Jones Creek?" she asked me.

"Just a lucky guess."

That evening after everyone had gone to bed, I helped Don wash up the last of the supper dishes. Rachel stepped into the tent and asked if she could see me a minute. Out at the wood pile, she said, "I've got that gate tied good tonight. Thanks for your help this morning. I really appreciated it."

"You're welcome. Hey, just stand still a minute while I brush that chip off your shoulder."

"Yeah, okay. I see your point."

Back at the Crow Creek corrals after the hunt, the hunters had left for home. The rest of us were putting the last of our tack away and feeding the horses. Everyone was looking forward to two days off before our next group arrived when I asked Tad, "What do you think, Tad, shall I let Rachel go so you can get one of your buddies to wrangle the next hunt?"

"Hell, no. Why would you do a fool thing like that? We'd just have to teach him all the horses' names. Besides, Rachel cowboyed up and brought all those horses back from Jones Creek by herself, she always has the right horses ready for us. Hell, after the big runaway, she even built our fire and brought hot coffee to our tent every morning. We've never had such a good wrangler."

Even though I had some very good men cooks, like Don Juby and Don McConnell, I have always preferred the cleanliness, flavor, and presentation of the meals by my good women cooks. Cooking in hunting camp is a very tough job, and it's hard to get really good women to leave the comforts of their own home kitchens to carry water, cook on a wood stove, play nurse-maid to whiney hunters, and fight bears at night.

Rachel's account in town of her experiences with Cabin Creek Outfitters encouraged other women to trust me. In time, I was fortunate enough to hire three of the very best. Loretta Ehnes was known as "The Wild Woman," and a more personable, energetic, attractive, forty-plus year old, in my opinion, does not exist. Loretta cooked at Jones Creek, and besides our large crew of hunters and hands, she fed and medicated dozens of U.S. Forest Rangers, Wyoming Game Wardens and Biologists, lost hunters and hikers. Sitting between the forks of two main trails, there was never a dull moment at Jones Creek.

Caitlyn Dallinger, a young vivacious woman with long thick dark hair, had a special flair for seasonings. In fact, she produced most of her own and built a successful spice cottage business. She was an excellent horsewoman, so efficient and well-organized that during her three-year tenure at Camp Monaco, she not only cooked but wrangled horses as well.

Karla, my guide Griz's wife, cooked at the original Cabin Creek Camp on the Elk Fork. Having cooked in other camps that Griz guided in, Karla had more experience than the other two gals. She, too, cooked and wrangled—an excellent horsewoman and packer.

When those three women were on the job, mine was a lot easier. They were darn sure top hands. I paid them more than the guides. They were still underpaid, as we all were, but going to the high country every fall never was about the money.

Three of the best camp cooks ever. From left: Caitlyn on Sage Fire, Carla, Loretta, Duane.

WOMEN & WILDFIRES

By 1985, Stephanie and John were in their early twenties and away to college or work most of the time. Stephanie would be married in 1987. That left Elizabeth and me pretty much home alone. It seemed that even when were together, we were alone. I spent most of my time working the business but blundered badly the spring of 1987.

Yes, it's true that since 1981, when I mentally and emotionally gave up on Elizabeth, she had poured on the verbal abuse. I may have unwittingly contributed to it by accepting it in a futile attempt to keep peace in the family. As the children grew into their teens, it became impossible to shield them from it. They also became the brunt of it. To my deepening despair, they all began to leave home at an early age. I was a grandfather at forty and totally unprepared emotionally for my children to be having children.

I no longer sought peace through appeasement. If I contended with the verbal abuse or didn't leave the house, Elizabeth's seething anger sometimes erupted into physical abuse as well. I just wish I possessed the strength of character to have dealt with our problems in a more positive manner. Instead, my reaction to our mutual frustrations and heartache was to have an affair with a younger woman during the summer of 1987. I sucked up the flattery and physical attention like a Hoover with an empty dust bag.

Over a period of four months, the relationship moved from verbal stroking to hugging, kissing, and hot, intense sexual escapism. It was a lose-lose situation for everyone. I might as well have been driving ninety miles an hour down a dead-end street. My perspective was barely six inches long.

Elizabeth soon found out and the proverbial shit hit the fan. I was crushed by my guilt and wanted to make up for it. Elizabeth was crushed by my betrayal and wanted revenge. We belatedly began weekly marriage counseling in July of 1987. By that September, Elizabeth insisted I move out of the house. Rejecting the marriage counselor's advice, she decided she was going to have the divorce she had been threatening me with for over thirty years. She just wanted six months to prepare herself for it.

I had finally screwed up big time. I practically handed her my head on a silver platter. Now she could have her coveted divorce and heap the blame on me for all the world to see. It was a once-in-a-lifetime opportunity for her.

While she was lamenting one day about how much she had given up for me, she revealed how six months before our marriage while still in college, she met the love of her life. Because our wedding invitations were already printed and paid for, she broke it off with him. Besides, she added, she knew I'd be a good provider. Yet she often thought about how much better her life would have been had she followed her heart. I felt sorry for her and guilty for having kept her from realizing her dreams of love and career.

I continued to see the counselor alone. One day he spoke earnestly to me. "Duane, I believe your affair was more a cry for help then anything. During the six months we've been talking, we have been totally unable to discuss the root cause of your and Elizabeth's unhappiness, which I believe to be wrapped up in her long-time anger. I'm not sure she even knows what she's angry about, because as you know, she not only refuses to talk about it, she refuses to even acknowledge it exists. Having gotten to know you, in my professional opinion, you would be better off divorced. You've been separated now for several months. It's time you accepted the inevitable and got on with your life."

At the time, I was living alone in a small apartment in Cody, keeping up with my work every day and taking long hikes each evening up Spirit Mountain, barely five minutes from downtown. It was late winter, so many evenings it was dark before I completed my tension-reducing hikes.

One evening in February of 1988, as had been my long-time habit, I was reading "Western Horseman" magazine. I always read until I got to the last several pages of display and classified ads, then no further. For some unknown reason that evening, I continued to thumb through the last half dozen or so pages of ads. That's when I saw this column of personal ads. I thought, *Holy cow, people really do this? They put ads in magazines looking for companions?*

As I continued reading I discovered eight or ten ads there. Some were from men, some from dating agencies, and three or four from women. One caught my eye. I read it over two or three times before putting the magazine aside and going to bed.

"Triple AAA rated, SWF, tall, slim, athletic NS. Seeking unencumbered NS rancher/horseman 45–55. Reply Box 128, c/o Western Horseman."

During the next evening's hike as I was sweating away some of my guilt and anxiety, the message in that one ad came back to me. After a TV dinner for supper that night, I reread the ad that had attached itself to my brain.

After the last year of tongue lashings from Elizabeth, my spirit was slowly sinking into a void as dark as the coal bin of my youth. I felt a strong need to talk to someone who knew nothing of my past—none of the good stuff, none of the bad stuff—to see if they agreed I was as bad as Elizabeth and her attorney were insisting.

I figured this intriguing ad would be a safe bet. First, she would probably never respond anyway. If she did, it would be a long-distance phone call and/or letter that I would deal with in my own time, not a real live person. So I sent a letter and picture of myself to the address in the Western Horseman.

After finishing my hike and returning to my apartment one night a couple of weeks later, I noticed my lonesome answering machine blinking. I punched the button. I was astonished at the pleasant, articulate, female voice that was responding to my letter and sincerely inviting me to call her back at her home in Tampa, Florida. The call I made to Jan Bailey in Tampa that evening opened a whole new world for me.

In addition to what became regular phone calls, Jan and I wrote cards and letters to each other, sharing our heartaches of the past and our hopes and dreams of the future. Over the next several weeks, I was amazed and thrilled to discover how much we had in common.

She had been born and raised on a farm near Swartz Creek, Michigan, barely thirty miles from where I'd grown up in Flint. She had ridden and shown Tennessee Walking Horses as a kid and young woman. As a young girl, her family spent summer vacations with friends in Lander, Wyoming. As an adult, she continued to spend her two-week vacations from her job with General Motors in Wyoming on horse pack trips. She had even ridden from Cody through the fabled Thorofare country to Dubois with my outfitter neighbor, Glen Fales.

We were not only from the same area but from the same era as well. I was fifty-two years old; Jan was forty-nine. I had five grown children and was about to be divorced. Jan had one grown son and had been divorced for twenty years. As a single parent and with a career as District Manager of Parts & Service for General Motors, Jan considered her life two-thirds full. The missing third was a soul mate.

For many years, she had been asking GM for a field position in the West, and had recently been thinking about finding a companion to share her life with. Hence, her ad in Western Horseman

She was, however, concerned that I was not unencumbered. I explained Elizabeth's intention that we would be divorced by late spring or early summer. Also that I, with my counselor's blessings, was looking forward to getting beyond that and on with the rest of my life.

As we continued to become better acquainted over the phone and through the mail, I was deeply impressed at her honesty and intellect. By the picture of herself she sent me, I could see that she was also tall, trim, athletic and very attractive with short blond hair, mischievous blue eyes and an infectious "what you see is what you get" smile.

So, where do we go from here? I wondered. *Is it really possible this woman is as good as she appears? After all these years and all the recent heartache, can it be so simple to find your soul mate by answering an ad in a magazine? I doubt it!*

There is only one way to find out, I decided. *I'll just go to Florida and see for myself.*

◆   ◆   ◆

Cody is a small town, and I was sensitive to other people knowing my business, so when making flight arrangements at the local travel agency, I made it plain I didn't want anyone to know my travel plans. At the time, I really didn't know what difference it made. I just had a gut feeling that I had learned to pay attention to in the high country. So I made it a point to make my arrangements with an agent I knew and trusted there.

Jan met me at the Tampa airport. She was even more animated, vibrant and energetic in person. We had a grand time together that weekend. She was a gracious host. I slept in her guest room and she showed me the big city of Tampa. She drove through bumper-to-bumper traffic like a race car driver, right foot on the accelerator, left on the brake, calling offending drivers "Bozos." About scared me to death!

We ate at wonderful local places and visited Sea World, where the crowds bothered me. We looked at her family picture albums and talked and talked far into Saturday night. She prepared us a scrumptious breakfast Sunday morning, with fresh Florida fruit followed by bacon, eggs and toast. We did a little yard work around her neat, well-kept three bedroom suburban home.

Then she innocently suggested we go to the beach for the afternoon and watch the sun go down over the Gulf of Mexico. Sounded good to me. I looked forward to seeing the Big Water. I was barely calming down from the forty-five minute white-knuckle ride when Jan began laughing so hard she nearly fell in the sand, at my reaction to my first sight of girls in thong bathing suits. I kept a close watch for more thong-clad hard bellies while we sat on the beach and watched the sun set into the Gulf.

As I prepared to board the plane for Cody on Monday morning, Jan and I both were a bit somber and reluctant to part, as we realized that we shared mutual respect and strong feelings for each other. I sensed a thirty-year void in my life being filled. I could literally feel Jan's invigorating spirit in my chest. I recognized immediately our connection was something mystical and rare, something I had sought all my adult life, like finding a once-in-a-lifetime treasure of untold wealth. In life's game of chance, I had drawn the Queen of Hearts to my Royal Flush. I felt if I ever lost this connection, my life would decline into a morass of quiet desperation.

◆   ◆   ◆

Tuesday morning, my travel agent called to tell me that on the previous Friday afternoon, the day I left for Florida, a private investigator tried to bluff her into telling him where I had gone and why. I was surprised and confused. Why should anyone care where I'd gone for the weekend?

"What did you tell him?" I asked.

"I told him it was none of his business. He tried twice, Duane. First by phone, then in person. Duane?"

"Yes."

"There is something fishy going on. Watch your back. Okay?"

"You bet. Thanks for your help."

"You're welcome. Good luck."

There was in fact something fishy going on. I was to learn much later that even though we had been separated on and off for the last year, and our divorce proceedings were to begin in a couple of months, Elizabeth was having me followed by a PI. Frustrated by his inability to come up with any dirt on me, she had gotten into my apartment by crawling through a window while I was in Florida but still couldn't find anything. There simply wasn't anything to find.

Shortly after my return from Florida, Elizabeth insisted I move back into my house so I could take care of the yard and spring work, and she would move into town. Jan and I continued to write and visit with each other by telephone. Even though we were miles apart, we were drawing ever closer in spirit.

Then Elizabeth dropped another bomb. She had hidden a voice-activated cassette recorder in the bookshelves near my phone and had been secretly sneaking into the house while I was working to retrieve the tapes. Now she was threatening to use my friendship with Jan to ruin me financially and emotionally during the divorce proceedings. I truly believe that she sent away to some shyster outfit for some sort of self-destruct divorce kit.

Even though I knew in my heart I loved Jan, I didn't feel worthy of her. Plus, I felt an enormous responsibility to Betsy and my children to honor my marriage vows of 1956. So with a heavy heart, I suggested since we had spent the last six months preparing ourselves emotionally for our divorce yet neither of us seemed ready for it, why not spend the next six months working to put the relationship back together? She agreed.

I knew it would not be fair to anyone, especially Jan, to maintain any contact with her. My subsequent phone conversation with her was a profound low point in my life. Her voice choking with disbelief and emotion, Jan whispered after all it was my life and decision. If trying to get back with Betsy was what I wanted to do, then that was what I should be doing full-time, and she didn't want any further contact with me whatsoever.

As I hung up the telephone, I literally felt a deep sad pain in my chest. I felt a vitality and a new-found zest for life draining out of my spirit. I felt hollow. I went to the barn and wept.

Elizabeth and I continued to live apart while we talked about the symptoms but never the real tough issues. We went to a different counselor. The days turned into weeks, the weeks into months. I anesthetized my chronic chest pain with hard work and diligent efforts to rebuild my marriage.

◆   ◆   ◆

Right in the middle of all this havoc, during the summer of 1988, Yellowstone Park's "let burn" policy resulted in the historic forest fires that consumed nearly two million acres of forest in and around the Park.

The smell of wood smoke was strong in the hazy air around Cody all summer. Some days, if the wind was just right, everything got covered with a dusting of fine white ash. I became concerned about my camp equipment, which I had packed into Camp Monaco a week earlier in preparation for our upcoming fall hunts. I decided late one afternoon, just to be on the safe side, to drive up to my cabin across the river from Pahaska Teepee, spend the night, then pick up a couple of my hands that were wrangling yellow-shirted fire fighters and their gear into hot spots just outside of Yellowstone. We'd lead our empty pack string the twelve miles up country and retrieve my equipment in case the Situation Commanders were wrong and the fire did come out of Yellowstone and hit us.

About forty miles into the fifty-mile drive from Cody, I could see an ominous red glow in the night sky in front of me. The closer I got, the angrier the glow looked. Soon, I needed the windshield wipers to remove the falling ash and dead embers so I could see. I didn't bother to stop at the drive to my cabin but continued the couple of miles up the river to my corrals and tack sheds at Crow Creek.

The corrals were a swirling mass of spooky horse flesh. Peering through the dust, smoke, darkness and falling ash, I could see fright-widened eyes and flaring nostrils. The mules had been the first to come in—Singer, Waco, Alamo, and Durango; followed all afternoon by the saddle horses—Boots, Stetson, Tomahawk, Bad News, Surprise, Plenty Horse—blacks, paints, sorrels and bays. Sixty altogether.

The remuda had been turned up Crow Creek the day before to feed and rest between forest-fighting assignments with the U.S. Forest Service. It was 8 p.m., September 6, 1988. The horses already knew what we were about to learn. We had lost!

In the darkness, the might, power and appetite of the biblical monster was absolutely awesome. The relentless march of the two hundred foot high, reddish-orange flames, the angry roar, the smoke and dust were terrifying to man and beast.

Because of the risk to human life created by the surrounding timber and location of our corrals, barns, haystack, and tack shed, all fire fighters and equipment had been pulled back to the main lodge a mile downstream. We were expendable.

By the time my four hands and I had shuttled the tack and equipment from three tack sheds and a cabin approximately eight miles downstream to Eagle Creek Trail Head, it looked like the only way to save the horses was to open the corral gates and let them run for it.

At that point, Jay Carlson, the new Shoshone Forest Wapiti District Supervisor, volunteered Forest Service hands, trucks, and trailers to help us transport the horses out of the area swiftly and safely. I worried that we didn't have time to wait for extra trucks and trailers to come. The advancing wall of flame, barely four hundred yards away, was raining hot embers and ash all over us. It was a nerve-wracking thirty minutes of trying to keep the hands and horses calm while the monster raged closer and closer.

Our gamble paid off in spades. About the same time the Forest Service trucks and trailers arrived, two outfitter friends, Gary Fales and Don Schmalz, showed up with their trucks and trailers. No one had called them. They just knew I was probably in a jackpot, so independent of each other, they gassed up and drove nearly forty miles to see if they could help out.

With that kind of experienced horse-handling help, we had the horses safely evacuated to the Eagle Creek Trail Head corrals and were spreading our sleeping bags on the ground for much needed rest by 3:30 a.m., September 7, 1988.

A month earlier, the Clover Mist fire had burned past just west of us in Yellowstone Park. Now, it had slopped out of the park north of us and was threatening Cooke City, Montana. About a week earlier, due to a quirk of nature and wind, some hot sparks from its southeast flank had blown over the line and set the Shoshone Forest ablaze at Stone Cup Lake, the heart of my big game hunting area.

My horses, four hands and I packed sixty firefighters fourteen miles uphill into the burned-out basin at Stone Cup Lake in early September. Forest Service policy is to establish fire camp in an area already burned if possible, assuring that the camp will not be overrun with flames. It works great, except for two minor hitches. We had to lead sixty dude horses with sixty dudes on them through the ring of fire surrounding the proposed campsite. And, there was not a single blade of grass left for the tired, hungry horses. So in the dark, we had to jingle those same sixty hair-singed horses through four inches of hot ash to the trail head fourteen miles away.

Since all air support was committed to saving Cooke City, it only took a couple of days for the fire to spot itself across the Jones Creek drainage and begin devouring down-country. Our hotshot crews had to be airlifted out of the potentially explosive situation at Stone Cup, which was deteriorating daily.

The Shoshone River valley was forever changed by the Yellowstone fires. Viewing the smoldering, blackened aftermath of the fire created a grief in the pit of my stomach that I hadn't felt since watching my Dad starve to death. There was absolutely no life of any kind left. From the Yellowstone Highway, eighteen miles upstream to Silver Tip Basin, the majestic river's birthplace, she was burnt bare from rimrock to rimrock. All the grass, all the trees, all the birds, all the animals. Gone!

No one knows how many animals and birds perished in the holocaust. The firestorm created such intense heat that the temperature of the glacier-fed river rose to the point that fish were killed. Rotting whitefish and trout lined the river banks. Dead elk, deer, moose, grizzly and black bear were everywhere. In the river along the horse trails and in the hills, the smell of death was heavy on the ash-laden breezes.

Wyoming Game & Fish Biologists and Wardens were emotionally spent and visibly shaken as they sat in my camp after hiking along Jones Creek, surveying the game losses. Disfigured mounds of burnt flesh offered mute testimony to the countless struggles for life lost by so many proud animals.

Forest Rangers and Range Biologists tried to cheer me up by insisting within three years the grasses would return in such dramatic fashion that I would have the best elk and deer hunting in the United States. I was skeptical and angry. I just lost two of the best hunting camps in Northwest Wyoming to a fire I figured was unnecessary and unfair.

I was mad as hell.

At least we saved all our horses and tack that night. I'm glad I missed the fireworks at Monaco that night when four twenty-pound propane tanks exploded from the same intense heat that killed the huge fir tree Buffalo Bill had carved the camp's name on.

Just before the flames were about to engulf my cabin and other buildings at the trail head, the wind changed and slowed the fire up enough for our annual Equinox storm to arrive with a couple of inches of rain and snow, which finally put the summer-long fire out.

◆   ◆   ◆

Slowly, things grew less tense and hostile between Elizabeth and me. By December, she decided she wasn't angry anymore and moved back in so we could have all the family together for the holidays. She even went to a sport show in San Antonio with me in February of 1989.

Suddenly, something snapped in her as we were driving home. For no apparent reason, she began screaming at me and pounding me with her fists. I had to pull off the Interstate to prevent an accident. Obviously, Elizabeth was not over her ancestral anger. She moved out again and began divorce proceedings shortly after we returned to Cody.

By now, I was resigned to the fact Elizabeth was never going to deal with the root cause of her anger and that a divorce was inevitable. I spent the spring and summer working my team and saddle horse concession in Cody and at Pahaska Teepee, while the legal process proceeded.

One windy July day, my team, Tom and Jerry, were uneasy and nervous. For some reason, windy days always have that affect on horses. On this particular afternoon, I had a full wagon-load of Taiwanese to pick up from a shopping trip. I had dropped them off earlier that morning. As usual, I was working the trip alone and needed to rely on the people getting up the steps and seating themselves, because Tom and Jerry's jitters required my full two-handed attention. I talked to them softly and soothingly. I cussed them and I threatened them. Still, I could barely keep their minds on our business ever since a passing car of rowdy teenagers on Main Street shot Tom in the side with a bottle rocket.

All of the Taiwanese were older folks with cameras around their necks who moved kind of slow, except the three thirty-somethings—beautiful girls who always sat in the front seat just behind me. None of them could speak a word of English, but that made us even, because I couldn't speak a word of Taiwanese.

I was holding the anxious team on a side street while all the shopping and sightseeing tourists slowly but surely got aboard and took their seats. Just as I was about to leave, everyone started jabbering loudly and gesturing up the street. Sure enough, half a block away, a couple of the lost souls were hurrying as fast as their short little legs could carry them, plastic sacks waving in the wind from their outstretched arms.

Tom and Jerry couldn't count, and besides, they didn't care if everyone was aboard or not. As far as they were concerned, it was time to go. I had the brake set hard, my feet braced on the wagon boot, and both forearms bulging from holding the reins tight. Once the two lost shoppers were safely seated, one of the beauties behind me leaned up and spoke provocatively into my ear, "Alright, Cowboy, let's get these 'god-damn Taiwanese' back to their rooms."

Then the three of them had a big laugh as my face and neck grew crimson with embarrassment. They spoke better English than I did. I spent the twenty minute trip back to the Holiday Inn wondering and worrying what else I may have confided to Tom and Jerry over the last three days that they overheard.

At the hitching rail as I helped them down from the wagon, I tried to apologize for my rudeness, but they were not going to let me off the hook so easy. They insisted if I truly wanted to be forgiven, I must take the three of them out dancing that night—their last night in town. That was by far the best offer I'd had in months, but I explained I would not have time to go home and change after taking care of my team. Their response was they had time to clean up and change, and besides, they liked me just the way I was.

Clean up and change, they did! Their narrow silk dresses set off their beautiful creamy complexions and glittering jewelry like nothing I'd ever seen before. We all fit comfortably in the front bench seat of my ten dually. I pushed my hat back and cruised down Main Street as I headed for the only dance floor around, Cassie's.

Cassie's is the place all the hands go to shoot pool, drink, meet girls and dance to live bands. It is also the place all the tourists go to shoot pool, drink and meet cowboys.

Well, let me tell you, when those three tall slender Oriental beauties in their high heels and pastel silk dresses walked in, Cassie's about came to a halt. The girls took turns dancing with me and only me for the entire evening, much to the chagrin of many disappointed hands I knew there. About 1:00 a.m., we left the dance hall and returned to the motel. In the lobby, each gave me a big full-body hug, thanked me for my most enjoyable apology, and invited me to return to Taiwan with them.

I declined and returned to my beloved Wyoming high country.

PLENTY WOMAN

If you want a good hunting horse, you'd best get to my Crow Creek corrals early the morning we're packing rifle hunters into elk camp.

Horses and guides exhaled clouds of frosty breath as I tied Plenty Horse securely to my pickup. Looking up, I could see the sky beginning to lighten, but down here on the timbered river bottom where we were working, it was still dark enough for some good old-fashioned Indian horse thievery.

You see, in Wyoming high country, there is an unwritten yet clearly understood practice that once you get a saddle on a horse in your string, he's off limits to the other guides. But for the next ten minutes or so, those guides are going to look like a herd of pack rats stealing horses from the poor devil who just ducked into the tack shed to get a saddle. The chatter of awakening Canadian Jays was interrupted by plenty of good-natured, profane ribbing, until all the horses and mules were wearing the appropriate riding or pack saddle.

Everyone was in a "Saturday night mood" and anxious to get started. We rode out of the trail head with our hats tipped back, sleeves rolled up, and sweaty shirts plastered to our shoulder blades.

There is no finer adventure than hunting high-country elk. This would be our first rifle hunt since the historic forest fires of 1988. The sky was blue and our spirits as high as the mid-morning sun. Some of the fellows were going to spike camp, near the high basin that usually hid elk. Some of us would stay at the base camp on the river. Everyone thought he had the best place. But there are no sure things when you hunt elk. The big question this year was, were there even going to be any elk to hunt?

The two inches of fresh snow that fell during the night would be a welcome help in finding out. We had left camp an hour before daylight when suddenly the majestic challenge of a big herd bull pierced the gray dawn. Accumulated snow fell from our wool hats and yellow slickers as Jeff and I dismounted simultaneously. Jeff pulled Jerry's rifle out of his scabbard and hurried him off his horse as I began tying horses to fire-blackened trees.

Jerry Stodghill from Kentucky was the first hunter to dismount. Jeff quickly helped him out of his slicker and handed him his rifle as they melted into the swirling snow and river-bottom fog.

The elk bugled again as I dispatched guide Jim Larsen and Jerry's hunting partners slightly upstream of the direction taken by Jeff and Jerry. Our hunting plan for that day had been to ride together as far as Hughes Creek, with some of us splitting to the left into Hughes Basin and the rest to the right into Silvertip Basin to check for sign of elk activity. That strategy would have to wait.

We had been horseback about an hour. It wasn't quite light enough for good shooting yet, but I never like to ride past this spot before daylight. Too much chance for elk here. There are a half dozen small, secluded, lush meadows across the river at the mountain base, lots of screening timber between the meadows and our horse trail, plus a well-used elk escape route out the backside.

The bull hadn't seen or scented us. He'd heard our horses' hooves on the rocky trail and was challenging what he thought were additional elk in his territory.

As I collected dropped, noisy rain gear and tied the horses, I heard Jeff answering the bull's bugles. I knew Jeff and Jerry would be crouched low to the ground, scurrying from tree to tree, straining to see that patch of yellow elk hair or antler beam through the fog and snow.

BLAM! BLAM! Two rifle shots unexpectedly echoed off the rimrock above. I nearly jumped out of my skin. God, I hate it when all the action starts while I'm doing chores. But I'm happy we got—

What the heck, the bull just bugled again! Darn, must've missed him.

BLAM! There, that third shot has to be the kill shot. Well, finally—

What the? The bull just bugled again! Far up the mountain, this time.

"That's it! I can't stand any more of this!" I grabbed my rifle and headed off towards the river, a little downstream from everyone else.

I had no more gotten to where I could see a little bench, about two-hundred-fifty yards up the other side, when I saw two cows nearly across the opening, heading for black timber. I immediately turned my attention to the left and saw a heavy-antlered herd bull as he started across the thirty-yard avalanche-cleared area.

Through my 2/7 Leopold scope I scrutinized his movements intently, looking for some sign of injury, my finger resting lightly on the trigger of my 270. But, nothing! No justification for me to shoot. *Darn, he's going to make a clean getaway. He's halfway across.* Head high and tipped back, six point beams straddling his flanks.

BLAM! To my left, Jerry fired again. BLAM!

I had my cross hairs right on his neck. But no hits! No stumble, no hump, no hesitation, no nothing. No reason for me to squeeze the trigger.

BLAM! Suddenly, the bull was sliding down the mountain right at me. After all the missed shots, Jerry had finally hit him! Rocks and branches and elk were coming down together. Then it was quiet. Nothing moved. I really couldn't see the bull, just the spot where everything stopped. *If he gets up, I'll have one shot before he disappears forever.* Talk about pressure and adrenalin. *God, I hope he doesn't get up.*

Two minutes—three minutes—nothing. Then, I heard Jeff and Jerry coming.

"Hey, Dad, can you see where he quit rolling?" Jeff asked breathlessly.

"Sort of," I answered.

"He's sure a dandy," declared Jeff. "Will you watch the spot in case he moves while we climb on up to him?"

The bull never moved. Jerry had made a good clean one-shot kill on an especially heavy-beamed, mature, six-point bull elk.

Jerry had been most fortunate to have harvested a mature bull. No wonder the bull bugled at us. He and his two cows were the only elk or sign of elk we saw during seven days of intense hunting in my burnt-out country. No squirrels or songbirds had appeared yet, either. It was painfully clear several more years would pass before enough wildlife returned to make outfitting a viable enterprise.

After they left for home, I was cleaning up around the cabin and making plans to head back in to pack our camp out the next day. My divorce had automatically become final two days earlier.

◆   ◆   ◆

While heating up some chicken noodle soup on the kitchen stove, I heard a car drive up the hill to the cabin. *Another lost tourist,* I thought as I looked out the window. Sure enough, a little red sports car had just stopped in the yard. The driver's door opened, and a long-legged blonde uncoiled from behind the wheel, looked around, and strode confidently toward the front porch.

Then it hit me. *My God. That's Jan!*

I got to the front door just before she did and opened it to see her effervescent smile.

"Hey, Cowboy. I wondered if I might find you here."

Boy! Talk about being surprised and confused. Here was this woman I hadn't seen or talked to in well over a year, a woman I loved very much, a woman I turned my back on sixteen months ago. Here was the woman that caused my chest to ache if I sneaked even the smallest thought of her. I hoped my nervousness didn't show, as I asked if she'd like some lunch.

"Sure," she replied. She walked around the little cabin, checking things out.

I served the hot soup with some crackers and cold bologna sandwiches. "What brings you all the way out here from Florida?" I asked.

"I'm not from Florida any more. Finally got transferred out west to Boise. My territory runs all the way to Billings. That's where I've been. I had a couple of days to spare, so thought I'd cut through the Park on my way home. I recall you mentioned having a cabin up this way somewhere, so I stopped at Pahaska Tee-pee to see if they might know where it was. They did, and here I am. Here you are too. Sorta good timing, don't you think?"

What do you mean "don't I think," I thought. I could hardly think at all. I was a bundle of nerves. I could hardly eat, let alone think. This was happening too fast. I've been officially divorced only two days, when out of the blue, the love of my life—who I thought I had lost forever—shows up in the middle of nowhere. In she comes, all bubbly and chatty, talking a mile a minute, calm and normal as can be, as if I'd been down to Tampa just last weekend.

She hadn't found a new house in Boise yet but liked the town, her new territory, and best of all, after all the years of trying, she was finally in the West. When she stopped to take a breath, I asked, "You haven't heard the latest, have you?"

As usual, she answered my question with a couple of her own. "What 'latest' are you talking about?"

"My divorce was final two days ago."

With a loud whoop, she threw her arms around me and gave me a big smooch. "I had a feeling," she said, followed by, "Where are we going to dinner tonight, Handsome?"

Dinner? My God, I can't go out in public with "another woman," I thought. Nobody even knows I'm divorced. I don't know how to act or anything.

"Is there a place a girl can shower around here?"

Shower? Oh boy, is she serious? She's bringing her suitcase in! She is going to want to stay here tonight. Oh boy. Oh boy. What do I do now? I darned sure can't just hang up the phone. I better cowboy up and get with the program. Dad always said, "Faint heart never won Fair Lady. I want this lady. But this is so sudden, I haven't had time to make and remake any plans yet.

"What about that shower, Cowboy?"

Jeez, she's already sorting through her overnight bag. I've got to calm down, get to thinking straight, one crisis at a time. Okay, the shower. Right! Handle that one first.

Worry about dinner later. "There's no plumbing in the cabin, but I can heat up some water, fill the sun shower bag, and hang it from a beam on the porch."

"Great, that'll work. But—no peeking, Mr. Wiltse."

"I wouldn't think of it," I lied, but I agreed to no peeking—and kept my word.

I was thrilled to see her again, to hear her voice, see her infectious smile. We spent the afternoon bringing each other up-to-date on our lives. Jan's urge to be in the West was so strong she even accepted a lower management position to move to Boise. She sold her place in Tampa and had been renting while looking for a new home.

The last couple of years of emotional roller coaster had left me pretty much screwed up in the head. To say the least, I was having trouble being logical and analytical. *I mean, here is the long-lost love of my life, wanting to go to dinner with me, and I'm worried what people are going to say. Hello?*

There is a small steak house about halfway to Cody from Pahaska Teepee. I figured that would be a safe bet. Business would probably be slow and touristy, with small chance of anyone there knowing me. I had no clue how wrong I could be.

When we arrived, the place was hopping and half full of locals. Three couples there I knew well, all of whom took turns coming over to our table to chat and eyeball Jan. The worst was our waitress, whom I knew from the Irma Hotel in Cody. If looks could kill, I'd sure have been a dead duck. When she brought our ice water, she "accidentally" spilled my glass into my lap. Jan loved every minute of it and made a big show of wiping me dry. I was darn sure the live entertainment for the night was me.

My initial apprehension about Jan spending the night at the cabin turned out to be totally uncalled for. We enjoyed a very pleasant, comfortable time together. What were the odds of the two of us ever meeting in the first place? Whatever that astronomical number was, it had to be at least double for us to have reconnected.

And reconnect we did. Even though Jan had to leave the next morning, again we both knew there was something special between us—something that comes along once in a person's life, something precious worth working and sacrificing for. Yes, it was love, but that term doesn't fully describe the trust, mutual respect, emotional and spiritual bonding that was renewing itself. We were soul mates. From that time on, Jan would be known as "Plenty Woman" to me.

The day after she left, I led my pack string back into the high country to pack out camp. When I thought about Plenty Woman's return, my spirit soared like the ravens in the deep blue sky above me. Yet on the other hand, I remained troubled by my current financial crisis. I had not objected when Elizabeth claimed all our assets in the property settlement. I was left with nothing but the burnt-out hunting camps and $17,000 of debt. Little did I realize how much things were about to change.

While I was at a sport show in Anaheim, California the first of January, I was offered a well-paying ranch management job on a big elk ranch in New Mexico. The new owners were looking for someone single with my experience. They even agreed to my maintaining some limited elk hunts in Cody, to retain my government permits while the burn country regenerated itself.

Though Plenty Woman and I were unhappy about being separated again, we knew it was a sacrifice we must make.

GRINGO

I would have liked to have seen Cubero, New Mexico, before it slid into a sorry resemblance of an old Clint Eastwood spaghetti western town. The remains of the town sat forlornly among the wind-blown sage and cactus along old Route 66, halfway between Grants and Albuquerque. I would soon find that even though Interstate 40 bypassed Cubero a couple miles to the south, and the platinum mining had petered out in the early sixties, there was more going on around there than you would suspect.

This was a cold, wet day in March, 1990. The forest fires of 1988 had roared out of Yellowstone Park and consumed my hunting country, my camps, and my business. Elizabeth had burned out on me the next year. So, after fourteen years outfitting big game hunts in the Cody country and thirty-three years of marriage, I found myself out of business, divorced, broke, and in a strange and hostile community—and it was raining like a cow pissing on a flat rock.

The new Eastern owners of the ranch I had hired on to manage left a red Chevy four wheel drive pickup at the Albuquerque airport for me. As there was no phone at the ranch, they had made prior arrangements with a local excavator to meet me at The Last Chance. This bar at the west end of town and Diablo's at the east end were the two largest buildings still standing and reasonably intact in Cubero. There were a half dozen faded adobe houses, the U.S. post office building shaded by a couple of weary elm trees, and the homemade, oft-added on to convenience store/gas station called Villa de Cubero. The other dozen or so buildings and old trailer houses with discarded tire-anchored roofs were pretty much weathered away.

The heavy wooden front door scraped on an uneven plank floor as I pushed my way into The Last Chance. The room was surprisingly large. I stood for a moment as my eyes slowly adjusted to the dim, smoky light. Even if it had been pitch dark in there, the smell of spilled beer and stale tobacco would have given the room's use away right off. Hanging on the walls were the obligatory red chili peppers and velvet pictures of bull fighters and dancing señoritas.

Drinking at a table to my right were three young Mexican men, all looking surly and half-crocked. None looked or dressed like an excavator. Glaring at me from behind the far end of the bar to my left was a slightly older Mexican man. As the bartender slowly made his way toward me, he kept his hands below the bar. His dingy, slept-in T-shirt read something I didn't understand. But I understood the message in his hot black eyes as his bearded face parted just enough for him to hiss at me. "What do you want, Gringo?"

I could feel the other three sets of black eyes boring into my back. I didn't understand why all the hostility, but I immediately understood that if I didn't want to become a premature organ donor, I should remove myself from the premises.

"Tell Carlos I'll catch him later," I replied as I jerked the front door open. *Damn, these are bullet holes in this damn door.*

By the time I reached the locked ranch gate some ten miles upcountry from Cubero, the cold rain had turned to a cold, wet snow. A mile from The Last Chance I needed the four-wheel drive when I dropped off the blacktop onto the muddy ranch road. It was dark before I made the last five slippery miles to the adobe cabin at 9,000 foot elevation—my home for the next two years.

This was an elk ranch, and I had agreed to spend two years getting the herd in shape for hunting, fixing up the big Spanish-style lodge, and implementing a Corporate Retreat program, which would involve getting telephone service up the mountain and a more serviceable road built. Oh, and almost as an afterthought, owner Doug had mentioned it would be nice if I could foster good relations with the locals as well.

"Just see Keith down at the Cubero store for whatever you need. He'll let you use his phone, and we'll leave you messages there," he had said a month earlier, during my fifteen-minute job interview. I had never interviewed for a job before. Somehow, I thought there would be more to it.

Wearing my longjohns and wool socks, I lay in my sleeping bag trying to blow "smoke rings" with my frosty breath. I decided that come first light, I'd cut firewood for the fireplace and warm up this four-room cabin.

My next couple of months were consumed with getting familiar with the seven-thousand-acre, high mountain ranch and hiking the twenty miles of eight-foot-high game fence to ensure its integrity, and scouting sites to install new water guzzlers to catch and save precious rainwater for the game animals to drink. In addition to my little adobe cabin and the big twenty-bedroom lodge, there were two other houses and a big shop to care for. This was the rainy season in New Mexico. There was much to do before the dry winds would begin to blow. Ranching of any kind is always a race with the changing seasons, and I was starting a couple of years in the hole.

By June, the country had warmed and dried up quite a bit. The phone company promised service by fall. Not having a phone was not so bad right now anyway. Elizabeth couldn't call to tell me how worthless I was. I tended to messages such as a call from the local Sheriff during my weekly trip to Keith's for supplies.

Keith was a talkative, successful businessman who loved golf and flew his own plane. He welcomed me to use his desk and telephone whenever I needed. He also offered me good counsel regarding implementing the ranch owners' policies, with respect to local customs and perceptions.

It was enlightening for me to watch Keith from the back corner of his office as he traded with many of the Navajo, Acoma, and Laguna people. I realized there was more to this ramshackle old convenience store the first time I glimpsed the treasures Keith had squirreled away in his hidden big old Victor safe.

Without his willingness to buy their handmade Kachina dolls, silver and turquoise jewelry and pottery, life would have been a lot harder on many of them than it was. Some of the items were truly exquisite works of art. Some were very crude. Some Keith bought with cash, some he bought with gas and beer.

Even though everyone was treated courteously after the wrangling that is part of every deal in this culture, I would often hear Keith muttering to himself how "those damn Indians were always trying to rob him." At the same time, I could look out the window and watch the recent "tradee" waving his arms, shaking his head, and talking to himself as he filled his dog and kid-laden, rusty pickup truck with gas.

"Marie is the best Mexican cook in the country" was Keith's reply to my question. I needed someone to cook for the retreats and workshops I had booked for the ranch. As he scribbled directions to her trailer, he added, "I don't know if she will cook for you or not, but it wouldn't hurt to ask. Just watch out for the dogs and her husband. Okay?"

"What do you mean, her husband? I understand about the dogs, but why should I have to watch out for her husband? I don't even know him."

"Yeah, but he knows you. You'll recognize him too if you see him. He's a big 6'4" Laguna, friend of Ricky Sanchez. And you better call the Sheriff before you go back up to the ranch, too."

Sheesh! What's with these people down here, and who is Ricky Sanchez, anyway? I thought as I climbed into the ranch pickup. And what in the world does the Sheriff want?

Ten minutes later, I pulled into Marie's well-kept yard and was relieved to find that Geronimo and the killer dogs were not home. Marie turned out to be a gracious, middle-aged lady who kept a neat house, and she had just received a phone call from Keith encouraging her to talk with me. After reassuring me she could cook "mild enough" for the owners, the ranch guests and myself, she challenged me to come over for dinner and see for myself.

I humbly explained that would not be necessary. She had been highly recommended. Slightly miffed by my questions, she courteously thanked me for my offer. Said she would take it up with her husband and leave word with Keith.

As I headed back toward Cubero, I remembered Keith's admonition about returning the Sheriff's call. I couldn't imagine him having any good news, but it could be something about my family. I decided to stop at the store and give him a call.

On the second ring, I heard a cheerful "Buenos Dias."

"Hi. This is Duane Wiltse. I'm returning Sheriff Richards' call. Is he available?"

From the phone pressed to my left ear, the pleasant female Mexican voice replied as if she were expecting my call "Ah. Si, Señor Wiltse, uno momento."

"Señor Wiltse?" a gruff voice asked.

"Yes."

"This is Sheriff Richards. I have an official-looking letter I am supposed to deliver to you. I don't suppose you would leave the ranch gate unlocked for me?" he asked politely.

"Who and where is the letter from?"

"It's from an attorney in Cody, Wyoming—name of Sommers. Looks like something you wouldn't care to drive into Grants and pick up either, huh?"

As far as I was concerned, any letter from Elizabeth's attorney, Meg Sommers, would be unnecessary grief. "No, sir."

"And the gate?"

"No, sir."

"And you're too busy to wait an hour at Keith's for me to drive out there. Right?"

"Yes, sir."

"That's what I thought. I'll just return it stamped 'undeliverable.' I appreciate you returning my call. Good luck out there".

Click.

That was an interesting conversation, I muttered to myself. *I don't know why Elizabeth and her damn attorney don't leave me alone.* How much revenge was it going to take, anyway? She had already taken more than her pound of flesh—besides, the divorce was final better than six months ago. Elizabeth had started threatening me with that divorce back in 1956, barely six months into our marriage. That was the first time in my young life I remember feeling genuine panic. I mean, that was just not an option. No one in my family had ever divorced. No matter what it took, there was just no way I could let that happen.

I wasn't quite twenty years old when we married. I hadn't even left home. I was a virgin in more ways than one. When we got married, after a turbulent on-again and off-again two-year courtship, I moved from my parents' home into a little starter house with Elizabeth. I bought the house the winter before, and Dad helped me fix it up. At least we wisely waited a year before Elizabeth became pregnant. Now here I was, some thirty-three years later, my five children grown and gone, and I had never taken the time to discover who I was.

What kind of person did I want to grow into? Not what my strong-willed father expected, not what my angry wife expected, not what my self-serving church expected, not even what my children had come to expect. But me. What was I going to expect of myself from here on out? It takes time and much honest, painful soul searching to answer that question. There were many days when I simply ignored the question, but it wouldn't go away.

The bloodbath that Elizabeth drenched my personal life in during and after our divorce was the most humiliating experience of my life. She spared no one. She poured out her thirty-three years of pent-up venomous anger over family and friend alike. One day, I had to excuse myself from an intensely accusatory session with her and her attorney and go to the restroom and vomit.

One positive thing this siege did accomplish was to strip me of the pretenses of my long-cultivated image. One by one, the skeletons in my closet had been yanked out for all to judge.

◆   ◆   ◆

A couple of weeks later while at the store, I was greatly relieved when Keith said Marie had decided to give me a try. I wanted to call her right up and get together to discuss a menu for our first retreat, coming up in barely two weeks. Keith told me to back off a little. "Just tell her how many people and when. She'll ask you anything she needs to know."

The big day arrived with a rush, and I worried we were not really prepared. I know how important first impressions are, especially in a small community. I needed this workshop to be one hundred per cent successful in order to build future business for the lodge.

For twenty minutes or so, I had been busily filling plates with rice, refried beans and burritos, topped with Marie's home-made sauce. There were twenty-eight hungry people in the lodge's spacious dining hall. The teachers and administrative staff of the Grants Community College were holding their first of several workshops here.

Even at 9,000 foot elevation, the kitchen in early July was hot. Marie handed me a plate of food and waved me out the back door to eat in the shade of the porch. I knew disaster had struck by the time my first bite seared its way to my stomach. I could just see all the educators in the dining room nibbling around the edges of their plates, looking for a lower-octane morsel. It was plain to me my efforts to create a workshop and retreat program were going down in flames.

I doused the fire in my belly with a glass of lemonade and went to fire Marie. I spied her in the back of the dining hall laughing with a small group of guests.

"Mr. Wiltse. Mr. Wiltse," a man called out from behind me.

Oh boy, here it comes, I thought.

A man with beads of sweat on his forehead began shaking my hand as he exclaimed, "I've always heard Marie was an excellent cook. Now I know what everyone's been raving about."

Behind him, I saw tables of empty plates and contented guests, all with sweaty foreheads. As my gaze found Marie, she looked at me with a knowing smile. Later during cleanup, Marie said to me, "I knew if I let you taste the food first, like you wanted to, you'd screw things up. Don't worry. I'll teach you to appreciate Mexican food, Amigo. And by the way, if you haven't found someone to fix that crummy road yet, my husband Del says you should see Bad Eyes over at the Laguna Council office."

I spent the rest of that first summer booking several more successful retreats from Albuquerque and Grants, getting ready for our first hunters in September, and trying to get someone interested in upgrading our road. I never did hear from Carlos. Keith said I was better off without him anyway. Once, I almost had a logger talked into improving the road in exchange for the timber on the place, but he decided $50,000 worth of road building for $25,000 worth of timber didn't compute. He's the one who told me Laguna Pueblo had some of the best machinery and operators around. If I could get them to come up there, they would be my best bet.

"They can be hard to figure, though," he added. "They may not even talk to you or they could charge you an arm and a leg. Or, if the mood strikes them just right, they might bring a whole crew up here and charge you next to nothing. I don't know. Maybe it's the moon or something. Anyway, it wouldn't hurt to stop over there and ask."

Keith had said about the same thing a couple of times, and I remembered Marie's earlier comments about seeing Bad Eyes, so I decided that after hunting season, I'd go over and see what I could stir up.

DAN'S DREAM

Dan Williams was a good example of the type of hunters I was guiding for the ranch. Dan was eighty-seven years old, a small, wiry fellow in good physical condition. Sharp mind. Hard of hearing and a little slow of movement.

Dan had worked as a civil engineer throughout the western United States for over thirty years, and he was very personable, with a lot of great stories to share. He didn't take himself too seriously and was devoted to Laura, his wife of sixty-two years. Laura felt the same about Dan and accompanied him on all his adventures. Laura was a sweet, patient companion.

During the four days they spent with me, I bet if I heard this exchange once, I heard it fifty times.

"WHAT DID HE SAY, MA?"

"HE SAID," Laura would automatically reply, and then her condensed version of my statement would follow. Dan would always nod his head in understanding.

Dan loved to hunt and had done so all his life. He recognized his inability to ride horseback in the western high country or even make long, exhausting hikes afield, or live in a tent camp any more. Still, he dreamed of harvesting the one major hunting trophy that had eluded him for so many years—a mature, trophy-class six-point bull elk.

When Laura first called me on the phone a couple months earlier to inquire about our hunts, I sensed something about this couple. I could hear Dan in the background ask a question, then Laura would repeat it to me. She would relay my answer to Dan, who would follow with another question. After several minutes of this disjointed conversation, I heard Dan ask, "WELL, WHAT DO YOU THINK, MA? CAN HE HELP US GET A BIG BULL?"

"I think so, Dear. He sounds honest."

"GOOD. SEND HIM THE MONEY."

Lodge at Mt. Tayor New Mexico.

When they got out of their Buick at the lodge, they reminded me of a couple of kids at Christmas time going to visit Santa. What worried me was they viewed me as their Santa for the next four days. As usual, Marie prepared and served us all a very nice dinner. The rest of the evening was spent sipping wine and getting acquainted around the roaring fire in the lodge's massive fireplace. Before turning in early, we stepped out on the upper balcony deck and shivered in the chilly September night as we listened to the challenging bugles of bull elk in the distance.

The next morning, our timing couldn't have been better. Dan, Laura and I left the lodge an hour before sunup. I drove the ranch's old white Jeep Cherokee. Dan hung on in the passenger seat, and Laura braced across the back seat. I was taking the so-called Jeep trail up the backside of the mountain. Sometimes, the light from the headlights reflected off the tops of the tall pines before being swallowed by the inky sky. Sometimes, they were lost in the emptiness of the abyss beside us.

While we bounced and jerked over the rocks and washed-out ruts, Dan and Laura weren't talking—just hanging on. I was thinking, *Boy, it's a good thing it's still dark. If the folks could see where we are, they would surely be scared to death.*

As the first hint of dawn pushed the darkness out of the pines, I braked the antique Cherokee and cut the engine. I had doused the lights a hundred yards back, as we clawed our way to the top of the grassy bench. From our vantage point, we would be able to see a vast panorama of great elk country and hopefully some elk as well.

"I'm sure glad you're driving," Dan muttered. I looked back to check on Laura. She didn't speak, just smiled weakly and motioned for me to look for elk. I had already seen a group of spots where I expected to see elk that morning.

Sure enough. As the world continued to awaken around us, with the stirring of birds and breezes, the spots slowly grew into elk. They were about fifteen hundred yards in front and below us. I tried to point them out to Dan. He was having a little difficulty separating the elk spots on the ridge below from the fly spots on the windshield we were peering through.

As I studied them with my binoculars, I could see one was sure enough a big six-point bull. For some reason known only to him, the bull raised his head, laid his antlers along his back, and started up the crest of the ridge, headed right at our hiding spot. He wasn't spooked but was certainly traveling with some purpose in mind. I couldn't believe how lucky we were. The bull didn't know we were there, and in three or four minutes he would be right on top of us.

"You see that big bull coming our way, Dan?"

"WHAT DID HE SAY, MA?"

"DO YOU SEE THAT BIG BULL?"

"WHAT BIG BULL? WHERE?"

The first tinges of concern began to flicker around the edges of my stomach. Even though I felt we had lots of time before the bull reached our bench, there was no need spending it trying to show him to Dan. He didn't need to see the bull until he was in range to shoot, anyway.

"Let's get out and get ready to shoot," I said.

"WHAT DID HE SAY, MA?"

"HE SAID GET OUT AND GET READY TO SHOOT."

"And be quiet," I added hopefully.

"WHAT?"

"AND BE QUIET!!!"

"Oh, right," Dan responded as he slammed the front door. Then carefully he made his way to the rear door.

"Hand me my rifle, Ma," he said as he opened the rear door.

Laura handed him his cased rifle. The bull was of very nice quality and closing fast. He was already better than halfway to us. I dropped my binoculars around my neck and went around the Cherokee to help Dan. Laura wisely stayed in the back seat. We got the old 30/06 bolt action Winchester out of the case and loaded just as the bull appeared on our bench, about one hundred yards in front of us. The range was good. The light was good. The breeze was light. And best of all, Dan now, for the first time in his life, saw a big six-point bull elk.

I could tell the bull was concentrating on something beyond us. He either didn't see us or he didn't care about us. By now, he was barely forty yards away and on a line to pass within twenty yards of us. I practically dragged Dan the two or three steps to the front of the Cherokee and motioned for him to get a solid rest over the hood for his shot.

Nodding his head, he drew down on the magnificent bull. Standing behind Dan with my fingers in my ears and holding my breath, I watched the muzzle of the old 06 follow the bull. I knew Dan would squeeze the trigger any moment. My body involuntarily tensed in anticipation of the loud explosion of gunpowder.

My eyes were now riveted on the single-footing bull as he drew abreast of us. His rippling muscles and his frosty breath reminded me of the slow motion scene in "Dances With Wolves," as Kevin Costner's character, John Dunbar, rode his horse across the front of the Rebel lines. In the movie, the Rebs fired unsuccessfully.

On the mountain that morning, the energy in Dan's small body seemed to be expelled with his out-rushing breath. His eyes stayed riveted on a patch of timber as the bull disappeared into it. He turned and jacked the unfired shell out of his rifle as he asked, "He sure was a nice one, wasn't he?"

"He sure was."

"I'm sorry, Duane. I just wasn't mentally prepared to see such an animal so close and so soon into our hunt."

"I know, Dan. It happens to a lot of guys."

Laura had gotten out of the back seat and was standing reassuringly close to the long-faced Dan, who said, "Well, I guess this means my hunt's over."

"Hell no, Dan. There's lots of elk around. We'll find another bull."

"But not like that one."

"You never know," I said, trying to sound more confident than I felt at the moment.

"I suppose we might as well head back to the lodge," Dan said. Laura asked if we had to go down the same way we came up.

"No, Laura. In fact, I think we should go on hunting. We can ease on down this open ridge and drop off the south end of the ranch to the main road. That will give us lots of good country to glass."

"Well, whatever you think," Dan said glumly.

We spent a couple of hours slowly driving down the ridge, stopping regularly to glass the cuts and coulees on both sides, but to no avail. The sun was high in the clear, blue sky now, and the temperature had warmed considerably. Any self-respecting bull elk would be bedded in the shade, chewing his cud by now. I drove with my window open, hoping to hear something I couldn't see. Neither Dan nor Laura had spoken a half-dozen words since we left the high bench.

Shortly after entering the timber below where we had seen the elk first thing this morning, I hit the brakes hard, killed the engine, and started furiously cranking my window up.

"What's the matter?" Dan asked.

I didn't answer until I had the window all the way up. "I think I heard a bull chuckle," I said with my hand on the door handle. I knew better than to open it just yet.

"WHAT DID HE SAY, MA?"

"HE SAID HE HEARD AN ELK."

"HOW? WHERE?"

I put my finger to my lips as I whispered to Laura I would go afoot to see if I could locate the bull and be right back. "Don't let Dan get out of the Jeep. Okay?"

She nodded.

As I slipped out of the Cherokee and quietly pressed my door shut, Dan looked at me and asked, "Where are you going?"

I was grateful to see Laura reach up and lay a hand on his left shoulder. I moved quickly and quietly along the game trail I discovered just a few yards from the Jeep. I knew if I was going to find the bull, it would be within ten to fifteen minutes. In this timber it was going to be a long shot to find the bull at all. If I did find him, there would only be two chances of getting Dan on him—slim and none.

A moment later, I froze in my tracks. I saw elk legs. A half step to my right, with some bobbing and weaving on my part, I could make out beautiful, ivory-tipped antlers above a nose nibbling grass at the base of a pine tree. Holding my breath, I backed up several steps before hurrying up the game trail toward the Jeep and Dan. I was calculating the bull should be about one hundred fifty yards from the Jeep. I didn't know what direction he was working. I knew I'd be very lucky to find the bull again without spooking him.

Getting Dan out of the Jeep and quietly back to the bull sounds like a Mission Impossible episode, I thought.

Next thing I knew, I spotted Dan hustling down the game trail toward me. "Did you find him?"

With my finger to my lips, I nodded and motioned for him to follow. Maybe we did have a chance, after all. It had been about ten minutes since I first saw the bull. Dan and I sneaked about halfway back to where I had left him. When I stopped abruptly, Dan ran into the back of me.

We were approaching a little grassy opening in the timber, and a small pine tree to the right of the opening was shaking unnaturally. I took a careful step forward and peered around a scrub oak. There he was, right out in the open, barely thirty-five yards away, polishing his beautiful six-point rack on that poor pine tree!

I stepped back, took hold of both Dan's shoulders, placed him in my tracks, and pushed him ahead. Dan immediately got the message. He took another step to his left for a rest aim in the fork of a small oak tree. His mind was right, this time. There was no hesitation. Shortly after the echo of his well-placed shot died out, Laura appeared with their camera.

A couple of days later, when I had their fresh elk meat and trophy prepared for travel, they expressed their heartfelt appreciation with goodbye hugs all around. Dan looked me in the eye as I held the door of the Buick open for him. "I still say that first bull was bigger, Duane."

I smiled, closed the door, and waved.

He was right.

BAD EYES

Bad Eyes—that's all I need, I thought as I parked in front of the gaily painted Council Office at the Laguna Pueblo. *At least his name isn't "Bad Ass."*

"Just call me Jack, Mr. Wiltse. I heard you may be coming over. Need that road fixed up, huh? Come on in. By the way, my given name is 'Sees At Night.' Del probably gave you that Bad-Eyes name, didn't he?" Jack added, with a smile.

Boy, I'm off on the wrong foot again. I began to sputter an apology. *I wonder how it is everybody knows so much about my business.* Jack waved off my apology, saying, "Aah, Del and I go way back."

Jack was a handsome fellow, looked to be in his early to mid-thirties, built and moved with the fluid confidence of a marathon runner.

"I can't promise you anything" was his reply to my question regarding the availability or interest of their road-building crew for my project. "I know they have a couple of weeks, maybe a month or two, depending on weather and stuff, to finish some work on our own roads. As Pueblo Secretary, the best I can do is get you a couple minutes with the Council."

"That would be great. I really appreciate your time and help."

"Okay, then come back next Monday."

"Fine. Monday, aaah, what time?"

"Time? What's good for you?"

"Umm, morning."

"Yeah, morning is good. You want a doughnut?"

"Sure."

"Okay, see you next Monday morning then." Jack rose from his chair, shook my hand, and handed me the half-empty doughnut box.

On the appointed Monday, I was extra careful driving off the mountain on our treacherous road. It had snowed the night before, and the gumbo surface was as slick as snot on a doorknob. I was a bundle of nerves, anyway, worrying about my first Council meeting. I didn't know what to expect or what was expected of me. I hadn't slept well the night before and was up extra early showering and shaving. I put on clean, freshly ironed clothes and brushed my hat and boots well. I wasn't sure I had given a very good account of myself with my Mexican neighbors the first year. I had already stepped in it with Sees At Night, thanks to Del, who I hadn't even met. At the very least, an audience with the Council was going to be educational.

I descended from the tall, dark pines to the lower piñon and juniper habitat just in time to see one of New Mexico's trademark sunrises—indescribably brilliant. While last night's wet snow had made the road ugly, it had washed the sky crystal clear. By the time I reached Laguna Pueblo, my mind had cleared also. It was 8:00 a.m.—time to go in.

I decided my presentation would be short, polite, and respectful—hoping for some questions that would allow me to expand, and then play it by ear. Jack met me at the front desk with a smile and a handshake. He led me down a short corridor through double doors carved with "Life" symbols, and into an attractive, wood-paneled sunlit room.

There were twelve well-dressed, mature-looking men, no women, sitting around a large, oval, heavy wood table. Everyone had papers on the table in front of them. Jack directed me to an empty chair as he introduced me. Some of the men looked up from their papers, some didn't. A few nodded. No one shared their name with me. I sensed they were not being rude, just busy with matters of importance to their people. My road was not one of them.

Everyone was attentive to my three-minute presentation, though no one asked any questions. Then the mood seemed to relax a bit, and someone passed a box of doughnuts around. As we all munched on doughnuts, the man next to me asked where I was from and why I was in New Mexico. I kept my answers short, as it seemed to me the others were restlessly waiting for me to leave. So, thanking them for their time and consideration, I got up and left.

As I passed through the outer office, without getting out of his chair, Jack spoke matter-of-factly. "See you in two weeks."

"What do you mean, in two weeks?"

"Oh yeah. You gotta come back."

"Oh. Uh, I'll see you in a couple of weeks then."

When you are tending twenty miles of fence by yourself, busting thirty-inch snow drifts with a chained up 4X4 loaded with thirty bales of hay and four hundred pounds of grain cubes for the one-hundred-fifty head of elk you are feeding each day, you work from can to can't. A couple of weeks passed quickly.

When I arrived at the Council building that morning, Jack was primed with several questions. Mostly it was small talk about the weather, elk and deer on the ranch, some about me, and some about the struggle of the Laguna people to get an effective game management program established on their Pueblo.

When I entered the Council chambers, some of the men were standing and visiting. We nodded as I removed my hat and sat in the same chair as before. Two or three of the men asked me questions as to just how much road construction would be required and how much time I thought it would take.

Again, they responded only with nodding heads as I explained I was looking for a minimum of actual construction, a couple of culverts, widening of three or four areas, and a top dressing of gravel so the road could be graded. Shouldn't take more than three or four days. Besides, the ranch couldn't afford more than that. That's when somebody started the box of doughnuts around again.

I was thinking, *It's sure a long drive over here every two weeks just for a doughnut.* I stopped to ask Jack about this process. He assured me all was going well and that I definitely needed to return in two weeks.

"But when can I get someone to come up and look at the project and give me a price?"

"Aren't you going to be up there all winter?" he asked.

"Well sure, but—"

"So, relax. Don't get an ulcer over this project." He smiled.

"I'm going to get an ulcer eating doughnuts with you guys," I said.

Jack laughed and waved goodbye.

Third Council—same drill! A couple of questions, polite nodding of heads, box of doughnuts passed around. Somewhat exasperated, I told Jack I couldn't keep coming over here every two weeks just to eat doughnuts.

"You haven't been," he replied. "You got a phone up there yet?"

"Sort of."

"Well, give me your number. I'll call you when I hear something."

◆   ◆   ◆

The time I had spent alone working on the ranch afforded me lots of time to think, to wonder about who I am and who I wanted to become. It slowly dawned on me that before I could answer these questions, there were other questions to be answered first. Such as, who have I been? How did I get to the place in my life where divorce was the answer? How could I be guilty of infidelity? I had always considered myself a man of integrity, yet I could not escape the fact I was guilty. From childhood I had been taught by family and church that divorce was unacceptable. How could this have happened?

I had been active in the church where I was baptized at eight years of age. I worked hard and came straight home after work every day. I didn't drink or chase other women, and I didn't appreciate men who did. I loved my family and enjoyed teaching and doing things with them. So what went wrong?

I studied hard to understand my failures of the past so as to not repeat them in the future Through painful reflection, I began to understand some things. I had heard of mid-life crisis but always considered that a malady of weak hearted wanna-be's. Most men handle their mid-life crisis better than I did. They change jobs, buy sports cars, etc. I had a train wreck! I clearly remember that shortly after our twenty-fifth wedding anniversary, I gave up on our relationship. That began the process where I became less accountable to myself, avoiding full responsibility for my behavior.

That was then, this is now. I am no longer okay with any lack of accountability on my part.

For the first time in my life, I understood my grandmother's admonition to "be good for goodness' sake." And I resolved to do just that. I realized how the choices I made every day, by my actions or inactions, dictate the quality of my life. My future choices would not be governed by fear of consequences but rather what positive results would be natural to occur.

I was immersed in a seven-day-a-week effort to bring the Mount Taylor Ranch back from several years of neglect. Plenty Woman was living in Boise, Idaho, traveling to her GM dealerships from Billings, Montana, and over into Oregon. We both found time and looked forward to writing each other. Jan's no-nonsense, down-to-earth counsel regarding what I was actually responsible for and what I could do about it, was like springtime in the Rockies to me—fresh, clean, invigorating, and full of promise.

During her occasional long weekend visits, I tried to impress her with my cooking and horsemanship skills. I soon found that compared to her cooking and horsemanship skills, I needed to hustle to keep up. We enjoyed learning from each other and were quick to recognize strengths in one another. Our growing love flowed easily, and like the spring at the base of the glacier in Silver Tip Basin becomes a sparkling stream, feeding and nurturing the mountain flowers, our love nourished our bruised and lonely spirits.

There was total respect and acceptance of each other. Early on, I was concerned that I needed to be brutally honest about my transgressions. At times I would begin an explanation with the words, "There is something you should know," to which Jan would reply, "That was then, this is now. It doesn't matter who you were or what mistakes you made before we met. What is important now is us—how we treat each other."

By September, 1990, the telephone company had intermittent service as far as our shop, three miles below the lodge and house. If I was working on the upper end or back side of the ranch, it could be two or three days before I would be around the shop to check the answering machine. Unfortunately, that was the case when Jan tried to reach me from the Boise Hospital. When I finally got the message two days later, she was still in the hospital and quite distraught.

She was almost as upset about not being able to get in touch with me as she was about her medical problem, which turned out to be a serious case of internal bleeding brought on by a ruptured vein in her esophagus.

In 1985, Jan was diagnosed with primary biliary cirrhosis and was told by her doctors a liver transplant was probable. This malady strikes mostly women in their early forties. There is no known cause and no cure except transplant. PBC has side effects such as portal hypertension, enlarging of the spleen, varices, fatigue, etc.

Jan spent five anxious days in the hospital before her system was stabilized and the bleeding stopped. Even though her condition was delicate, the doctor sent her home with the admonition of no travel whatsoever. She worked from home, but the demands of her job tended to overstress her fatigued condition, and shortly, the doctor ordered a medical leave of absence.

I was relieved when she accepted my invitation to come to the ranch to convalesce. This was the beginning of a new experience for Jan and me. Neither of us had to leave in a few days. The continuity of this arrangement fostered feelings of permanence and security that was strengthening for both of us.

During her analysis at Mayo Clinic in February 1991, it was determined that she must accept full-time medical retirement, as a transplant was likely in the next two years. Her reply was, "The hell you say. I'll see you guys."

By now, I knew without a shadow of a doubt that Plenty Woman and I were soul mates. We had taken a long time to find each other. Our separate journeys had taken many twists and turns, but now we were finally together. Come hell, high water, or liver transplants, we were determined to stay together. On Valentine's Day that year, I asked her to marry me.

"You betcha, Cow Buddy. I was beginning to wonder if you were ever going to make an honest woman of me."

We set the date for July 20, 1991.

♦   ♦   ♦

It ran on about three months, and one day ol' Jack called up and asked about the weather and snow conditions on the mountain. When I told him things were pretty clear and dry, he said "Good. Can you meet the road crew and unlock the gate for them Monday morning about 8:00 a.m.?"

"Well, sure I can," I answered. "But what will this cost? I can't just okay fixing the road without knowing what it will cost, Jack."

"It won't be much" he said.

"I appreciate that, Jack, but I got to have a number."

"Oohhh, well, okay, uh, how about $5000?"

"That's way more than fair, Jack. Are you sure you can do it for that? No one has even come up here and looked at the job."

"Don't worry about it! Can you meet us at the gate or not?" Jack asked impatiently.

"You bet, looking forward to working with you. Should I have a box of doughnuts?"

Jack laughed and hung up.

Come Monday morning, I no more than got the big, black wrought-iron double gates open when a whole convoy of orange trucks came thundering around the bend. They shot through that gate like green grass through a goose. You'd have thought it was 1876 and they were on their way to the Little Big Horn.

There were four pickups loaded with hand tools, two small five-yard dump trucks with twelve foot of galvanized culvert sticking out of each of them, one pulling a trailer loaded with a backhoe, the other pulling a trailer dwarfed by a big 4-wheel-drive articulating loader. Then came a ten-yard belly dump loaded with road gravel and a grader, followed by a big fuel truck. Choking in their dust, I closed the gate.

Half the convoy roared on to the upper end of the road to begin work back. The other half started at the gate and worked up. The pickups relayed information, men and hand tools back and forth as well as ferried the twelve-plus men home at night. They didn't spent a lot of time with transits, chalk line and such. They did exactly what I wanted—used the existing grade and made the road carworthy. They did an excellent job.

By the end of the fourth ten-hour day, as everyone was preparing to leave the completed job, Sees At Night crawled stiffly out of his pickup. Brown eyes beaming, he asked, "Well, Boss, what do you think?"

"I think you damn Indians been having a lot of fun with me," I answered.

He laughed, threw his arm around my shoulder and whispered loudly in my ear, "You got that right, White Man."

"I've got one more favor to ask of you, Jack," I said.

"Shoot," he replied.

"I'd like you to invite every member of the Council and every man that worked on this road to bring his wife and children up here for a cookout when it gets warmer this summer."

"That will be very much appreciated, Boss," he answered earnestly. Then he added with a mischievous smile, "Can we fish?"

"The kids can fish. Catch and release only," I answered firmly.

"Fair enough," he said, adding a thumbs up. "Better get that gate."

The revving trucks were raring to go. I locked the gate and watched their cloud of dust disappear around the bend. I couldn't help but think, *I'm going to miss that wild-ass bunch of Indians.*

But they had one more surprise for me.

I received a couple of "attaboys" from the owners for the good job on the road. They weren't too sure about the cookout, though. I finally convinced them it would be good public relations and an ideal time for them to meet some locals. Besides, I would be inviting Keith and his family, and there would be some people here they knew.

Sunday afternoon, July 21, was selected as the big feast day. When I called Sees At Night with the date, I asked how many of his people I should expect.

"Oh, maybe twenty-five or thirty. We really appreciate you doing this, Boss."

"You're welcome. I'm looking forward to it. See you the 21st," I said, hanging up the new telephone in my office at the lodge.

Two of Jan's close friends, Charlene and Kelly from Florida, flew in on Thursday, July 18, to be part of our wedding. The three girls had a grand time together, and Jan and I were married in a simple ceremony that we wrote. Frank Young, a minister friend of mine from Cody, flew down and officiated in front of the huge fireplace in the great room of the lodge. Our personal vows were not exchanged with aprehension this time. But rather with a welling up of emotion born of experience and true commitment.

The three owners and their families were in for the big cookout the next day. So all in all, we had twenty wedding guests. Marie cooked a fine dinner for us, and we all sat up til midnight, visiting and enjoying some fine wine. Jan and I never did take time for a honeymoon.

By 12:30 p.m. on Sunday, July 21, our cookout guests began to arrive. The owners and Jan and I were cooking and serving so the other ranch hands could enjoy the cookout and a day off. We were grilling beef tri-tips over white-hot charcoal. Potato salad, baked beans, iced tea and Kool Aid rounded out the menu. We started serving around 1:00 p.m.. There were already more than twenty-five or thirty Indians there, and a steady stream of them could be seen through the pines, still coming up the road.

By 1:30 p.m., the crowd had really swelled. The people I knew were being swallowed up by lots and lots of people I had never seen before. Women and kids were running everywhere. I could see the veins on Arthur's forehead bulging with tension. He was the principal owner. About that time, Sees At Night apologetically said to me, "I'm sorry, Boss. That damn Ralph stood up in church this morning and told everyone they were invited to a cookout up here."

"Who's Ralph?"

Sees At Night pointed to a guy sitting at the base of a big shady pine with a heaping plate of food. "That damn fat Indian over there. Didn't even work on the road either." The gentle breeze carried puffs of dust across Ralph's food as Sees At Night muttered unmentionables to himself, intentionally dragging the heels of his Tony Lamas in the dirt, and walked away.

Fortunately, the traffic dried up about the same time we exhausted all the personal reserves from the lodge's kitchen. However, Arthur was quite unhappy with me over the number of guests that had arrived. As I hurriedly washed dishes for reuse, he told me bluntly he counted over a hundred people here, and I had done a very poor job of planning. I was just glad he wasn't aware of all the Indian kids down at the lower pond catching the heck out of his trout.

A couple of weeks later, during one of my stops at Keith's, he was delighted to tell me what a success the community considered the cookout to have been. Everyone was talking about it and what a big improvement had taken place at the ranch since the new owners had arrived.

"What big improvement you talking about?" I asked.

"Well, you know. The way you've hired all local help for your projects. And then the cookout, which everyone knows got out of hand, but you still welcomed and fed everyone," Keith answered. Then he added, "You know, everyone's been suspicious of the ranch since the shooting a few years ago."

This was news to me. "What shooting?"

"You don't know about the shooting? You mean the owners didn't tell you about it when you took this job?"

"No. What happened?"

"Well." He seemed to hesitate. "Jesus, Duane. Before you showed up, one of the managers up there thought he was Rambo or something. Carried a gun with him all the time. He was an arrogant, disrespectful, paranoid sonofabitch. He just pushed things too far, and one day ol' Ricky shot him dead."

"My neighbor—Ricky Sanchez?"

"Yeah. Acquitted, too. I can't believe they didn't tell you."

CRAZY FRENCHMAN

With each passing day, my yearnings for Wyoming grew stronger. I missed the Rockies' high-country habitat. I missed Cody and the cowboy/outfitter culture. I was glad my two-year commitment to the Mt. Taylor Ranch would be completed in a few months. At the same time, I was hesitant to leave the many new friendships that had been forged. Jan and I were getting along great with all the locals, Indian and Mexican alike—even Ricky Sanchez. It's amazing what a little mutual respect among neighbors will accomplish. The owners were paying me good money, too—but Cody's mystique and magnetic pull was strong, and I wanted to go home. I was anxious to see my children. But it was not to be.

While Jan and I were in Las Vegas at the Safari Club Convention in early 1992, booking future business for the ranch, I received an offer from a man who owned a ranch in southern Colorado, and I couldn't turn it down. He was a Frenchman, who inherited a large fortune his father had made in the Paris grocery business. He didn't seem to appreciate my attempt at humor when I commented that the way to make a small fortune in the ranching business was to start with a large one. Mark Jung was his name, and since he needed to travel back and forth to Paris regularly, I was to be his personal representative during his absences.

In addition to overseeing the other four ranch employees, my three additional responsibilities were to get the ranch qualified and included in the Colorado Wildlife Department's attractive Ranching for Wildlife program, and foster good relations with neighboring ranches—because Mark wanted to enlarge his three thousand acres of mostly mountain terrain by buying all of the low-lying ranches surrounding him. But it was the third responsibility that puzzled me and made me uncomfortable, and that was to escort his younger, attractive mistress, Evelyn, during her trips to town.

Evelyn and her French ways had a habit of scandalizing the little western town of Trinidad, such as sunbathing topless at the local Holiday Inn pool, where she liked to swim on Sunday afternoons. She had short dark hair and a great figure and enjoyed flaunting her considerable sensuality. Why else would she wear skimpy tank tops with no bra when Mark was not around? No one wore tighter pants or shorter miniskirts than Evelyn.

Her desk in the ranch office sat against an outside wall under a large window. When just the two of us were in the office, discussing ranch business or going over paperwork, she would sit on the swivel chair at her desk while I stood or sat in a chair to her side. At least once a week, she would have me in there for an hour or two, going over maps, invoices, insurance papers, taxes, and whatever, while she displayed her ample tanned cleavage and her panties.

She would swivel her chair toward me with her miniskirt hiked up slightly, parted thighs exposing a white panty-clad crotch, crossing and uncrossing long legs with a smoldering look in her devilish black eyes.

Some days, the panties were red. Some days black, blue, lavender, and even yellow. I don't know why the yellow ones were so tantalizing to me. Maybe it was the way wisps of her black pubic hair contrasted with the bright color. Who knows what her real intentions were. Maybe she just enjoyed teasing me. I never asked. I had decided a year before that I would be totally accountable to myself for my choices, and I chose to honor my commitments to myself and Plenty Woman, but Evelyn never tired of the game.

Mark's personality and habits presented a more complex challenge. Trinidad is a small town, and the ranch is located barely twenty miles south of town along Raton Pass, just north of the New Mexico state line. It turned out Mark was well-known by the Sheriff and everyone else in town for his excessive drinking and fast, reckless driving. The Sheriff had pulled his driver's license and tried to mediate some "minor disagreements," as Mark referred to them, with his neighbors.

I began to understand why the community dubbed him "the crazy Frenchman." He was so impressed with his American nickname that he christened his ranch "The Crazy French Ranch."

It didn't take me long to question what I had gotten us into. At least I was comforted by the thought that Jan and I were a day's drive closer to Cody. I immediately began discussions, negotiations and paper work to comply with Colorado's Ranching for Wildlife program requirements.

At first, I didn't understand many of the customs and traditions of the older landowners in the area. The Sheriff had cautioned me to tread softly when approaching the neighboring ranchers, as many of their places were part of the old Spanish Land Grant era.

Luckily, I met a fellow hunting guide, Louie Osola. Louie's father was Italian, his mother Mexican. Louie had been born and raised in these parts. He had a magnetic personality that served him well in any situation. Even though he was in his late thirties now, he still loved to raise hell and stick a chunk under it.

Louie's intimate knowledge of the people, their feuds with each other, and their distrust of the crazy Frenchman was invaluable in helping me soothe relations and hurt feelings.

Unfortunately, modern surveyed property lines sometimes conflicted with the locals' age-old land and water usage habits. When Mark had bought his property a couple of years earlier, it was not a real ranch by any means. It was just a piece of beautiful mountain country consisting of tall Ponderosa pine, lots of scrub oak, and a little early summer grass. There were no fences or buildings. There were a couple small streams and natural ponds that generations of neighbors' cattle drank from. Cattle from all three neighboring ranches were accustomed to wandering around the place. They enjoyed the higher elevations during the hot summer months, cool shade, fewer flies, fresh grass, cooler water.

Things began to get a little testy when Mark decided to fence his place along the legal property lines, which he did the year before I arrived. Mark didn't like cows and flew into a rage on the numerous occasions when thirsty bovine haybalers trespassed. He wanted a private game ranch and resented competition from the cattle for the resources.

The biggest bone of contention was along Mark's north line. There is an age-old water hole at the base of a small draw just inside the new fence. Three deeply worn cow paths approach the water hole from different directions. Today's cows were brought there by their mothers, who were brought there by their mothers, and so on as far back as there were thirsty cows in the country.

When hot, thirsty mountain cattle have walked a couple of miles under southern Colorado's summer sun and can see and smell cool water just a few yards beyond a three-strand barb wire fence, property damage is sure to occur. Mark claimed the old rancher was cutting the fence to allow his cattle to water in his pond.

I suspected Mark was right, but I didn't blame the rancher, either. Mark wouldn't or couldn't appreciate old traditions. He strode hard-heeled throughout the community. Because he had money, there were many who cut him a lot of slack.

It was a different story with the old-timers, though. They lived by the code of honor, honesty and respect. Men who didn't were not welcome. The crazy Frenchman was viewed with suspicion and distrust by his neighbors. Fortunately, I was able to convince Mark the only way he could begin purchase negotiations with his neighbors was to allow me to make peace with them.

The day Mark left for his customary three month return to Paris, I asked Louie to set up a visit with the Martinez family.

Louie drove us, but he made no attempt to get out of his pickup when he shut off the engine in the cluttered yard of a weathered, crooked house half hidden by underbrush and juniper. No one came out of the front door. Shortly, an older Mexican man appeared at Louie's window and spoke Spanish pleasantly with him for a few minutes.

Meanwhile, I noticed in the side mirror a couple of men in their thirties standing at the rear of the truck. By then, the older man invited us to get out of the truck. Louie introduced me to Mr. Martinez and his sons, Richard and Chad.

As we shook hands and exchanged pleasantries, I noticed a shade being edged over through one of the cracked windows in the house behind them. Mr. Martinez welcomed me to the community and hoped I enjoyed it there.

He went on to say, "My grandfather watered his cattle at the water hole in Lobo Draw and his grandfather before him. And now this crazy Frenchman fences off the water and my cows go thirsty. What is the matter with this man? Has he no respect?"

"He is a strange man, Señor, and he wants the grass for his elk. He has asked me to solve this problem."

"He can have the grass for his elk, but we need the water for our cows."

"I know, and I have an idea. If I buy the fencing material, will your sons help me move the fence to the back side of the pond? I think if we use new barbed wire, it won't 'break so easily' and let your cows onto Mr. Mark's grass."

"You would do that?"

"I will do it tomorrow, if you agree."

All of a sudden, everyone was all smiles and earnestly shaking my hand.

"Si, Señor. We will meet you at Lobo Draw mañana."

"Louie, so there is no misunderstanding, please explain in Spanish to these fellows I will have the fence material at the water hole 10:00 tomorrow morning. Okay?"

"You bet."

As we drove away, Louie asked, "Don't you think Mark's going to be mad at you for moving that fence?"

"If he gets mad, he gets mad. He's the one who told me to make peace with the neighbors. Besides, I don't blame Mr. Martinez for being upset. For crying out loud, his cows need that water. Mark doesn't. When Mark gets back this fall, the folks will be in a much better mood when he offers to buy them out. And, it won't make any difference which side of the water hole the fence is on if Mark owns both places anyway."

Sure enough, later that summer Mark had his attorney present the three neighboring ranchers generous offers. He also asked me to personally visit with each of them to convey his earnest intentions and assure them they could stay on their places for a year or two, if need be.

These neighbors were all older folks who were looking forward to a less demanding lifestyle. They welcomed me, Mark's offer, and were excited about their upcoming retirement and eagerly looking forward to closing in September when Mark returned from France.

However, when Mark arrived in September, we were all in for some major disappointments. Instead of honoring his previous buy offers, he insisted on starting the whole negotiating process over at much lower figures. The neighbors' dreams of a reasonable deal were shattered. They felt betrayed—as did I.

When I confronted Mark about his unscrupulous manipulation of these people's financial needs, he shouted. "How dare you speak to me in that tone of voice! I'll do business my way and if you don't like it, you can go to hell! I haven't gotten to where I am today by listening to the likes of you. You better understand something, Mr. Wiltse. There are a lot of people in this town, even on this ranch, that would like to have your job, and just to make it easy for you to understand, it WILL be my way, or the highway!"

"As long as we're making things easy to understand," I said, "understand this. That highway out front runs all the way to Cody, Wyoming, and Jan and I'll be on it in the morning. I'll be expecting my $5,000 back wages when I leave."

"And good riddance to you. You're nothing but a troublemaker, anyway," he shouted at my back as I left his Main Street office and stepped into the bright Colorado sunshine. As I headed for my truck I wondered, *Did I just quit or did I get fired?* It didn't matter. *I'm out of a job again, but I'm headed back to Cody. And that ain't all bad!*

When I got back to the double-wide that Plenty Woman and I were living in, she had supper on the stove and was full of questions about my day. After I washed up and sat down at the table she said, "Don't give me that one-word 'Fine' answer to my question about your day, Cowbuddy. I know that when Mark is around here, nothing goes 'Fine.' I had lunch with Evelyn today, and she's sporting a fresh black eye. I'm telling you, Hon, there's something counterfeit about that jerk."

I told her about the dishonest real estate negotiations that afternoon. "Why, that no good sonofabitch. What can you do about it?" she asked.

"Nothing I can do about it. It's his business. Besides I don't know if I quit or just got fired, but I told him we'd be heading for Cody in the morning."

"Good for you. I don't think these are our kind of people anyway."

"Au Revoir!"

Plenty Woman with her favorite pleasure horse, Gentleman Jack.

HOME AGAIN

There was no way we could actually leave for Cody the next morning. However, after a week of packing, we were on the road. Mark refused to pay the money he owed me. I don't know if he ever got any of the neighbor's ranches stolen.

A couple of years earlier, Jan and I had bought ten acres of land on the Yellowstone Highway about halfway between Cody and Yellowstone Park, a perfect location for our outfitting and horse-selling business.

We spent the winter designing and drawing plans for our dream home. It would be a log house at the location I had always wanted. In the spring of 1994, we began an ambitious building program that would include a large equipment and tack shed and corrals for our rapidly expanding horse herd.

Having built and remodeled a couple of houses before, Jan was right in the thick of things. She is the sharpest, most alert and aware person I have ever met. Her sense of hearing, smell and sight are finely tuned. Her mind is quick and analytical. She can retain and recall an immense amount of information. She has no college degree but made herself indispensable to General Motors. Jan continued to advance in a male-dominated corporate arena. There is a natural exuberance about her that people and animals are drawn to. She speaks three languages—English, horse, and corporatese.

Plenty Woman has the ability to converse with veterinarians or doctors intelligently regarding injuries, illness, treatment, medication and cures, plus the expertise and discipline to follow through with the treatment required by sick or injured horse or human. Neither I nor my horses enjoyed such good care before she came into our lives. I was about to benefit greatly from her intuition when she asked, "How you feeling, Cowbuddy?"

"Not good."

"I'm not surprised. You don't look good, either. You been flat on your back on that couch for three days now, and it's high time you went to the doctor."

"Oh, I'll be better tomorrow."

"Yeah, or dead."

"Probably take a week to get an appointment with the doctor anyway."

"Wrong! I already called, told them it was an emergency. Receptionist said to come on and they would fit you in."

"Emergency! Why did you tell them it's an emergency?"

"Hey, you have any idea how long I looked for you? We lost each other for a year and a half once already, didn't we? So, if I feel it's an emergency, it's an emergency. Get your cute little cowboy butt off that couch and into the truck while I go get ready, or my next call will be to the ambulance and we'll pack you out of here on a stretcher."

It was thirty miles to the doctor's office. The ride over there about did me in.

"Just let me lay here on the lawn til the doctor can see me, okay, Hon?"

"Why?"

"I don't feel up to waiting in a room full of strangers for the doctor."

"You promise to stay right here?"

"I couldn't go any where if I wanted to. I'll just lay here in the shade."

"Okay, I'll check you in and come for you when the doctor can see you."

"Thanks, Hon."

◆   ◆   ◆

Upon completing his preliminary examination, Dr. Prevost said, "Well, Duane, here's the deal. I've sent your blood and urine samples to the lab. I have some suspicions, but I won't know for sure until I get the lab results back tomorrow afternoon. Meanwhile, we need to get some antibiotics and liquids into you, get your temperature down, and work on that headache. I've already called the hospital. They're waiting for you. Just have Jan take you into Emergency and—"

"Hospital! Wait a minute. I've never been in a hospital before."

"Believe me, Duane. You need to go to the hospital right now."

It felt good to lay down, even if it was a hospital bed. I couldn't get much sleep that night, as nurses were checking vital signs and changing IV bottles every couple hours. Late the next afternoon, Dr. Prevost studied my chart and asked, "How do you feel today, Mr. Duane?"

"A little better. I still have the headache."

"Yes, and some fever, I see. Have you been bitten by a tick recently?"

"Yeah. Last week I was at the sawmill, picking out logs for our new house, and that evening I found one of the little beggars bored into my back. I've been bitten before. So what?"

"I got the lab report back. My suspicions were confirmed. You have Rocky Mountain Spotted Fever, and now I know how you got it."

"So what does that mean?"

"That means you're going to be with us for a few days."

"A few days? Do you have any idea how long?"

"It all depends on your system. Now that we know for sure what the problem is, we can get more aggressive and selective with your treatment. Duane, I don't think you know how sick you were when you first came in. Your body was on the verge of shutting down. When that happens, it is hard to reverse the process. You can thank your lucky stars you came in when you did."

"Lucky stars had nothing to do with it, Doc. Plenty Woman there, she's my lucky charm."

"Well, you better hang on to her then. I'll see you tomorrow."

"Okay, Doc. Thanks again."

◆　　　◆　　　◆

That damn tick set our building schedule back almost two weeks. Soon we were back up to speed, and we moved into our new house in time to head for the high country for the 1994 elk-hunting season. Before I left to set up camps, I got a phone call from my old bud in Colorado, Louie.

"Fine thing—you come down to Colorado varmint hunting and don't even stop in and see your old buddy."

"What are you talking about, Louie? I haven't been to Colorado since I left the Crazy French Ranch."

"You sure you weren't down here last week?"

"Hell, no. I told you I hadn't been to Trinidad since the blowup with Mark. Why?"

"Has the Sheriff called you?"

"No, the Sheriff hasn't called me. Why should he?"

"Old Mark's dead."

"Dead? How can he be dead, somebody shoot him?"

"Aha, you were down here last week."

"Dammit, Louie, tell me what happened."

"Like I said, Mark's dead. Shot in the head. Sheriff says self-inflicted gunshot wound. When I asked him about the bullet hole in the corner of the kitchen window, he tells me its probably another one of those Spanish Land Grant mysteries that we'll never solve."

"I don't know, Louie, but as far as I'm concerned, it couldn't have happened to a more deserving fellow."

"That's what folks around here are saying, too. Just thought you would like to know. Tell Jan 'Hi.' And next time you're prowling around the mountains down here, stop in for coffee."

"Dammit, Louie!"

"See you around, Pard."

Click.

◆   ◆   ◆

My cold feet had not yet responded to the coziness of my down sleeping bag. The October wind slapping the sides of my tent promised to blow in more good elk-hunting weather. As I lay there on my army cot, clips of the two previous elk hunts flashed old-newsreel-style through my mind's eye. One of my hunting guides, snoring on the cot next to me, was oblivious to my muttered question, "Seven bulls in seven days? How are we ever going to do that again? After all the bulls we've already taken during the last two seven-day hunts?"

In my twenty-plus years of big game outfitting, we'd never experienced a year as awesome as 1994. Oh, we'd had a lot of good years, even a few remarkable years, but this year was shaping up to become one for the books. I remembered back in January and February, predicting a barn-burner of a year. Forty-three nonresident elk hunters believed in my prediction and booked with us before the February 1 deadline for Wyoming tags. Thirty-eight of those guys got lucky and drew licenses, and now we were down to the last week of hunting season and the last seven excited elk hunters, and we'd already harvested twenty-six big bulls!

My feet were beginning to toast up a little as I thought, *Even if we get two or three more bulls this last hunt, that's not too bad. I mean, let's be honest—how much luck can we expect?* We had already harvested seven bulls in seven days on our first hunt, but to do that again the same year on the last hunt? *Come on, this is real life, not a sporting magazine story. We have a lot of elements we can't control. First, how many more bulls can be left up here? I let the country rest for five years. This is the first year I've reopened both camps and really hunted.* So I had three big questions on my mind this evening: "How many bulls can still be around?" "Will we get at least a little snow and nasty weather out of this blow?" And, "How many of this group of hunters are capable of getting on a bull and getting him shot?"

Tim and Duane leading a heavy-laden pack string through the burnt out
Jones Creek.

Regardless of what happened during the next seven days, the previous two hunts had been packed with fun, excitement, and success. In years past, we'd struggled with our archer success. Lots of shooting arrows into trees, over backs, under bellies, through antlers, but only a very few into the boiler room. However, this year was to be different.

Jim Fisk of Idaho received the 1994 archery hunt I donated to North American Hunt Club. Now, Jim had never hunted elk with a bow before. In fact, he never hunted anything with a bow before—PERIOD. So in January, Jim bought himself a bow and commenced practicing. On the morning of September 18, the first day of Jim's archery hunt, he and guide Andy Johnson unsuccessfully worked two bulls for a couple of hours. When that stalk fizzled, they rode a couple more hours horseback up the trail within earshot of three more bulls bugling at each other.

After tying their horses and sneaking in closer to the preoccupied bulls, they set up and began cow talking. Immediately, a big 5x6[1] bull materialized in front of Jim at about thirty yards and headed straight at him. The bull dropped out of sight for a few seconds as he crossed a small wash. Jim came to full draw. The bull reappeared at about twenty yards, still coming straight as a string right at Jim. Camouflaged and hugging the dirt, Andy gave him one quick chirp. The bull froze; Jim released. The arrow penetrated the bull's brisket. In the blink of an eye, the bull whirled and disappeared in the wash. There was a moment of stunned silence with Jim and Andy blinking at each other.

"What happened?" Jim asked.

"Hell of a shot, Jim, but damn tough to kill a bull that way," Andy answered. "Let's just sit tight for thirty minutes or so. In fact, let's eat our lunch."

"Eat our lunch?? Are you crazy?" Jim asked in a hoarse whisper. "My stomach is still playing leapfrog with my tonsils! Did you see the size of that bull? I think I hit him good, though. Duane said when the shot is there, take it. It was there, and I took it. Come on, Andy, let's go see."

"Whoa, Jim. Wait a minute," Andy insisted. "We don't want to screw up now. Best to wait. Be patient. I'm going to eat my lunch."

By and by, the boys eased out to pick up the track. Shortly thereafter, Andy spotted through his binoculars a big antler sticking up at a crazy angle. Sure enough, within seventy-five yards lay the big bull with only about six inches of feather visible, dead center of his brisket.

---

1.   5x6 = one five-pronged and one six-pronged antler

During the next few days, each first-time archer scored kills on bull elk—one 4x4 and one really big, heavy-beamed 6x6 that would probably score[2] 330.

So our hunt season got off to a grand start. We were looking forward to a good rifle season, as well. With all the bulls that we had seen during our archery hunt, the riflemen should have an exceptional hunt. Plus, my one guide Richard Mason—assigned to scouting trophies—had already located a nice Big Horn sheep and a Shiras moose for the two sheep/elk and moose/elk combo hunters we had.

Dr. Jim Smith of Virginia, our sheep hunter, arrived in late September in time for a couple days sheep hunting before elk season opened. This was Jim's first sheep hunt. The first day out, the big ram was relocated in the late afternoon, with not enough time for a careful stalk that evening.

So, well before daylight the next day, Jim and Richard were horseback, making their way toward the hidden basin where the ram was hanging out. The boys did a good job of glassing, locating and crawling to within about 175 yards of the bedded ram. But Nature took over as the suspicious ram began moving off. High altitude, exertion and excitement produced short, raspy gasps for air as Jim tried in vain to steady his cross hairs on the ram's rippling shoulder. The shot echoed loud and long off the surrounding granite crags. The bullet ricocheted off a rock slightly below and to the right of the disappearing ram. For a moment, all was still again. Disappointed, Jim looked questioningly into the knowing eyes of his guide.

"Don't worry, we'll find him another day." Richard spat a long stream of pent-up tobacco juice downhill. "What do you say we hunt elk a couple days? Give ourselves and this ole ram a bit of a rest."

"Suits me" was Jim's tired response.

A couple days later, Jim made a fine two-hundred-yard shot on a massive 350+ six-point bull elk. Even though packing out an elk is a lot of hard work, it's also a fun time full of laughing, joking, and picture taking. Anyone not otherwise occupied around camp will volunteer to go along. In the case of Jim's elk, Ron Mohnke of Big Rapids, Michigan, rode along to help.

Ron and his wife Carol were cooking and tending camp for me this year at Camp Monaco. If you look in the dictionary for a description of "salt of the earth," there will be a picture of Ron and Carol. Great people. Carol owns and operates a busy family restaurant, and Ron owns and operates the local mortuary in Big Rapids. Ron is quiet and unassuming, as you'd expect of a mortician, and

---

2.   score = the method by which trophy animals are judged for size

he is also a good hand in the outdoors. Whether it's with rifle, axe, saw, or deck of cards, Ron made a good account of his fifty-five years of experience.

This packing job proceeded smoothly enough, with elk quarters and antlers secured by double diamonds[3] to two pack horses, one that Richard was leading up front from his long-legged red roan, and Jim following, riding a big-boned chestnut horse named Wapiti. Ron brought up the rear, astride a muscular sorrel horse called Predator and leading the other pack horse, Teton, a half-Belgian mare loaded with the hinds and antlers.

The pack string was making good time and was within three miles of Camp Monaco when suddenly Richard began to shout and holler, and his horses began to rear and paw. Curious, Ron stood up in his stirrups to see what was the matter. Just as Richard's horses took to opposite sides of the rocky horse trail, Ron saw the object of their objection. A big grizzly sow and her half-grown cub were bearing down on them in full charge. By now, all the horses were fixing to quit the country.

Abruptly, like a flock of pigeons wheeling in unison over a November corn field, all the horses whirled in their tracks and began galloping back up the trail. Now, neither Jim nor Ron had ever ridden a galloping horse. They told us later how amazed they were at how fast they were traveling, and how effortlessly the horses were gliding in and out over the rocks in the trail. They went on to relate how they were not overly concerned about the bear, because Richard and the elk meat were between them and the hungry griz.

In the about-face maneuver, Jim's Wapiti had stayed in the middle of the string. That left Ron on Predator in front, traveling like hell. Both men were hanging on for dear life but enjoying the adrenaline rush of riding racing horses. About this time, Ron became aware of some movement in the timber to his left. He chanced a quick look away from the rushing horse trail.

"Oh, my God! The bears are passing us!"

Now, Predator was well aware of the grizzlies' progress, and as the bears angled to cut them off, the about-face maneuver was performed again—this time in full stride. Sparks were flying from their iron shoes, their hoof beats shattering the quiet afternoon, their lungs now straining for oxygen through flared nostrils as they raced back down the trail toward camp. Ron received another jolt of adrenaline when he realized that he and his meat horse were closest to the stubborn, hungry bears. Thoughts raced through his mind faster than the galloping horses.

---

3.   double diamonds = a lash rope hitch to secure an unwieldy pack to a pack mule or horse, as compared to a single diamond, a box hitch, a square hitch, etc.

What's the matter with this damn bear? How far is it to camp? Oh, damn, almost fell off—can't fall off! No matter what happens, I gotta stay on this horse! Oh, why did I leave camp? Why did I even leave home? Why are these horses slowing down?

The bears were winded, too. They trailed the meat for about another mile—hoping, I'm sure, that one of the diamonds would slip and they'd get an easy meal. The sweaty horses kept a knowing eye on them and finally outdistanced Mama Griz and her cub about a mile from camp.

The next day was a much-deserved rest day for horses and people. The following day, Jim and Richard were crawling through the rocks after the ram again. This time, Jim made the shot and collected a fine trophy to fill out both his tags.

◆   ◆   ◆

While all this was going on at Camp Monaco, it was not exactly "Dullsville" at Jones Creek.

For the most part in hunting camps, most of the excitement and story materials take place during the actual hunting and shooting. 1994 was unique in that respect, also. It all started when Byron Ramsing and his guide, John Davis, came in late one evening early in the first hunt. The rest of us were sitting around the dining tent, talking over the events of the day while waiting for them for supper. As we heard the hoof beats of their horses on the frozen ground, we grabbed our flashlights and ducked out into the cold darkness to see what luck they had.

John, an experienced, thirty-eight-year-old top hand, strode purposefully toward me. "We need fresh horses. Byron broke his arm."

Two overlapping scenes flooded my mind—one of Byron's horse doing something stupid, and the other of me in a courtroom full of nasty lawyers. It turned out that the fellows had indeed gotten on a nice 6x5 in some steep country just before dark. Byron made a clean one-shot kill. As they were preparing to field dress the bull, Byron tripped over his antlers and took a bad fall, snapping his right wrist.

A couple of the hands administered first aid while the rest saddled fresh horses and packed Byron's duffle on a pack mule. John spent most of the night getting Byron to the hospital in Cody.

The next morning, well before daylight, all the rest of the hunters and guides headed out for the day's hunt. In the glow of early dawn, I was helping John saddle pack mules to retrieve Byron's elk when gunfire clearly cracked through the frosty air. The insistent shots continued until it became almost comical to us—fifteen reports, all told, from one of our obviously excited hunters upstream

A couple of hours after John rode up Jones Creek, Dave Stull of Pennsylvania, and his guide, Marlon Richardson, rode into camp all smiles. This was Dave's first elk hunt, and he was understandably proud of his first kill. It had not been quick and easy, however. In fact, during the fifteen-shot barrage, he had shot one tine off one beam and about eight inches of beam itself off the other side of his 6x6 bull's rack. But the bad part was over now, he thought. All we had to do was take a pack horse up and pack him in, since the bull was only about seventy-five yards off the horse trail. So, after coffee, they confidently headed up the trail, each leading a pack horse.

As the October sun burned away the morning, I began to wonder if Tony was going to make it in on time and okay. Tony was one of my Monaco hunters who liked to get involved and help out around camp. Yesterday, he'd volunteered to bring four pack horses from the trail head back to Jones Creek. It's only a little over an hour's ride, and he should have been getting in around 11:30 to noon. It was now after 11:00, and I broke away from my camp chores regularly to peer through the burned-out trees at the river crossing, about three hundred yards from camp, for some sign of Tony.

Presently, I saw the pack string snaking its way through the rocks and down timber toward the crossing. I sighed, relieved. *Well, Tony's going to make it okay after all,* I thought.

WRONG!

A few minutes later, the pack string—following a riderless saddle horse—walked up to the hitching rail. The packs were all neat and secure on the pack animals; lead ropes and reins were all done up properly on the saddle horse. The horses were all calm, with no cuts or blood anywhere, no sign of a wreck or struggle of any kind. But where was Tony, and why had the horses come in without him?

Guide Matt Taton happened to be in camp with his hunters for lunch at that time. Matt is about 130 pounds of appetite stretched over a wiry frame and can effortlessly mount a horse in a heartbeat. He sized up the situation, mounted his horse, and reaching for the reins of the empty saddle horse, said softly over his shoulder, "I'll check it out."

Within fifteen minutes, Matt was back with Tony. It seems Tony had stepped off his saddle horse to relieve himself. Ole Yukon, not sharing the same urge, simply walked the last mile into camp himself, and the pack mules dutifully followed, knowing their job well—a bit embarrassing for Tony, but a big relief for me.

Best of the best: The hands at Jones Creek camp led by the indomitable "Wild Woman" Loretta. All Cabin Creek Outfitter hands were wild, wooly and full of tease, but were never curried below the knees.

As we sat around after lunch, discussing where Matt and his hunters would hunt that afternoon, we were startled by thundering hoof beats. We bolted out of the dining tent just as Frick, one of Dave and Marlin's pack horses, went galloping by.

"Look out!" someone shouted.

We all hit the ground to keep from being clothes-lined by a muddy empty canvas pannier on the end of about twenty foot of lash rope arcing out behind the runaway horse. In seconds, Frick was approaching a small band of the loose horses resting at the upper end of the camp meadow. I expected him to stop once he reached the safety of his buddies. WRONG again!

A big bay horse we call Trooper came prancing out to meet him, and now they were both gleefully circling the camp at full speed. Sod divots splattered all around us. We ducked helplessly as Frick thundered by the second time with ole Troop racing him, neck and neck. They seemed to be slowing down a little as they approached the band of amused horses, and just as the winded Troop broke off, a long-legged white horse named Shadow took up the challenge and around the camp they came again, just barely far enough from the tents that the bouncing pannier that was driving Frick to his SeaBiscuit-like speeds was not also leveling camp.

Before they could make another pass, we rushed out and turned them into the timber, where the demon pannier wrapped itself around a stout tree and anchored the sweaty Frick. Shadow, throwing his head and prancing around, wanted to go on with the race. But Frick's heavy breathing and trembling legs made him a willing candidate for unsaddling and a soothing rubdown.

About that time, an embarrassed Marlon came into camp looking for Frick. John got back with what he could salvage of Byron's bull. A griz had eaten some of it during the night. After a brief rest, John volunteered to help Marlon gather the meat Frick had scattered when the antler jabbed him and he blew. Finally, everything settled down and seemed to be under control again.

WRONG!

Everyone had been gone about thirty minutes when I heard a horse whinny. I headed over to the corrals to check, and sure enough, there were two fully saddled, riderless horses standing there. During all my years of outfitting, I remember only one other riderless horse coming into camp. Yet today, there seemed to be a steady stream of them. In the dark confusion that usually accompanies hunters leaving camp in the early morning, it's not always possible to know who is riding which horse. In this case, I recognized my guide Toad Body's rig on one of the runaways.

That meant Toad Body was afoot with his hunter Harry Levesque, who doesn't think much of walking in these mountains anyway. They'd have a mighty long walk, too. They had headed for the East Fork of Red Creek way before daylight, which is a two-hour horseback ride from camp. Curiously, these horses' lead ropes were dragging and their bridles had been removed and neatly secured to the saddle horns. As I saddled Black Jack, Plenty Woman's big black Tennessee Walker, for the ride up to Red Creek, I thought, *I'll bet Toad Body will have a good story about this deal.*

Sure enough. About an hour out of camp, I met the two footsore, grouchy elk hunters. "Did those sonsabitches just get back to camp?" Toad Body muttered. "They left us like their tails were on fire at noon," he added.

It seems as the fellows took their lunch break, they felt sorry for the horses and decided to let them graze a while in the meadow. The horses were only a few yards away, grazing as the hunters sat comfortably on a log in the noonday sun, eating their sandwiches. Suddenly, both horses' heads jerked up as they snorted and looked intently behind the relaxing men. Sandwiches flew as Toad Body and Harry scrambled for their rifles and turned around, fully expecting to see a hungry griz bearing down on them. But nothing. No movement, no nothing. They looked questioningly at each other for a moment. Then back at the horses.

What horses? There was nothing in the little meadow in front of them either.

"What the hell?"

Then they heard the splashing of horses crossing the stream fifty yards to their right and got a glimpse through the burnt timber of their butts as they headed off down the trail.

"We've been had" was all Toad Body could say.

It's hard to believe that all this fun and excitement would happen in any one season, let alone in one twenty-four hour period. And yet the last seven days proved to be as challenging and rewarding as any of the other 1994 hunts. Mother Nature responded with some wintry weather. There were still plenty of elk around. The hunters worked hard and long to get some shooting. Of the seven hunters on the last hunt, four of them were two teams of father and son. I always like that kind of combination. When those hunts work, the bonding and memories achieved are the very essence of what hunting is all about.

In fact, there were three teams of father and sons on a single hunt. Paul and Greg Klose of Florida and Oregon not only filled their elk tags with heavy-beamed five and six-point bulls, but each one also took a mule deer buck. Tennesseans Troy Stubbs and his son, Michael, were on their first elk hunt with us. Michael took his first bull, a massive five-point, and Troy took the biggest bull of the year, a seven-point with heavy thirteen-inch bases. The bull's beams were so massive that one 270 round passed completely through the left and lodged in the right beam.

Also, for the second year running, we enjoyed the company and stories of Phil Land and his non-hunting father, Major. Major kept the fires going and Phil harvested a fine 6x6 bull midway through the hunt.

That left the team of Joe Cascarelli of Colorado and Joe Brooks of Tennessee, who had been pounding and getting pounded by the mountain for five solid days with no shooting. On the morning of their last full day to hunt, they were sore, tired, and understandably a bit disappointed. They were debating whether to even go out that morning or not.

Their guide, Toad Body, tipped the balance with a promise of an easier hunt along the river bottom. Barely forty-five minutes out of camp, Toad Body spotted a 5x5 grazing on the hillside across the river, less than a 200-yard shot. Joe C. dismounted only a heartbeat before Joe B. He quickly dropped his right elbow on his right knee and settled the cross hairs on the shoulders of the unsuspecting bull. A deep breath, a slight pause, his left index finger gently squeezed the 300 Mag's trigger.

BLAM!

"Missed him!" Toad Body exclaimed. "He's moving out—get some lead in—"

BLAM!

From his rest on a dead tree, Joe B. interrupted Toad Body's excited discourse.

"You got him, Joe! He's down!" Toad Body yelled.

"Bull shit!" Joe C. replied. "He's been down all the time. What are you shooting at?"

"At that bull what was leaving the country, that's what!" Joe B. stated emphatically.

The confusion is probably best explained by Toad Body's poem describing the experience:

> "Two big bulls, standing side by side,
> That's how they lived; that's how they died.
> One had five points, six on the other,
> Those bulls died, facing one another.
> Two shots, each right thru the heart,
> Them bulls died, not fifty feet apart."

And that gave us our seven bulls in seven days.

After evening chores it's staring into campfire, story-telling time. Better than TV!

RANGERS & RADIATION

"So, Mr. Run Around the Mountains Half Your Life, how long have we known each other?"

I'd known Plenty Woman long enough to know that when she speaks to me in that manner, it's a loaded question. It's best if I answer briefly. She's about to deliver one hard and fast right down the middle, and I better not strike out.

"Including the time before we were married, about four years," I said.

"Right. And in those four years I've never heard you mention going to the doctor for a complete physical checkup, have I?"

"Nope."

"Have you ever had a complete physical checkup? I mean with blood work and everything?"

"Of course."

"You have? What did the doctor say?"

"He said I didn't need to come back for five years."

"Five years? That's hard to believe. How long ago was that?"

"Uhmmm, about ten years, I guess."

"Ten years ago. You are so bad. Didn't that tick last summer teach you that you aren't bulletproof? Here you are, sixty years old. Don't you think you should be getting regular checkups?"

"I'm only fifty-eight."

"Okay. So you're only fifty-eight. Big deal. You know you should be getting regular checkups, don't you?"

"Yeah, I guess so."

"SO?"

"So, I'll go see the doctor when I get back from the sports show. Okay?"

"Good. I'm glad you decided. I'll make an appointment for you."

Dr. Prevost and I share a common affliction—hunting elk in Cody's high country. Later, in his office, he said, "Well, Duane, for a man sixty years old, you're in very good shape. Must be a result of all the time you spend in the hills."

"I'm only fifty-eight years old."

"Right. Sorry. There is just one thing that concerns me. It's probably nothing. Your PSA numbers are a little high, but without previous tests, we have nothing to compare. That may be a red flag. There is a little rough spot on your prostate, so I would like you to see a specialist, Dr. Wade. Okay?"

"Sure. When?"

"Right away. I'll call for an appointment."

"Fine."

Unfortunately, Dr. Wade agreed with Dr. Prevost.

"I detect a slight rough spot on your prostate. With the apparent elevated PSA numbers, I recommend we do a biopsy. It's probably nothing, but that way we'll know for sure."

"Okay. When do we do the biopsy?"

"I'm only in Cody on Thursday each week. Can you come to my office in Billings on Monday?"

"Sure. What time?"

"You'll have to drive down from Cody that morning, right?"

"Right."

"How about 10:00 a.m., then?"

"That'll work."

◆   ◆   ◆

"You'll feel just a little sting when I pull this trigger. That will be the needle taking a microscopic sample of the rough spot. I'll just take two or three quick samples. Okay?"

"Sure."

SNAP!—SNAP!—"Hmm." SNAP! "Hmmmmm."—SNAP! "Oooohhh-hhh."—SNAP!

"Dammit, Doc. A couple more of those and I'm afraid I'll lose my cookies!"

"Sorry. I just want to be sure. One more."

"Let me get a better holt of this table first. Okay, fire away!"

SNAP! "You can get dressed now."

"Boy, I'm glad that's over."

"If you'll come to my office in Cody next Thursday, I'll have the lab results by then. Just call the receptionist for an appointment."

Thursday came quickly. "I think I'll go to the doctor's office with you this afternoon," Jan said.

"Sure. Any particular reason?"

"No. I just want to hear what he has to say. I may have a question or two. Okay with you?"

"Of course. I have a 3:30 appointment."

Dr. Wade raised Tennessee Walking horses as a hobby, and usually we spent the first ten minutes or so talking horses. That afternoon, he was different. He was serious, businesslike. No horse talk. Straight to the lab results.

He matter-of-factly told me I had cancer and kept right on talking. I know because I could see his lips moving, but I didn't hear anything after the word "cancer." He must be mistaken. How could I have cancer? That shit kills people. It killed Dad, and now he says I got it.

"Wait! Wait!" I interrupted. "Go back. Start over and go slower."

That's when I realized Plenty Woman had my hand in hers. Then the damn doctor said it again. Said I had cancer. But this time, I could hear the rest of what he was saying. Dr. Wade spent the biggest share of an hour explaining the diagnosis and choice of treatments. Plenty Woman asked several clarifying questions. I was glad she came along that day. Dr. Wade was confident the cancer was detected early, before it spread to any surrounding tissue, but we needed to decide on a treatment and begin as soon as possible. We might be able to take a chance and treat it with radiation. Surgery would be more decisive but carried the risk of unpleasant side effects such as incontinence and/or impotence. The possible side effects scared me, but living with them was a damn sight better than dying of cancer.

The way I see it, life is not for the namby-pamby. The minute you're born, something is trying to kill you—disease, nature, accidents, or predators. I've decided when the Grim Reaper comes for me, he better be well-mounted, cause he's in for a helluva race.

Before we left his office, we opted for the more reliable cure of surgery. It was scheduled for August 7 in Billings, in thirty days. To my question about what I could do to prepare for surgery and recovery, Dr. Wade answered, "Be in as good physical condition and frame of mind as possible. And don't worry. You're only fifty-eight years old. You'll do fine."

We had been home from the doctor's office barely an hour when a neighbor, Lee Livingston, pulled in. Lee had guided for me his first year out of high school. He was in his mid-thirties now, married with a couple young children. Lee recently decided to get back in the business and had been pestering me to sell him Cabin Creek Outfitters for a couple of years. Having a lot to think about, I promised to answer him in a couple days.

♦   ♦   ♦

It seems when a man begins to get a little older, the younger generation is eager to push him aside and take over. I had been strenuously resisting that process. If I sold my outfitting business, what would I do? I started out in Michigan, trained only as a brick mason, but I had long cherished a romantic dream of the West. Once I saw the country of snow-capped peaks, bugling elk, and screaming eagles, I put everything on the line to be a part of it. I was in the right place at the right time, and my gamble paid off in spades. During the last 20 years, I'd learned to be a wilderness outfitter, big game hunting guide, and horseman. If I sold out, who would I be? I seemed to exist only in my mind and old photos. Brown spots were showing up on the parchment-like skin on the back of my hands from too many years in the sun. When I caught a glimpse of myself in a store window, I was surprised to see my Dad looking back at me.

I didn't have an answer to my question, "If I am no longer an outfitter, who am I?" but again, circumstances beyond my control were about to impact my lifestyle and income. The Federal Government had reintroduced wolves into Yellowstone Park that previous winter. I had learned not to expect Yellowstone Park to be a responsible neighbor.

First, they turned their grizzly bears loose on me. Then they burnt me out with their "let burn" policy. Now they were adding wolves to my burden. The wolves weren't going to stay inside the Park boundaries any better than the fires did, and they were the biggest threat yet to my business and way of life. It's risky and hard to accurately foretell the future, but by looking at history, sometimes a person can identify a trend.

When I started outfitting in 1974, unlimited nonresident elk licenses—ninety-nine percent of my business—were sold over the counter. Hunting season was from September 10 to November 21. I could also hunt moose, grizzly, and black bear. By 1995, nonresident elk licenses were issued through a very limited, sometimes corrupt computer drawing system eliminating sixty-five percent of my client base. Elk season now opened October 1 and closed October 21, reducing my business operating days by seventy percent. Black bear baiting was one hundred percent eliminated. Grizzly bear and moose hunting were both gone, too.

In the old days, large ranchers dealt with trespassers and squatters in their own way. As a large outfitter of three camps within a 200 square mile hunting area, I dealt with similar problems. In my hunting area, Forest Service policy allows the general public unlimited access to the entire forest. Because there is no permit system for the general public, the bureaucracy has no idea how many people are on it at any time, where they are, or who they are. It's estimated only ten percent of forest usage is by permittees like myself. The other ninety percent is by people with little to no management by the Forest Service.

This is National Forest, yet all my guests pay a user fee. I pay a pasture fee for each horse, a permit fee, a license fee, a site fee, and a premium for the minimum $1,000,000 liability insurance required by the Forest Service. Plus, I must operate in strict compliance with a two-inch-thick regulation manual that includes not tying my horse to a green tree. Another reg is to disperse all horse manure. However, it was not uncommon for a wet-behind-the-ear Forest Ranger to ride into my camp for a weekly inspection, tie his horse to a green tree, ride out when he's through, and leave me a pile of horse manure to disperse.

Many Wyoming residents who pay no usage fees think they own all the game and National Forest. They resent the presence of the nonresident sportsmen and the outfitters who serve them. Yet at least once every year, we will save two or three of their asses up there. They'll be lost, hypothermic, injured, or left afoot by their runaway horses. They stumble into our camp, or we find them wandering aimlessly about, hopelessly lost. We warm them up, dry them off, feed them, give medical treatment if needed, and sometimes take them back to the trail head. Usually they are so embarrassed by their incompetence, we seldom get so much as a thank you.

On rare occasions, one of our clients will turn out to be just such a scissorbill[1] also. Operating three camps simultaneously, it was possible for me to spend only a couple of days in each during a given seven day hunt. Prior to each hunt, I gave detailed instructions to all hands on how the hunt was to proceed, who was to guide whom, and the admonition to never, under any circumstance, allow one of the guests to start running the show.

In Monaco one hunt, a prominent surgeon insisted on doing just that. His first mistake was not to recognize that his Grand Rapids, Michigan importance did not transfer to Monaco. Dr. W's unsuccessful attempts to coerce or bribe the guides into giving him special treatment caused stress and frustration to all in camp, including his hunting partners.

The day before I arrived, in a fit of anger he hit one of my best mules in the face with bear pepper spray. That did it for the guides. Dr. W was in camp when I arrived. For everyone's safety, the guides refused to take him hunting. Of

---

1.   scissorbill = a shirker, incompetent person

course, he became upset when I refused to fire my guides on his say-so. I don't know what made him madder—me not firing my guides; or when he refused to pay his bill, me telling him he was the kind of stingy phony that wouldn't pay five dollars to watch a piss ant eat a bale of hay.

At any rate, that winter I got a letter from the Outfitter Board reprimanding me for being unprofessional in my treatment of Dr. W. Seems the good doctor was looking for sympathy and wanted my license revoked. He had written to the U.S. Forest Service, Wyoming Game & Fish, the Outfitter Board, and even the Governor.

I replied to the Board as professionally as I knew how, that I never have and never would tolerate rude behavior or unruly people in my camps. I don't care how important they think they are someplace else. As usual, the bureaucracy had the last word. Damned if *they* didn't put me on probation, too.

Then there's always the renegade outfitter, some guy with a few head of horses and camp gear who wants to make extra money from unsuspecting nonresident hunters by sneaking them into my country. The renegades have no license, no permits, no assigned camp sites and no insurance. Yet it is almost impossible to get the Forest Service to hunt these guys down and prosecute them.

So if I'm not tough enough to protect my own hunt country, little by little the renegades will take the best of it. I try to work through the Forest Service first, but that usually works out like the last time I called them.

Bill Oliver was my Wilderness Ranger then. Bill and I go way back, to when he first came to this country in the mid-80s, right after his high-school graduation in California. Bill did well, rode a lot of rough stock for me in those years, and developed into a top hand. He became one of my best hunting guides and learned most of my old Indian tricks. Then, like so many of the good ones, he got married and got a real job. Only his job was with the Forest Service. Again, Bill did well and in a few years became my ninth Wilderness Ranger.

I had enough confidence in our relationship that I rode twelve miles after dark to a telephone to report a renegade outfitter camp to him. There was no snow yet, but I had tracked these guys for half a day before finding their hidden camp. Without dismounting, I identified four grizzly-country Forest Service violations.

Bill agreed to meet me at Camp Monaco the next day, so I could guide him to the trespassers. Noon came and went. No Bill. I worked around camp all afternoon. Bill never showed. Right after breakfast the next morning, I was at the corral saddling my horse to tend to the renegades myself as Bill and another guy came riding in, leading two pack horses for their camp gear.

"Good morning, Duane. Looks like you're getting ready to go somewhere." Bill said, as the two of them dismounted without being invited to do so and walked over to where I leaned on the corral.

"Yup."

"Duane, I'd like you to meet Tim Eckerd. Tim is the new Federal officer in charge of investigating wolf and grizzly bear violations."

I shook Tim's hand and said, "Pleased to meet you."

He didn't answer. Just looked at me. Bill spoke up and said, "Duane, I'm afraid I've got some bad news for you."

"Oh?"

"I'm going to have give you a ticket. I hate to do it but I have no choice."

"How do you figure that?"

"The reason we didn't get up here yesterday was because we got held up at your Jones Creek Camp."

"How so? That camp is between hunts. There's nobody there but Matt."

"Matt wasn't there. No one was there, and the ladder was leaning up against the bear stand. A bear could've climbed up there."

"There's nothing up there for a bear to get, except some diesel in antifreeze jugs."

"That's what I want to talk to you about." Tim spoke for the first time. "You say it's diesel in those antifreeze jugs?"

"Yeah."

"What do you do with the diesel, and why antifreeze jugs?"

"We soak sawdust and pine cones in the diesel for fire starter. I use the antifreeze jugs because they seal so well, and I don't have seepage when we pack the diesel in on our mules."

"You sure that's not antifreeze."

"No, it's diesel. What's the big deal about antifreeze, anyway?"

"I have intelligence reports that some of you outfitters are using antifreeze to poison raiding grizzlies."

Sounded like a crock to me! "I hope you guys will do me a favor when you go back down. Pour some of that stuff out of the antifreeze jugs on the ground, toss a lighted match into it. I'll guaran-damn-tee you it'll burn."

"Don't worry. We will."

"So what's this ticket you're talking about, Bill?"

"The ladder up against the bear stand gave us probable cause, so we searched the rest of your camp."

"You searched my camp?"

"I'm sorry, Duane. I had to do it. It's my job."

"You searched my camp? Bull shit it's your job!"

"Anyway, we found cosmetics in the cook's tent—that's a bear attractant. We found half a fifth of Jack Daniels in one of the guides tents—that's a bear attractant. And we found a tube of toothpaste in the other guide's tent. Those are all bear attractant violations, plus the ladder. I have to write you a ticket, Duane. I'm sorry."

"Bill, you know in all the years I've outfitted this country, even before you came, I've never had a ticket."

"I know, Duane. I'm sorry."

"So write your sorry damn ticket and let's ride on up to the renegade camp."

As Bill handed me the ticket, he said "Well, that's just it, Duane. We don't have time to go any further. Sorry, but we've got to get back tonight. You know how the Government is about overtime."

◆   ◆   ◆

Well, I'm here to tell you, that afternoon while the renegades were out hunting, a little Jewish lightning[2] struck a big dead pine and it fell the full length of their damn tent, tearing it open and busting everything in it.

The low clouds scrubbing the mountain peaks obscured the toenail moon that night as the five trespassers huddled dejectedly around their fire. Six heavily armed riders unexpectedly appeared in a semicircle at the edge of their fire's glow. The sound of Toad Body racking his 30/30 Winchester grabbed their attention.

Twenty years of pent-up anger and frustration resounded in my voice as I stated, "My name is Wiltse. I own Cabin Creek Outfitters. This is my hunting country. You guys are here illegally, and you're not welcome. Be gone by tomorrow noon."

One of the demoralized dudes spoke up and said, "We'll go tonight if you'll help us, Mr. Wiltse."

The renegade and his partner glared at me.

"Be gone by tomorrow noon, or I'll damn sure help you." We backed our horses out of the firelight and rode silently back to Monaco. Our sleeping hunters didn't even know we'd been gone.

When we left camp a couple days later, I checked and sure enough, there were their tracks leaving the country. Two hours later, we pulled into Jones Creek

---

2.   Jewish lightning = a term of self-induced misfortune for profit or revenge

Camp to allow our hunters a few minutes to stretch their legs. Matt was cutting firewood in preparation for the new hunters coming in tomorrow. The bright October sun was just beginning to melt last night's heavy frost. It felt good to get off the cold, shaded trail and warm up around his campfire.

Matt motioned for me to follow him over to the bear stand. "I'm sure sorry about that ticket, Boss. It was my fault."

"So what's the deal?"

"I didn't think it would hurt if I rode down to Pahaska in the middle of the day for a shower. I was only gone a couple of hours."

"More like four hours, probably."

"Yeah, I guess. But what's with Oliver these days?"

"What do you mean?"

"Well, he rides in here yesterday with that old Silent Sam guy he's with, didn't say howdy, go to hell, or nothing. Just climbs up on the bear stand, gets some of our diesel, pours it on the ground and sets a match to it. Then he gives me a ration about having to give you a ticket about all the bear violations. I told him you wouldn't mind if I went down for a shower in the middle of the day, when the bears are holed up in their day beds. If there were bear violations, they were my fault and he ought not be giving you tickets for something I did. He allowed as I didn't know for sure that all the bears were sleeping while I showered, and as long as I admitted to the violations, he was going to write me a ticket too. And the sorry bastard did."

Later that afternoon, when I stopped at the Forest Service to object to Matt and I both getting tickets for the same offense, I was informed that Monty Barker, the District Ranger, wanted to see me. Seems the nice renegade man had been in a couple days earlier and filed a complaint against me for harassing him and his "friends."

"Duane, you can't be taking these matters into your own hands any more. One of these days, somebody's gonna call your bluff."

"I wasn't bluffing. I called Oliver first, but he was too damn busy searching my camp. Be a cold day in hell before I call him again."

"Meanwhile, your file keeps getting thicker."

"After hunting season, I'll write you a letter about my side of the story. You can stick that in my file, too."

◆   ◆   ◆

The reintroduction of wolves and the adverse impact they would have on the game herds caused great concern among the Cody Country Outfitters. Unfortunately, the Government in the form of the Wyoming Game & Fish Department and the U. S. Forest Service did not share my dream of my three sons joining me in a profitable family outfitting business.

With hunters taking the mature animals out of the herds and the wolves taking the calves, how long before there was a big collision right in the middle? Five years? Seven years? Impossible to say. The Government bureaucracy would survive at any cost. Wyoming Game & Fish's main source of revenue is the sale of hunting licenses. They will continue to need their new computers and pickup trucks, to say nothing of their pensions. Wolf packs will need more and more elk and moose calves to feed their burgeoning numbers.

I don't know how the Game & Fish will respond to this impending crisis, but according to the trend over the last twenty years, it will not be good for the outfitting industry in Cody.

The first week after Dr. Wade told me I had cancer passed agonizingly slow. After long discussions with Plenty Woman and sleepless nights, I realized the time to sell Cabin Creek Outfitters was like selling a horse—before he got too old to have any value, and when you had an interested buyer.

I decided that before the wolves eroded the value of my business and the cancer eroded my ability to run it, and while I had an interested buyer offering me an earnest money check, I needed to set my fears of the unknown aside, accept his check, and move on. I called Lee.

The deal was struck. Upon receipt of the full amount, I would turn over Cabin Creek Outfitters, lock, stock, and barrel, the first of January 1997.

◆   ◆   ◆

Jan had begun researching health supplements and settled on Usana, a solid company that produced high-quality vitamin and mineral supplements designed to provide optimum nutrition at the cellular level, thereby strengthening one's immune system. I took the supplements morning and night to help withstand the trauma of the upcoming prostate surgery.

Soon, PS (prostate surgery) day arrived. Surgery was scheduled for early morning, so Plenty Woman and I spent the previous night in a Billings motel. After a passionate, "tear each other's clothes off" lovemaking session, I slept like a baby. Instead of breakfast, the next morning began with a short briefing with Dr. Wade. To reduce the chance of blood clots, he stressed how important it was for me to get up and walk as soon as possible after the surgery. I was worried that every day I spent in the hospital exposed me to risk of infection or contamination by somebody's mistake or incompetence. I may have offended Dr. Wade when I insisted every medication and procedure be approved by Jan as my last line of defense against screw-ups. Nevertheless, he agreed and so noted on my chart.

When they took me into the prep room, I was self-conscious about having my private parts shaved. The anesthesiologist said he was going to insert the needle in my back for the painkillers. Then they would prep me for surgery.

The next thing I knew, I was struggling to get up out of a deep dark hole. I could see some light above and hear voices in the distance. But I had to stop and rest a moment. Then I tried again. Still couldn't get out. Something was wrong. I couldn't focus my mind or coordinate my body. I rested again. Then, with a mighty effort, I broke out and found myself in a hospital bed, with Jan and a nurse holding me in the bed and telling me to take it easy, everything was alright.

By hell, everything didn't seem alright to me. My legs were all trussed up in some sort of bulky leggings, and my mind was scattered in a dozen pieces. I finally realized that damn weasel anesthesiologist had sucker-punched me. When he put that needle in my back, he'd gone right on and knocked me out with no warning. The surgery was over. I remember Dr. Wade telling me it was important to get up and walk around. But something was definitely wrong, because even several hours after I woke up, I was so groggy and dizzy I couldn't even sit up in the bed, let alone get up and walk.

It was well into the first night after surgery that I figured out it was the painkillers that were killing me. I asked Jan to call the nurse and remove the needle from my back. The nurse arrived and said she didn't have the authority to remove the needle, and besides, I needed the pain killers.

"No, I don't need the pain killers," I said. "I need to get up and walk."

"I'm sorry, Mr. Wiltse. You will just have to be patient and wait till morning for Dr. Wade or the anesthesiologist to remove the needle."

"Whichever one comes in first, please send him up right away."

"Of course."

I spent several more hours in la-la land til the weasel came in and asked, "What seems to be the problem, Mr. Wiltse?"

"There's no problem. I just need you to get this damn needle out of my back so I can get up and walk."

"Can't do that, Mr. Wiltse. You need the pain killers."

Nearly exhausted from trying to concentrate and exasperated at the hospital bureaucracy, I turned to Jan and said, "Hon, you've got to get this needle out of my back."

She invited the weasel out into the corridor. About thirty minutes later, he returned with a release for me to sign, and only then would he reluctantly remove the needle, warning me of the impending pain. Apparently, he'd never been kicked in the belly by a mule or on the elbow by a horse, cause I didn't think the pain was any worse than that.

Within an hour or so, my head cleared and I was hoofing it up and down the corridor. After four days in the hospital, I was glad to be going home. The next morning, I embarked on a walking exercise program to regain my strength and get ready for my twenty-first consecutive year as a professional big game outfitter.

I wish I could say it was my best year ever, but I can't. 1994 was. The main thing I remember about the 1995 season was the pain associated with many hours horseback too soon after the surgery.

The recurrence of the cancer took over my life the summer of 1996. There was indeed more cancer than Dr. Wade had suspected. Although he thought he got it all during surgery, rising PSA numbers indicated an ongoing problem. According to Dr. Wade, my only recourse was to hit it hard with radiation daily for thirty-six treatments at the Cancer Center in Billings, 110 miles from home. Luckily, a bus left the Cody Hospital at 6 a.m. and returned about 3 p.m.. The bus was for cancer patients only and quite depressing. Everyone on there was fighting for their life. There was some small talk on the way to Billings, but too much nausea and pain from chemo or radiation for conversation on the way home.

I felt sorry for every one of the ten people on the bus that summer, especially the young women bald from the side effects of their chemo treatments for breast cancer. Some of the folks died before I finished my treatments. The radiation technician kept telling me how strong my immune system was and how well I was doing. But I knew the radiation was making me weaker and sicker every day.

One of the people that helped me survive the bus trip was our driver, Doug, a crippled-up old cowboy who'd "seen the elephant.[3]" He kept my spirits up by

---

3.   seen the elephant = describes a man with considerable practical experience of life. In the old days, when a traveling circus came to town, its main attraction was its elephant. A man who had been to town and "seen the elephant" had, as far as the mountain men were concerned, seen the ultimate sight.

insisting I was doing better than any of the other male passengers he'd had. Some just gave up and quit the treatments.

I believe that five-hour bus trip every day took as much out of everybody as their treatments. I've been one of the fortunate ones. The combination of surgery and radiation seems to have eradicated my cancer.

For twenty-one years. I had eagerly anticipated every fall. The opportunity to ride the high country was intoxicating to me. It's what I lived for. I was addicted to the sights and smells of tall pines, wood smoke, elk rubs, and horses. By August, the radiation made this year different. After last year's experience of being horseback too soon after surgery, I was not looking forward to doing it again this fall.

The radiation had replaced my strength and endurance with painful exhaustion. By the time I'd rode into camp, I could do little more than doze in the shade. I grudgingly accepted the fact that it was time for me to move on.

I came to Wyoming when I was 35 years old. My only regret is that I didn't come when I was 25.

Duane and Plenty Woman.

TENNESSEE

After the sale of Cabin Creek Outfitters in January, the summer of 1997 found me recovered completely from the radiation and rigors of the '96 elk hunts. I was busy training and selling horses, doing masonry work, and pursuing my new career as a hunting consultant and booking agent. I came up with a plan where I could use my outfitting experience, contacts, and expertise to book summer pack trips and fall hunts for outfitters I knew in the Rocky Mountain West. I would host the trip to give the clients the security of professionalism they desire. The outfitter paid me fifteen percent for the extra clients, and I got to go back to the mountains regularly. Without the worries of management, I was having a ball. My long-time desire to own a well-bred stud horse to breed my mares with was realized when I bought a tricolor, triple-registered gaited stallion. I bought him from a man in Tennessee, and even though his registered name was Neal's Apache Brave, we called him "Tennessee." When he arrived in Cody he was a surly, undisciplined, sixteen-month-old delinquent. I suffered many bruises and abrasions during the next two years of his education.

Tennessee grew into a big, handsome, mischievous—even well-mannered—favorite member of our personal string. Well-mannered around people and under saddle, that is. Around other horses, he was the "Boss Hoss" and big enough and tough enough to enforce his will. When it came to breeding mares, he was aggressive and hard to manage. We had more than one rodeo during breeding season, but Tennessee sired some of the best colts for mountain work around.

Like most studs, Tennessee had a roving eye and found ingenious ways to escape his home corral. Sometimes, in his attempts to slip through the five strands of barbless wire that defined his home, he'd get impossibly tangled up. Usually, when a horse gets tangled in a fence, they panic and fight the wire til they cut or kill themselves in a futile attempt to escape. Not Tennessee. No-siree-bob. When he got hung up, he'd just stand there and whinny til I arrived with the wire cutters to free him. Then he'd insist on nuzzling me and playing with my tools while I made repairs.

"Boss Hoss" Tennessee full of heart and personality.

Tennessee didn't like the strand of electric wire I put around the top to cure his wandering ways. So, when I gave him a big red rubber horse ball to play with and relieve his boredom, he used it as a tool, hammering the electric wire into oblivion. He grew into a hard-working, dependable, lovable rogue, who kept us entertained and on our toes with his innovative antics and became a role model for the younger horses. We used Tennessee to teach our colts how to handle themselves on high-country mountain trails.

Jan's son, Tim, grew up without a father or other consistent mature male influence at home. Yet we hit it off right away in 1991, when Tim came to visit his Mom at Mt. Taylor in New Mexico. Tim was thirty years old and had done a very good job of teaching himself to fish and hunt. He was already planning to accept a job as service manager at a dealership in Billings, Montana. Once he got moved, he fit right in with my three sons and the other young men that were guiding for me then. Over the years, Tim became an excellent hunting guide and good with horses. We became quite close.

On an overnight orientation trip for a two-year-old filly called Dixie and her half-sister Echo in July 1999, Tim was leading the heavily packed Tennessee. Tennessee was leading the much lighter-packed Dixie. We were on the return leg and only a couple of hours from the trail head. So far, it had been a good work trip for all the horses.

Naturally, the young filly was tired and mentally irresponsible. For the last mile, she'd been wanting to quit; she didn't want to play pack horse any more. Yesterday was fun, but today was work. Dixie never had to work before and didn't care for the concept of sweat and sore muscles. Tim and Tennessee right-fully insisted she pay attention and do her job.

Riding behind them and leading the equally reluctant Echo, I would occasion-ally slap Dixie on the rump to motivate her. Even then, sometimes she would just lock up, as colts will do, and pop the breakaway twine used to safely tie her to Tennessee's pack saddle. Once she learned to do that, she began to make a ten-minute habit of it. Out of exasperation, Tim tied her hard and fast to Tennessee, so she would have to pay attention and follow no matter what.

The forest fires of 1988 led to massive erosions and washouts. The old Forest Service trail we would be riding on had been cut in four different places in the space of one mile. When I say cut, I mean cut. The four gullies were one hundred feet across and twenty to thirty feet deep. Horses could not traverse the sheer walls. The year after the erosion, a well-known Cody sportsman and accom-plished sheep hunter, Lloyd Zieman, lost his life trying to cross one horseback.

This was 1999. For ten years, we had been gingerly working our way around the deadly washouts on a small elk trail while the Forest Service studied what to do about their trail. I had just settled a minor mutiny with Echo and was trying desperately to make up the twenty yards that separated me from Tim, Tennessee, and the rebellious Dixie. This part of the elk trail ran around a steep hill that fell away sharply to the creek bottom, about twenty yards below and to the right of us. I was halfway to them when Dixie set her front legs and threw her head from side to side, trying to pop the nonexistent breakaway twine.

Tennessee just leaned into his breast collar, and even despite his heavy pack, Dixie was no match for his muscular hindquarters. I yelled "whoa" to Tim just as she stumbled over her locked-up front legs, but it was too late. I watched in horror as the wreck unfolded in apparent slow motion.

When Dixie's sore and tired right hind leg stumbled over the edge, as tired colts are prone to do, instead of scrambling back to good footing, she just gave up and sagged heavily on her stout lead rope, tied hard and fast to Tennessee's pack saddle. He never had a chance. She jerked him sideways over the edge with her. There was no way Tim's horse could hold both of the floundering pack horses. In a heart beat, it was either drop his dally or go over with them.

Watching your pack horse roll down the side of a mountain is never a good thing. But this was only about twenty yards, and as soon as they hit the bottom, Dixie got right up and stood innocently looking at Tennessee, who seemed to be pinned by his pack. Tim and I hustled down to them and tried to get him up. But the lazy old devil wouldn't even try. So, with our knives we cut his pack and saddle off. We knew he was strong enough to get up with his gear on if he wanted to. But something about him—his eyes—something wasn't right.

We worriedly cleared everything out of his way, including a medium-sized log he'd rolled over, before we asked him to get up again. He was sweating unnaturally but dutifully got his front end up and then with a mighty effort stood up on all fours.

The sound of the ends of his broken backbone grinding together sickened Tim and me as our magnificent Tennessee collapsed in a heap in the tall green grass and mountain flowers beside the swift-flowing Jones Creek. Tennessee was sweating profusely now. His once invincible body racked with convulsions.

Tim cradled his handsome head in his lap and cursed the flies and Dixie and the Forest Service's procrastination. I brought cool water from the creek in my hat to bathe Tennessee's face and head while Tim talked soothingly to him and kept the flies away. I knew we had to put him out of his misery. He was my horse—I had to shoot him.

As I asked Tim to lay Tennessee's head down and step back, he shuddered one last time and died in Tim's lap. I stood there, six-gun in hand, tears streaming down my cheeks. Tim looked up at me, unashamed of his own tears, and said, "If there is a horse heaven, they just got a new Boss Hoss."

Life is never easy or guaranteed. It's not so much a matter of right or wrong, but a matter of choices and consequences. We impatiently had tied Dixie hard and fast to Tennessee. He paid the consequences of our poor choice. We divided Tennessee's gear and pack between our two saddle horses and silently walked the remaining six dusty miles to the trail head.

When we stopped in town to report the incident to the Forest Service as required, they casually remarked that it was too bad about our accident. They were scheduled to begin rebuilding their trail next week.

◆   ◆   ◆

Jan's physical health couldn't tolerate the harsh weather of hunting season any more. However, she liked to accompany me on at least one or two pack trips each summer. Sometimes, just she and I would take some friends. It all helped me realize there was life after Cabin Creek Outfitters. We became fast friends with a group of Walking Horse owners and trainers from Middle Tennessee on just such a trip. In fact, they came three Julys in a row.

One was an excellent horseman named Troy Yokely. Troy had trained and traded the "big lick" Show Walking Horses for a living all his 30+ years. We had a little money left from the sale of Cabin Creek, so one evening around the campfire, I asked if he'd be interested in finding Jan and me a good walking horse colt to speculate on—something we could buy right, put about six months training on, and then sell for a profit.

"If you're not in a big sweat, I reckon I could come up with something," Troy said.

"Being in a big sweat is the main thing I'm not, Troy. Just take your time. You run across something with potential at a good price, call me. Doesn't matter when."

Troy just nodded, somewhat hypnotized by the cheery campfire at our snug little camp along the Elk Fork River.

The following March, Troy called and said, "I think I found what you're lookin' for"

"Tell me about it."

"Wal," he drawled, "I run onto this old boy who needs some money. He's got two pretty well bred fillies 'bout ready to start. He'll take $7,000 for the pair. I believe if they'll hit a lick just a little, you'll be able to sell the worst one for that and make a little on the other one."

I hadn't wanted to buy fillies. I'd had my heart set on a good-looking stud colt.

"You really think we can make some money on these fillies, Troy?"

"All you gotta do is take the profit when it's offered."

"Okay, you want me to send you a check?"

"Yup."

Jan had grown up with Tennessee Walkers and since a little girl had dreamed of attending the National Walking Horse Celebration in Shelbyville, Tennessee. The Celebration is a ten-day competition of all the best Walking Horses in the world. It was first held in 1939 and now attracts an attendance of approximately 100,000 people and 4,500 entries during late August each summer.

When Troy invited us to the Celebration, we decided this was the year to fulfill Jan's dream of attending the Celebration. By the time we got to Shelbyville, Tennessee, it had become obvious our filly Troy thought would be the best was a dud. It was costing money to feed and train her every day, so to cut our losses, we sold her for $1,250.00. However, the other filly—named "Poncho Impact"—was coming on like gangbusters and beginning to create a stir as a legitimate prospect for the show ring. People were making interesting offers to buy her—a number of them were in the $30–40,000 range. One was even for $50,000. Jan and I had planned to sell, until we saw her work ourselves. Then, I thought, *She is likely the only horse we will ever own that may be good enough to compete in the Celebration.*

Troy's expertise is in starting colts, not in finishing or showing them. He had taken Poncho as far as he could. Jan and I decided to gamble another year and see if a show horse trainer felt he could develop her into a contender. I sought out the Walking Horse Trainer of the Year, Rodney Dick. Rodney is a short, intense redneck who wears bib overalls and has a special touch with fillies and mares. Rodney knew of Poncho and liked her, saying if nothing bad happened to her, she damn sure would wear roses one day. He agreed with us to bring Poncho along slowly, with next year's Celebration our objective.

Rodney showed Poncho sparingly, just enough to get her used to crowds and competition. She thrived on it, was a crowd pleaser, and took blues whenever she showed.

◆   ◆   ◆

The year before, Jan and I sold a couple of nice gaited horses to Frank and Debbie Eichler of Denver, Colorado. We became friends, and they jumped at our invitation to join us for the Celebration.

I think they must've gotten bitten by a Tennessee horsefly, though, because they insisted on buying a large, beautiful horse farm just south of Shelbyville. They wanted Jan and me to run it for them. I tried to caution Frank that it was hard to make money in the horse business.

"Duane, if you make any money on that farm, shame on you. And if you clean any stalls, shame on you. I'm sick and tired of sending Uncle Sam over a million dollars a year for income tax. If I have to spend the money, at least I'm going to have some fun at it. But I want to stay in the background and learn from you and Troy how to train and trade horses. You just run the place like it was your own. I'll pay the bills and Debbie will have a place to ride. Okay?"

"But, Frank, I don't know anything about show horses."

"We won't do show horses. You and Troy pick out the best colts around, we'll buy them, train, and sell for a profit. We'll get some good mares and raise colts of our own. We'll take in other people's colts for training by the month. We've got room for a hundred head of horses there."

"We should go slow at first, Frank. It's always easier to buy horses than it is to sell them."

"What ever you're comfortable with, partner," he promised.

Jan and I talked it over for a week. Frank said we could leave anytime we wanted, just give him two months notice. So, we took the job.

The last few years Jan and I owned Cabin Creek Outfitters, we would drop down into Tennessee after our last sport show, enjoy some early spring weather, and buy a horse or two and even some mules for our string in Wyoming. We had met some really fine country folks, so we had a number of friends there when we moved down to Frank's farm in November 2000.

Between riders, grooms/legmen[1], and maintenance people, we soon had fifteen people working on the 120-acre farm. Jan ran the office, and I supervised

---

1.   legmen = young men or women who spend most of their workday on hands and knees, tending to the show horses' lower legs, ankles, knees, and tendons—massaging, doctoring, wrapping, applying liniment

everything else, from feed rations to buying colts to reseeding fields, plus riding a couple colts a day.

We named the farm "Rising Star Ranch" and designed a logo. Everything went well at first, but after a few months, Frank and Debbie wanted to be more a part of the politics and glamour of the show horse set. That was fine with me. I didn't care for that end of the business. Besides, it was their place and their money.

Even though it was all Frank's money, Jan and I became more and more uncomfortable writing checks for the impulsive deals Frank was making, and in which we felt people were taking advantage of him—like paying $20,000 for a mare that hadn't foaled in three years and the vet advised would likely never raise a colt. But Frank thought it was good politics. Then there was Frank and Debbie's inability to recognize when he should sell a colt, like the young, extremely well-bred colt I bought for $35,000, with the expressed intent of training and reselling in six months for profit.

We were offered $80,000 for the colt, but Debbie liked to pet the colt, so Frank wouldn't sell for less than $100,000. It seemed the more I tried to counsel Frank and get him to slow down, the more horses he bought. One day, we got a bill for $120,000 for six mares he'd bought sight unseen. Shortly after that came another bill for $90,000, for ten colts in Texas also bought unseen.

Aerial view of Rising Star Ranch, Shellbyville, Tennessee. 2001.

Tensions were building up between us. I didn't think impulsive buying for some intangible political capital in the future was any way to run a horse ranch. Frank insisted he knew what he was doing and was getting a little exasperated with me. Over the phone one day from Denver, about a month before the upcoming 2001 Celebration, Frank said he would prove it to me and write it all out on paper so I could see how at the end of Celebration we would have $420,000 in the bank.

A few hours later, his faxed plan arrived. I couldn't believe it. Eight short months ago, I was supposed to make all the deals. Now, I received a fax listing twenty head of colts he'd bought recently with their purchase price noted, plus a $10,000 profit added to each for the corresponding sale price he expected to receive. He planned to sell all twenty of them during the ten-day Celebration.

This from a man who had never sold a horse in his life, and these were the colts he didn't like after he bought them. That night at the supper table, I told Plenty Woman we needed to be planning to head back to Cody soon after Celebration.

"Why so soon? I thought we were going to stay a couple of years."

"I did, too. But Frank is expecting to sell twenty head of colts for $10,000 profit each during Celebration, and when that doesn't happen, I expect it's going to be a long, tough winter. Besides, I've had the same dream twice in the last two weeks. Kinda bothers me."

"What was it about?"

"It's hard to describe. You know how dreams go. It had to do with us staying away from Wyoming too long, and when we did return, the mountains were gone, the rivers were dried up, and there was nothing but desert left."

◆　　　◆　　　◆

A few days later, while Jan and I watched Rodney riding Poncho in preparation for Celebration, I was watching Jan's eyes. I could see the want in them. I knew she'd never ask Rodney if she could ride Poncho, so I asked Rodney.

He said, "Poncho is a lot of horse. Can Jan ride?"

I looked Rodney square in the eye. "Jan can damn sure ride."

During Jan's second lap on the track, Rodney turned and squinted at me, saying, "Jan can damn sure ride. We'll put her in the Amateur class at Celebration."

After another lap. when Jan stepped down, she was beaming. "Oh, Hon. She's a walking machine. She has unbelievable power and a good mind to go with it."

"Rodney says you should ride her in the Celebration."

"Duane, I can't do that. I haven't been in the show ring in twenty-five years."

"You sure can. Rodney said. Just come over for a few more practice rides, and you'll do fine."

Pulling off her gloves, Jan turned to Rodney. "But I don't want to mess her up for you, Rodney."

"Miss Jan, with your soft hands and balance, you're never going to mess up a horse. Y'all come back next week, you hear?"

Jan is tall and thin, Rodney is short and round. I thought she was going to kiss the top of his shiny head. Instead, she gave him a big hug and said, "We'll be here."

Under Rodney's watchful eye, Jan rode Poncho for the next three Wednesdays. She made arrangements to borrow one of Debbie's show saddles. Formal riding clothes are required to ride in the Celebration, so Jan decked herself out.

It is tradition in Walking Horse circles to wear a horseshoe-shaped diamond ring. Jan has always had a soft spot for horses, cowboys, and diamonds, so we splurged for a horseshoe diamond ring for her to wear in the Celebration.

The two-year-old amateur class that Jan and Poncho would be competing in is a longtime favorite with riders and trainers from all over the United States. Seventy-two of the very best two-year-olds the walking horse industry had to offer were entered that year. There were so many entries the class was divided into two nights. Jan rode the second night. The roar from the crowd raised the hair on the back of my neck, and my stomach did a flipflop, when the hometown horse with the Wyoming rider entered the ring. They were a sight to behold—the shiny, high stepping bay mare with the regal, cream-jacketed Plenty Woman aboard.

Then the announcer's voice came over the PA, "And here you have it, Ladies & Gentlemen. The Two Year Old Mares & Geldings Amateur Class of 2001. Riders, show at a walk, please."

There were five eagle-eyed judges intently watching the thirty-eight horses in this class. The trick is not to get buried in the pack, but to keep your horse in the open so the judges get a good look at you, but don't wear your horse out by showing everything before the cut. It's a huge, oval ring and after a couple of rounds, the judges called for the cut.

They call out the fifteen numbers of the horses they like for an additional workout. The rest are thanked and excused. Then the real competition begins. There are fifteen riders and horses vying for ten places. Now, the judges really want to see what you and your horse are made of. The laps are hard and grueling. After three laps at the walk and running walk, then three more on the reverse, some of the horses were beginning to lather up and riders were looking a little frazzled.

Poncho was showing a light sheen of sweat, but Jan was as cool as the other side of the pillow. The announcer called for the Running Walk. That's what Plenty Woman had been waiting for. She shifted Poncho into high gear and they commenced to put on a show. That ol' filly rared back and put on a clinic about steppin' and stickin', her head was a-bobbing, and she was the epitome of a big lick horse. The crowd began to chant "Poncho—Poncho—Poncho."

Rodney, who is not the least bit reserved when it comes to training or competing, was shouting into a mike that relayed instructions to Jan via an ear plug, "Ride the hair off her. Ride the hair off her!"

While we were waiting for the judge's decision, Rodney nodded at me and said, "They gotta give 'em a ribbon."

I knew Jan had made a helluva ride and was a favorite of the crowd, but none of the judges owed us any favors. Unfortunately, favors do play a large role in the show horse world, just like the rest of life. The judges' card had Jan and Poncho scored anywhere from 2nd to 10th, with a final award of 9th place. We were elated! To think a couple of gunsels from Cody, Wyoming, where cow ponies are king and mules wear diamonds, could have a horse good enough to place in the National Celebration was beyond anything either of us had ever dreamed. We celebrated that evening with Margaritas at Shelbyville's Mexican restaurant.

◆   ◆   ◆

Duane and Jan sharing final farewells with Poncho.

As I feared, by the end of Celebration, Frank had not sold the twenty cull colts for $10,000 profit apiece. In fact, he hadn't sold a single colt at any price. Celebration is always held the last week of August, so in keeping with Frank's requirement to give him two months notice, on the first of September I told him Jan and I would be heading back to Cody first of November. He wasn't in a very good mood, anyway, and our decision to leave didn't help. Again, I was short-changed when it came to settling up.

Just a day before we planned to leave, we got a call from Rodney. Some folks were making serious inquiries into buying Poncho. Could we come over to his barn and visit with them?

We liked the people right off. There were three generations present and were looking for a horse to adopt into their family and win blue ribbons with. They knew we had turned down $50,000 the summer before and hoped we'd give serious consideration to their offer of $60,000 with the promise Poncho would have a good home for life, and Rodney would remain the trainer.

Jan and I had no interest in being absentee owners and agreed to their offer. They would wire the money to our bank in Cody the next day. We all shook hands. Jan and I had one last picture taken with Poncho and said our emotional goodbyes to her.

We've never owned a cell phone, as our lifestyle usually keeps us out of range. So when we stopped for lunch at the Flying J truck stop the next day, Jan used the pay phone to call our bank in Cody to see if the money had arrived. She returned to our table all smiles and gave me a high-five.

As I pulled our furniture-laden horse trailer back onto the Interstate and pointed the nose of the pickup west, Plenty Woman turned to me with anticipation dancing in her talking blue eyes, and said, "Westward Ho, Cowbuddy."

Westward Ho? My God. That's what I said to Mark and Jeff when we left Michigan thirty years ago to begin our great American adventure in Wyoming. What a ride it's been! To prosper—hell, to even survive the lifestyle I've chosen—a man needs an Ace in the hole. Before I met Jan, I usually found a Joker in there. Nowadays, I'm finding more Aces. What helps keep me sharp are the days my horses, mules, or Plenty Woman call my bluff. I'll keep one eye on them while I roll up the corner of my hole card for a peek, to see if I'm holding that damn Joker again, cause you never know.

In the high country, things have a way of rapidly "gittin' western".

Mark keeping an eye on the skyline.

EPILOGUE

I miss hearing Dad's voice, talking with him and the familiarity that was his alone, and I still don't eat T-bone steaks.

Though Jan's liver problem has methodically eroded her tall, athletic body's boundless energy and steadily crowds her toward a transplant, she cowboys up every morning and keeps a full schedule of life, such as household chores, treating injured horses, family finances, etc.

As a youngster, I learned to be honest and accountable. Somewhere along the line, I forgot. Experiences surrounding my divorce brought me back to those basic principles of life.

In 2001, I received a sincere apology from Elizabeth for her debilitating anger that created so much grief and destruction in our family.

I've also learned to speak horse, and have many good friends in that society. I still enjoy my masonry work, plus nowadays I'm having a good time doing old rancher-type radio and TV commercials. I've always said it's easy to make money in America.

In my travels, I've seen first-hand that every area in this United States has its own unique beauty, charm, and culture. However, I feel most comfortable in the Cody country. I understand and appreciate the local culture, environment, and traditions as if I've lived here once before. Who knows? While it's true nobody gets to be a cowboy forever, many of us will think cowboy forever.

Cabin Creek Outfitters provided me with the opportunity to spend countless hours horseback in Wyoming's Rocky Mountains, where I met many interesting clients, hands, and horses who turned into good friends. I learned and taught my five children the lessons of Nature, animals, life and death, of honor, integrity, compassion, accountability, and self-worth. My children enjoyed experiences that very few children today know or even dream about. Now they are all married and have children of their own. Denise is an award-winning secretary of schools in Lovell, Wyoming; Stephanie and husband Trent operate their profitable trucking business from Billings, Montana. The girls and their families aren't much into horses and high country, but we always have a good time golfing together.

My three sons, Mark, Jeff, and John, and I still struggle to make a good living in Wyoming and Montana. However, we all set aside life's complexities and with our best horses, gather at Jones Creek the first week of October each fall. My vision of each son managing one of my outfitting camps was never realized. Yet the times, memories, and stories we share around our little tent camp, hidden away in Wyoming's high country, make up a very important part of who each of us has become. Yes, we still fight grizzly bears and hunt runaway horses, but we understand and confidently accept these challenges as a tribute we pay for the privilege of watching the ravens cavort in Wyoming's pristine blue sky, and listening to bull elk bugling at night, while resting tired minds and muscles in our warm sleeping bags.

The minister talks of a baptism of water, the general of a baptism of fire. I believe there can also be a baptism of wind. A wild, pine-scented Wyoming wind sounds like Mother Nature's violin, the currents swirling through the dead trees create an eerie wailing, as if the trees were mourning their premature demise during the forest fires of 1988.

One thing I know for sure, that high country wind will clear the cobwebs out of your mind. It has a cleansing, invigorating feel we've all become addicted to.

So please, if you don't mind, just send my mail to the end of the trail.

END

Jeff, Duane, Mark and John ready to pack two big 6x6 bulls out of our "hide out" camp in the head of Jones Creek, Wyoming. October 2004.

978-0-595-34722-3
0-595-34722-3

Printed in the United States
33650LVS00005B/67-102